PENNSYLVANIA BREWERIES

3RD EDITION

PENNSYLVANIA BREWERIES

LEW BRYSON

3RD EDITION

CHEERS!

LEW BRYSON

STACKPOLE
BOOKS

First edition published 1998. Second edition 2000
Third edition 2005

Published by
STACKPOLE BOOKS
5067 Ritter Road
Mechanicsburg, PA 17055
www.stackpolebooks.com

The author and publisher encourage readers to visit the breweries and sample their beers and recommend that those who consume alcoholic beverages travel with a nondrinking driver.

Printed in the United States of America

10 9 8 7 6 5 4 3 2 1

Cover design by Caroline Stover

Labels and logos used with the permission of the breweries

Library of Congress Cataloging-in-Publication Data

Bryson, Lew.
Pennsylvania breweries / Lew Bryson.–3rd ed.
p. cm.
ISBN 0-8117-3222-3 (pbk.)
1. Bars (Drinking establishments)–Pennsylvania–Guidebooks. 2. Microbreweries–Pennsylvania–Guidebooks. 3. Breweries–Pennsylvania–Guidebooks. I. Title.
TX950.57.P4B79 2005
647.95748–dc22
ISBN 978-0-8117-3222-2 2004026867

To my wife, Catherine
Heaven knows she deserves it

CONTENTS

ACKNOWLEDGMENTS

There are some people I need to thank for their help in making this book happen. First, Chris Trogner of Tröegs Brewing Company, who said to an editor friend of his, "Hey, I know a beer writer from Pennsylvania!" and got this whole series started back in 1997. My publishers, for putting me where Chris could see me: Tony Forder (*Ale Street News*) and John Hansell (*Malt Advocate*). My editor at Stackpole Books, Kyle Weaver, for all his help with this book and the others we've done.

For teaching me about beer, my thanks to Dr. Paul Thibault, who first put a good beer in my hand, and the late Wilhelm Lauzus, who put that beer in Paul's hand and so many more in mine. Again to John Hansell, who opened my eyes to how very little I knew about beer after ten years of learning about it. To Jack Curtin, who is a reliable source of info on the Philly beer scene and has been a great drinking companion. To the people who have strewn my path with excellent beers: Tom Peters of Monk's Café, Matt Guyer and Buzz Ordonio at the Beer Yard in Wayne, Eddie Friedland of Friedland's in Philly, Scoats at the Grey Lodge, Nima and the gang at Shangy's in Emmaus, Tony Knipling and the guys at Vecenie's in Pittsburgh, William Reed at Standard Tap, and my hometown beer store, Centre Beer in Newtown.

Beer is not just a drink, it's the people you drink it with. The Internet becomes more and more important in finding good beer and those people to drink it with. I've been drinking at the No Bull Inn on Friday nights at www.StarChat.net for more years than you'd believe: thanks to Okie Bob, RP, Mr. Lloyd, BlueBomber, and Mike the Sextuplet for plenty of advice. Thanks to www.Pubcrawler.com for excellent direction on finding bars and breweries—still the best site on the Net for it. Coming on strong is www.BeerAdvocate.com—tip of the hat to the guys in Pittsburgh. To the legions of beer lovers who have offered leads, tips, assistance, and even bought me a beer or two, thanks, and keep those e-mails coming! Finally, a wave to Woody Chandler, possibly the man who has used *Pennsylvania Breweries* the most, and who has given plenty back—thanks for the bar leads, Woody.

My thanks to all the brewers of Pennsylvania, who have never let me down, with particular thanks to the following: Ron Barchet and Bill Covaleski, whose freely given technical knowledge of brewing has helped me through many articles. Carol Stoudt, who laughs damn near as loudly as I do and knows how to do a beer fest the right way. Tom and Mary Beth Pastorius, who supplied never-failing hospitality and cheerful honesty. Brian O'Reilly, who never, ever hesitates to let me know when I'm wrong. Scott "Dude" Morrison, who opened up his brewhouse to me and let me help brew a batch of a wonderful beer I'd thought was lost. Bill Moore, who has given years to Pennsylvania brewing. Brandon Greenwood, who gave me a fearless interview and makes beers for drinking. Tom Kehoe, who brought an ancient brewery to life. Artie Tafoya, who spent an afternoon with me in Gettysburg drinking and laughing when we were supposed to be doing an interview. Sam Allen, who brought life and brewing to the wonderful bar where I spent so many hours in my younger days. Heather McNabb and Steve Leason, who prove every day that size doesn't matter at all. Dan Weirback, who never gives up and was great company on a trip to Albany. The whole crew at Iron Hill, who are a real band of brewers. Charlie Schnable, who didn't let a few bad reviews upset him when he was getting Otto's up to speed. And the master brewers of the five Old Guard breweries, whose stubborn determination makes me proud to be from Pennsylvania.

And special thanks once more to the people who have made me what I am. To my father, Lew, for help with the maps and for driving on my big western Pennsylvania tour. To my mother, Ruth, for proofing the manuscript. To my brother-in-law, Carl Childs, for lots of help with the Yuengling entry. To my big sister, Liz, who has shown me lots of Philadelphia (and answered lots of stupid questions). To my children, Thomas and Nora, who finally got to see their dad at work this time. And finally and again, to my wife, Catherine, who keeps me going when I wonder why I do this.

To all of you: Cheers!

INTRODUCTION

Welcome again to Pennsylvania and its breweries! You will find plenty of beer here these days, even though it's a far cry from the glory days of beermaking a hundred years ago. Almost every Pennsylvania town had a brewery then; some, like Philadelphia and Lancaster, had ten or more. You'll still find beautiful old bars in many small Pennsylvania towns, relics of the days when Pennsylvania's German and East European laborers crowded into taprooms in search of cool lager to relieve the heat of a day's hard work in forges and factories.

Pennsylvania still has five of its old breweries, but the state has grown a new crop of breweries today—more than fifty so far, and more are on the way. They are called microbreweries or craft breweries, and they are notable not for their size, but for the broad variety of beer they make. This variety is not really a new thing; it is a return to the way beer used to be in America.

To understand where these new breweries came from, we need to take a look at our country's history, during which American brewing went from a broad, vibrant industry to a fossilized oligopoly of brewers making one style of beer, take it or leave it. What happened?

The Rise and Fall of American Brewing

The history of the Europeans in America goes like much of human history since the discovery of alcohol. As soon as they got ashore, the early settlers started looking for something to ferment and distill: pumpkins, corn, pine needles—anything for a jolt. The most popular alcoholic drink in early America was cider, followed closely by rum brought in from the West Indies.

Americans drank a lot of these beverages and a lot of alcohol in general. Per capita annual consumption of alcohol was over ten gallons by the 1840s. That's gallons of pure alcohol, not gallons of rum at 40 percent alcohol or cider at 7 percent. Americans drank pretty much all the time.

When Americans did drink beer, they mostly drank imported British ales. And when Americans began brewing, they mimicked the English by producing similar unfiltered ales.

Cider was still the most popular drink through Andrew Jackson's presidency, but things changed rapidly in the 1840s. There were three complementary components to this change. In Philadelphia in 1840, a brewer named John Wagner is believed to have been the first to brew German-style lager beers in America. This refreshing beer became very popular with laborers because it could be drunk quickly to quench a thirst.

Paradoxically, the temperance movements that swept the nation in the 1840s accelerated the rise of lager beer. Temperance had strong effects on many suppliers, retailers, and drinkers. One of its major "successes" was wiping out America's cider-producing orchards almost entirely. The 1840s saw fields of stumps on many farms; woodcut illustrations of the devastated orchards are a bemusing legacy. The demand for drink did not go away, of course, and lager brewers picked up the shifting market.

The third thing that drove lager's popularity was the rise in immigration to America after the squashed German rebellions of 1848. Germans and other beer-drinking Europeans came to America by the thousands, and they wanted their beer. America was happy to supply it.

There were plenty of breweries in Pennsylvania, and some of the names survive in labels brewed by other brewers—Stegmaier, Schmidt's, Gibbon's—or merely in memory. You or your father may remember Old Reading, Koehler of Erie, F&S out of Shamokin, Ortlieb's from Philadelphia, Lancaster's Rieker-Star, or DuBois Budweiser.

There were more than two thousand breweries in America at the turn of the century, mostly small local breweries producing almost every style of beer, although lager was a clear favorite. The temperance movements, however, had not gone away. The Great Killer of breweries in America was the little social experiment called Prohibition (1920–33). By 1939, when this fanaticism had run its course and the industry had briefly boomed and settled down, only about five hundred breweries remained.

People didn't stop drinking during Prohibition, but the quality of the beer they drank was dramatically affected. Some drank "needle beer" (near beer injected with alcohol) or low-grade homebrew, made with anything they could get their hands on. They used cake yeast and the malt syrup that brewers were making to survive. Other beer generally available during Prohibition was low-quality and relatively weak, made from cheap ingredients with large amounts of corn or rice for fermentation. Illicit brewers used the high-gravity system, brewing very strong beer, then watering it down. This saved time and money, as did greatly shortened aging times. Federal enforcement agents knew that hops were a commodity really used only for brewing; brewers, therefore, decreased the amount of hops they used to avoid suspicion. For fourteen years, people drank literally anything that was called beer.

These changes brought about some long-term effects. The corn and rice and high-gravity brewing produced a distinctly lighter-bodied beer with an identifiable nonbarley taste. Low hopping rates made for a sweeter beer. Over Prohibition's fourteen years, people got used to light lager beer. The process continued over the next three decades as big brewers came to dominate the market.

The rise of big breweries and the decline of small breweries can be tracked to several important developments. World War II brought a need to get lots of beer to troops abroad. Huge contracts went to the brewers that were big enough to fill them. Hops and malt for home-front brewing were considered largely nonessential. Improvements in packaging, such as crimp-top bottlecaps and aluminum cans, made buying beer for home consumption easier. Refrigerated transportation enabled brewers to ship beer long distances to reach more customers. These improvements required large capital investments possible only for successful, growing breweries.

Mass-market advertising during broadcast sporting events got the national breweries in front of everyone. The advertising further convinced Americans that light lagers were the only type of beer out there. Advertising was expensive, but effective. The big breweries got bigger, and small ones went out of business.

Why did the rise of big national brewers necessarily mean that American beer would become all the same type of light lager? Simple reasons, really: Making it all the same is cheaper and easier. Success breeds imitation. Image is easier to advertise than flavor. A large national brand has to appeal to a broad audience of consumers.

This led to the situation in the 1970s in which one dominant style of beer was made by fewer than forty breweries. People who wanted something else had to seek out the increasingly rare exceptions made by smaller brewers (Stegmaier's and Yuengling's porters kept things going here in Pennsylvania) or buy pricey imports of unknown age and freshness. The varieties of beer styles were unknown to most Americans.

This is the real key to understanding the craft-brewing revolution. These beers are not better made than Budweiser; in fact, Budweiser is more consistent than many American craft-brewed beers. What craft-brewed beers offer is variety.

The American Brewing Revolution

How did microbreweries get started? Fritz Maytag bought the Anchor Brewery in San Francisco on a whim in the mid-1960s. He had heard they were going out of business and knew they brewed his favorite beer. Fritz was an heir to the Maytag appliance fortune and could afford to indulge his whims. But he got hooked on brewing, and Anchor led the return of beer variety in America. Fritz brewed Anchor's trademark "steam" beer, an ale and lager hybrid; he brewed the mightily hoppy Liberty Ale; and he brewed the strong, malty barley wine he called Old Foghorn. Things were off and . . . well, things were off and walking in the United States.

Next came the microbreweries. Ambitious homebrewers, maverick megabrewers, and military personnel or businesspeople who had been to Europe and wanted to have the same kinds of beer they drank there saw a need for better beer. They started these small breweries, cobbling them together like Frankenstein's monster from whatever pieces of equipment they could find. The beer was anything but uniform—sometimes excellent, sometimes awful—but even so, it found a receptive market.

The revolution started in the West and grew very slowly. New Albion, the first new brewery in America since World War II, opened in 1976 in Sonoma, California. Ten years later, Dock Street and Penn Brewing hired an existing brewery to brew their beers. The first new "brick and mortar" brewery in Pennsylvania, Stoudt's, opened in 1987. Progress was gradual in Pennsylvania until 1995.

By the end of 1994, there were twelve breweries in Pennsylvania, including the six "Old Guard" regional breweries. By the time the champagne popped again at the end of 1995, there were twice that many. In the next two years, the number doubled again. Brewpubs popped up like mushrooms after the rain, microbreweries opened on a loan and a wish. It was an optimistic time, and it seemed as if 40 percent growth would last forever.

Then the long-anticipated shakeout hit the industry, and the press has gleefully reported several times since then that microbrewing is dead. Independence and Red Bell crashed in spectacular fashion. Dock Street, the state's oldest brewpub, was ignominiously run into the ground less than six months after changing hands.

Things looked bad for a few years, and the nationwide slump in the hospitality and travel industries after September 11, 2001, didn't do breweries any favors either. On September 13, I was talking to John Trogner for my *Ale Street News* column. "John," I said, "I just don't know why I'm doing this. It seems so pointless and unimportant." "I know what you mean," he said. "I'm 'just making beer.' But you know, we still have jobs that need to be done, and people who are counting on us. We still have families that need to be fed, mortgages that need to be paid." It seems almost oversimplified as I write this three years later, on September 13, 2004.

But it was just what I needed at the time, and that simple statement of carrying on with the job was what the industry was doing. Craft breweries are part of the landscape now. Brewpubs are established in their communities, and more are opening. The area's smaller microbreweries are doing well. Victory is booming and developing a national reputation, Tröegs has a cultlike following, Penn is on the verge of a big expansion, and Yards' reformulated Philadelphia Pale Ale is a runaway hit.

People have discovered the many different ways beer can taste. No one thinks all wine comes in gallon jugs anymore, and everyone knows there are more types than red and white. Beer is on that same path.

How I Came to Love All Beer

A growing number of Pennsylvanians look for something a bit more stimulating than a mainstream mug o' suds these days. But even when it comes to those standbys, we have always been remarkably loyal to our local brewers. These were lessons I learned early, in a beer-drinking career reflective of America's beer revolution.

I had my first full beer as a freshman in college. When I was a kid, my father had often let me have sips of his beer with dinner. That was Duke Ale, from Duquesne Brewing of Pittsburgh, one of Pennsylvania's many defunct breweries. But I'd never had a beer of my own until Tim Turecek handed me a Genesee Cream Ale in that 16-ounce, solidly brown and green returnable, dripping with condensation. I drank it, and it was good.

I drank a lot more of them over the next three years. "Genny" Cream, Prior's Double Dark, Stroh's, and Rolling Rock were my staples, along with Stegmaier, National Bohemian, and National Premium when the money was tight.

Then one night in my senior year at Franklin and Marshall College, I met my medieval history professor for drinks, a special treat for a few legal-age students, at the Lauzus Hotel in Lancaster, Pennsylvania. Run by old Wilhelm Lauzus, an ex-German Navy man, the bar carried more 125 different beers in 1981, not too shabby at all in those days. I had no clue and grabbed my usual Stroh's. My professor laughed and slapped it out of my hand. He pulled a German beer, an Altenmünster, out of the cooler and popped the swingtop. "Try this," he said, and changed my life.

It was big, full in the mouth, and touched by a strange bitterness that I'd never tasted before. That bitterness made another sip the most natural thing in the world, like pepper on potatoes. I've been looking for beers outside the American mainstream ever since that night.

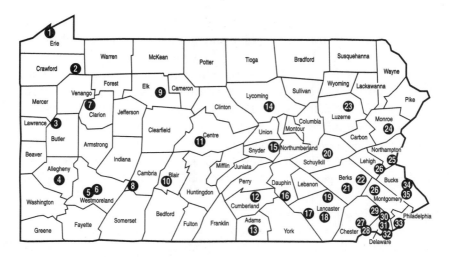

🔞 Appalachian Brewing Company, Gettysburg

🔟 Appalachian Brewing Company, Harrisburg

㉔ Barley Creek Brewing Company, Tannersville

㉖ Bethlehem Brew Works, Bethlehem

🔟 Bube's Brewery, Mount Joy

⑭ Bullfrog Brewery, Williamsport

④ Church Brew Works, Pittsburgh

㉟ Crabby Larry's Brewpub, Steak, and Crab House, Chalfont

① Erie Brewing Company, Erie

② Four Sons Brewing Company, Titusville

⑦ Foxburg Inn on the Allegheny, Foxburg

㉚ General Lafayette Inn, Lafayette Hill

🔞 Gettysbrew Restaurant and Brewery, Gettysburg

㉝ Independence Brew Pub, Philadelphia

㉛ Iron Hill Brewery and Restaurant, Media

㉗ Iron Hill Brewery and Restaurant, West Chester

㉟ Iron Hill Brewing Company, North Wales

㉜ John Harvard's Brew House, Springfield

㉚ John Harvard's Brew House, Wayne

④ John Harvard's Brew House, Wilkins Township

⑧ Johnstown Brewing Company, Johnstown

㉒ Kutztown Tavern/Golden Avalanche Brewing Company, Kutztown

🔟 Lancaster Brewing Company, Lancaster

⑥ Latrobe Brewing Company, Latrobe

㉑ Legacy Brewing Company, Reading

㉓ The Lion Brewery, Wilkes-Barre

㉝ Manayunk Brewing Company, Philadelphia

⑫ Market Cross Pub and Brewery, Carlisle

🔟 Marzoni's Brick Oven and Brewery, Duncansville

㉘ McKenzie Brew House, Glen Mills

㉝ Nodding Head Brewery and Restaurant, Philadelphia

③ North Country Brewing Company, Slippery Rock

⑪ Otto's Pub and Brewery, State College

④ Pennsylvania Brewing Company, Pittsburgh

④ Pittsburgh Brewing Company, Pittsburgh

㉞ Porterhouse Restaurant and Brewery, Lahaska

㉝ Red Bell Brewing Company, Philadelphia

⑤ Red Star Brewery and Grill, Greensburg

④ Rock Bottom, Homestead

㉚ Rock Bottom, King of Prussia

⑮ Selin's Grove Brewing Company, Selinsgrove

㉙ Sly Fox Brewery and Pub, Royersford

㉙ Sly Fox Brewhouse and Eatery, Phoenixville

⑲ Stoudt's Brewing Company, Adamstown

⑨ Straub Brewery, St. Marys

⑰ Swashbuckler Brewing Company, Ltd., Manheim

㉞ Triumph New Hope, New Hope

🔟 Troegs Brewing Company, Harrisburg

㉚ Valley Forge Brewing Company, Wayne

㉗ Victory Brewing Company, Downingtown

㉕ Weyerbacher Brewing Company, Easton

㉝ Yards Brewing Company, Philadelphia

⑳ D. G. Yuengling and Son, Pottsville

It's increasingly easy to find that kind of beer in Pennsylvania, where our breweries are turning out everything from whopping Imperial stouts to crisp, bitter pilsners to rippingly hoppy India pale ales to bubbly, spicy hefeweizens. Is that all I drink, beers like that? Well, no. When I mow my lawn in hot, humid southeastern Pennsylvania summers, sometimes I want a cold glass of something dashingly refreshing and fizzy. Then I keep it local and reach for one of Pennsylvania's regional brews or one of our many microbrewed Bavarian-style wheat beers.

My family and I have enjoyed traveling to Pennsylvania's breweries and sampling these beers at the source. My son took his first tour of the Yuengling brewery on his first birthday, and my daughter would rather have dinner at a brewpub than at McDonald's. My wife loves a good beer as much as I do and is always happy to see the brim-full growlers I bring home from my research trips. Beer traveling is a lot of fun, and this book will serve as a guide for your travels in Pennsylvania. Hoist one for me!

How to Use This Book

This book is a compendium of information about Pennsylvania's breweries. It also lists some of the interesting attractions and best bars in Pennsylvania. And it offers facts and opinions about brewing, brewing history in the United States and Pennsylvania, and beer-related subjects.

It does not present a comprehensive history of any brewery, nor is it one of the ubiquitous books that try to rate every single beer produced by every single brewery. It is not a conglomeration of beer jargon—original gravities, international bittering unit levels, apparent attenuations, and so on. And it's not about homebrewing. Other people have done a fine job on books like that, but it's not what I wanted to do.

It is a travel guide about breweries and Pennsylvania, home to startling natural beauty and man-made wonders. Sharing information has been a central part of the success of the rise of microbreweries in the United States. I've been sharing what I know for more than twenty years, and this book and its companion volumes, *New York Breweries* and the new *Virginia, Maryland, and Delaware Breweries*, represent my latest efforts to spread the good word.

The book is organized in alternating parts. The meat of the book, the brewery information, is presented in seven sections. The first section gives a general description of the large mainstream breweries that make up the Old Guard. Each of the six geographic sections—Philadelphia, Philadelphia suburbs, Pennsylvania Dutch Country, Capital region, Upstate Pennsylvania, and Pittsburgh—is prefaced with a description of the area for those unfamiliar with it. The "A word about . . ." sections are intended as instructional interludes on topics you may be curious about. There should be something there for almost everyone, whether novice, dabbler, or fanatic.

The history and character, highlights, my observations, and other information about the brewpub or brewery are presented in a narrative section. A brewpub sells beer to be enjoyed on location. A brewery sells its beer primarily off-premises. If any beers have won Great American Beer Festival (GABF) or Real Ale Festival (RAF) awards, those are noted, but not every brewery enters these competitions. The annual capacity in barrels, as listed for each brewery, is a function of the fermenting-tank capacity and the average time to mature a beer. Lagers take longer, so on two identical systems with the same fermenter setup, an all-lager brewery would have significantly lower annual capacity than an all-ale brewery.

The other area beer sites I've listed for most breweries may include multitaps, historic bars, or restaurants with good beer selections. Whenever possible, I visited these bars and had at least one beer there. A few of these descriptions are based on recommendations from brewers or beer geeks I know personally.

One final note: Where hunting or fishing is mentioned, your best bet is to contact the Pennsylvania Game Commission (717-787-4250) or Pennsylvania Fish and Boat Commission (717-657-4518) for license and season information. Enjoy yourself!

GRITTY SURVIVORS

The Old Guard

C all them fossils, call them smokestack breweries, call them beer
factories, these are the regional breweries that somehow survived
Prohibition, World War II, and three decades of brewery wars
between 1950 and 1980. They are not national breweries that pump out
oceans of beer supported by multimillion-dollar advertising campaigns.
They are not hip, trendy microbreweries that get tons of press coverage
for their tiny beer output. They are gritty survivors, working with old
plants, a fiercely loyal but aging customer base, and sheer guts.

Pennsylvania has five of these Old Guard brewers, more than any
other state. They include Yuengling, America's oldest brewery, and
Straub, the smallest pre-Prohibition brewery still open in Pennsylvania.
Pittsburgh Brewing is famous for its mainstream, blue-collar Iron City
Beer but has also brewed fine examples of the beers cherished by Pennsylvania's beer-aware. Latrobe is now owned by a Belgian-Brazilian brewing conglomerate, InBev, which has pumped a lot of money into the
brewery. The Lion survived the last twenty years mainly by brewing malt
soda for the Hispanic market.

Some of them managed to keep alive elements of American brewing
history. Yuengling and The Lion were the last pre-micro breweries in
America to brew porter, a dark, rich brew with roots in London. Although
porters are traditionally ales, these porters are lager-brewed, easier for
these breweries to produce. Recently, however, The Lion took a tradition-
alist step backward by once again brewing their porter as an ale.

For the most part, these breweries produce mainstream American
lager beers, brewed with adjuncts such as corn and rice. The beers are
not of great interest to a beer geek, but they are all well made and consistent in their high quality. When I'm in the mood for a sluicing,
sloshing, "lawn mower" beer, I always buy local and support Pennsylvania brewers, and so should you!

1

You should also go visit them. Yuengling and Straub give two of the best industrial brewery tours in the country. They take you right down on the floor. Until recently, you could actually climb the ladders and look into Straub's rare open lager fermenters, practically unheard of in these days of lawyerly precautions. Even if you don't go inside, simply viewing the architecture and the size of these buildings will give you a whole different angle on brewing.

There is a sixth large—very large—brewery in Pennsylvania, west of Allentown on I-78. This beautiful brewery was recently bought from Pabst by Diageo and converted to the production of "malternatives" such as Smirnoff Ice. It has continued Pabst's policy of not giving tours (as Pabst did after buying the plant from Stroh) and has no hospitality center. Therefore, it is not included in this book.

Pittsburgh Brewing Company

3340 Liberty Avenue, Pittsburgh, PA 15201
412-682-7400
www.ironcity-beer.com

Pittsburgh Brewing Company (PBC) is best known for its flagship Iron City brand, to the point that most people think that's the brewery's name. PBC is banking their future on Iron City and its strong spinoff, I.C. Light, and as I write this, it's still looking like a gamble. I've got my fingers crossed for this gritty scrapper of a brewery.

Much of this town's brewing heritage is reflected in PBC's brands and corporate lineage. The brewery stems from one started by Edward Frauenheim in 1861, which brewed Iron City Beer. In 1899, that brewery joined forces with the twenty-one other local brewers—including Eberhardt and Ober, whose old building now houses Penn Brewing—to form the consolidated Pittsburgh Brewing Company. That made a

Beers brewed: Iron City, I.C. Light (GABF Silver, 1994), Augustiner, Mustang Malt Liquor (Original and Melon), American, American Light, Keene's N.A., Sierra, Sierra Light.

big brewery, the largest in a state full of breweries. Until Yuengling took off like a rocket in the 1990s, PBC remained the biggest independent brewer in Pennsylvania, its annual production hovering consistently around one million barrels. That has dropped off a lot recently because of a combination of labor troubles, management malfeasance, and an assault by Coors Light.

The Pick: Gather round children, and listen closely: The Pick is Iron City. That's right, the much-maligned Iron City. Maybe it's because of my time in the 'Burgh, or maybe it's just because a survivor like this deserves it. The fact is, this is a mainstream American lager that's not bad for what it is, has no overt off flavors, and is loved by the local market. How can you argue with that?

PBC has issued commemorative cans featuring local sports teams, along with other collectible cans. Among those are the infamous Olde Frothingslosh cans, featuring the huge Miss Frothingslosh in all her cellulitic glory. PBC did this as a spoof of beer beauty queens like Miss Rheingold and touted the beer as "the pale, stale ale with the foam on the bottom." People loved it, and the brewery gave in to years of demand and released it again in 1999.

The brewery had great success with I.C. Light beer, which was popular in Pittsburgh when I was living there in 1982. But as that original market aged, and as the big Iron City drinkers aged, sales slipped. The company tried various things, including the fruit-flavored light beer I.C. Twist, but nothing worked.

A "City Living" branding campaign kicked off with a return to a retro Iron City label, and I.C. Light has been buffed up as well. A newer campaign, "Bring it!" is a feisty shot at defying the national brands; bring it on, the brewery says, we're Iron Men, we'll take you. It's a 'Burgh thing, to bring up a former Iron City ad campaign. I.C. Light's low carbs have taken center stage in the newest advertising: "More taste. Less waist." The brewery recently started bottling in advanced new aluminum "bottles," the largest brewery to launch this new technology nationwide, in a partnership with Pittsburgh-based Alcoa. And the brewery has taken on the challenge of the Chicago market. Feisty indeed.

But Iron City must win or lose in Pittsburgh, because, unfortunately, the brand has a terrible reputation outside southwestern Pennsylvania. I've heard people say Iron City tastes salty, rusty, sour, or oily. Some say it's the worst beer made in America. Balderdash! After spending time in the 'Burgh drinking my share of "Arn" and tasting similar beers from regional and national brewers all over the country, I have to say that Iron City is no

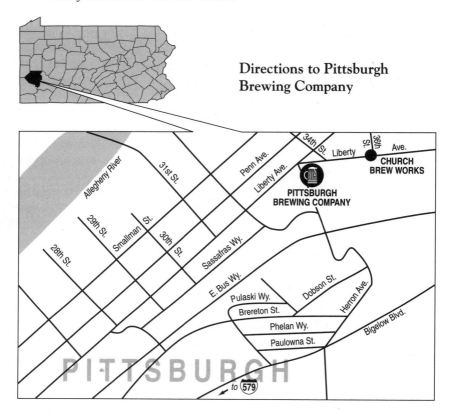

Directions to Pittsburgh Brewing Company

worse than most, and better than some. I have it whenever I go to Pittsburgh; it's a touchstone.

I hope the new campaign works, that Pittsburgh continues pumping Iron for years to come, and that the big old brewery on Liberty Avenue makes it for them. Stop in and take the tour; see the big twin brewkettles in their tiled setting, smoothly curving stacks reaching up through two stories of space. Hike the hill the brewery clings to and sense the size. Then go pump some Iron.

Opened: 1861.
Owner: Privately held partnership; chief executive officer, Jim Gehrig; vice chairman, Joe Piccirilli.
Brewers: Master brewer, Mike Carota; Greg Zalewski.
System: Two 600-barrel Enerfab brewkettles, 1 million barrels annual capacity.
Production: 425,000 barrels in 2003.
Tours: Tuesday and Thursday, 11 A.M. and 2 P.M., and by appointment.
Take-out beer: None available.

Special considerations: Tours for adults and children over twelve only. Handicapped-accessible.

Parking: Small lot; on-street parking usually available.

Lodging, Area attractions, Other area beer sites: See pages 222–227.

Latrobe Brewing Company

ℒATROBE BREWING Cº

119 Jefferson Street, Latrobe, PA 15650
724-537-5545
www.rollingrock.com

33. Think about that for a while; we'll come back to it.

You need an appointment to tour Latrobe. It was bought by Labatt and is now owned by InBev, a giant Belgian-Brazilian brewing conglomerate that is currently the world's largest brewer. More than 95 percent of Latrobe's output is a beer that once used the advertising slogan "Same as it ever was." So why should you visit?

Because it's so darned cool. Latrobe Brewing is better known in Pennsylvania (and everywhere else) as the brewer of Rolling Rock. With its mysterious "33" labeling, Rolling Rock is a beer that inspires great loyalty. Same as it ever was? Thousands of Rock fans say, "It had better be!" There is also a tremendous gift shop at the brewery, with some great-looking Rolling Rock stuff.

Latrobe Brewing was originally a cadet brewery of Pittsburgh Brewing. After Prohibition, Pittsburgh decided to drop some of its smaller breweries. Latrobe was sold to the Tito brothers, who ran it until the 1980s. One of the best moves they made was to create a new beer in 1939: Rolling Rock. On those very first silk-screened green bottles, the motto read as it does today: "Rolling Rock. From the glass-lined tanks of old Latrobe we tender this premium beer for your enjoyment, as a tribute to your good taste. It comes from the mountain springs to you." And at the end of the motto is the number 33.

What does it mean? Theories abound, although the owners of the brewery will admit that they don't actually know what it means. The number of

Beers brewed: Year-round: Rolling Rock, Rock Green Light, Loyalhanna Pennsylvania Lager.

words in the motto? Yes. The number of letters in the ingredients? Yes. The year Prohibition was repealed? Yes. Unfortunately, the Tito brothers sold only the brewery and the brands to Labatt, and not the company archives. The real meaning of 33 may be lost forever . . . though an unnamed Tito family member supposedly confirmed the words in the motto as the source of the number in an interview.

The Pick: Rolling Rock is one of the beers I grew up with, and I still think it's one of the best mainstream American lagers.

What has not been lost forever is the brewery. Labatt spent a lot of money on this brewery and renovated it to a fare-thee-well. There's a

new brewhouse, new fermentation hall, new valving system, fancy testing systems, and serious automation. Brewing is a one-person operation; fermentation is a no-person, remotely controlled operation. All the improvements make it look as though Labatt jacked up the building and slid in a new brewery. Latrobe even has two new beers, both introduced since 2002: Rock Green Light, a low-carb light beer, and Loyalhanna Pennsylvania Lager, apparently a shot at the Yuengling market.

But "same as it ever was" still holds sway at Latrobe. For example, brewmaster Joe Gruss went to college right there in town, at St. Vincent's. Guess what Joe's dad did? Yup, he was brewmaster at Latrobe. "There are lots of second-generation guys here," Joe told me with a smile; "even some third-generation guys." That's nice to think about.

Opened: 1933.

Owner: InBev (of Belgium).

Brewers: Joseph Gruss, Mark Ecker, Brad Bernas.

System: 500-barrel Acme Brewing brewhouse, 1.2 million barrels annual capacity.

Production: 1 million barrels estimated in 2004.

Tours: The brewery is now open for tours! Call in advance—"as far in advance as possible." Visitors must be at least twelve years old, and anyone between twelve and eighteen must be accompanied by a parent or guardian. The Rolling Rock visitors center has a twelve-minute video, a museum of collectibles, and a gift store. Call for current hours. 724-539-3394.

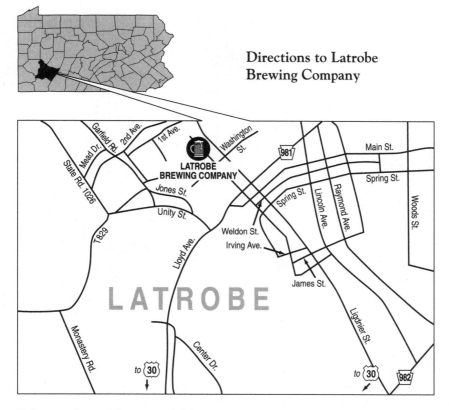

Directions to Latrobe Brewing Company

Take-out beer: None available.

Special considerations: Gift shop is handicapped-accessible.

Parking: Plenty of free off-street parking.

Lodging in the area: Comfort Inn Greensburg, 1129 East Pittsburgh Street, Route 30, Greensburg, 724-832-2600; Mountain View Inn, 1001 Village Drive, Greensburg, 724-834-5300; Knights Inn, 1215 South Main Street, Greensburg, 724-836-7100.

Area attractions: *St. Vincent's College* in Latrobe was the site of one of America's few monastic breweries, and some of the old brewery buildings still stand on the campus. *The Steelers* hold their training camp at St. Vincent's. Follow the signs to *Strickler's Drug Store* in Latrobe and stop in for a banana split; they were invented there about a hundred years ago. North of town, *Keystone State Park* (724-668-2939) offers camping, hiking, boating, fishing, swimming, skating, sledding, and cross-country ski trails. *Idlewild Amusement Park* (724-238-3666) in nearby Ligonier has rides, miniature golf, water rides, and Mister Rogers' Neighborhood, with a trolley ride and lifesize puppets; it recently was rated the second-best kids' park in the world. Latrobe is the hometown of Fred Rogers, Arnold Palmer, and professional football.

Other area beer sites: The locals drink their Rock in these Latrobe bars, recommended by Joe Gruss: *Dino's Sports Lounge,* U.S. Route 30 East, 724-539-2566; *Sharky's Café,* 201 U.S. Route 30 East, 724-532-1620

Straub
Brewery

303 Sorg Street, St. Marys, PA 15857
814-834-2875
www.straubbeer.com

SINCE 1872

BREWERY, INC.

Straub has a few small claims to fame. It is, by Straub family reckoning, the highest brewery in the East, sitting at an elevation between 1,900 and 2,000 feet above sea level. This puts the brewery just below the Eastern Continental Divide, which means, as Dan Straub laughingly put it, "We get to use the water first!" It is the smallest regional brewery still in operation, with an annual capacity of 35,000 barrels. Most appealingly, it is the home of the Eternal Tap, which I'll explain later. First, let's see where Straub came from and where it's going.

Peter Straub came to the United States from Germany in 1869. He came to St. Marys and soon married Sabina Sorg, whose father owned the local brewery. Peter started his own brewery in 1872, then bought and merged with his father-in-law's brewery in 1876. The copper brewkettle from Sorg's brewery was in continuous use until 1995, when it was finally replaced with a new 160-barrel stainless kettle. The fourth generation of the family is running the brewery now, and the fifth is working there. Dan Straub runs the operation, and Thomas Straub is the brewmaster. They're doing a good job, too. The main worry at Straub is how to control the brand's growth so they don't outgrow the brewery!

To hear the Straubs tell it, the real challenge is getting all their work done so that they still have time left for fun, mainly hunting and fishing. Dan

Beers brewed: Straub, Straub Light; Pymatuning Dam Beer brewed under contract.

said that was the main reason behind the upgrades made in 2000 to improve the brewery's efficiency. The rare open lager fermenters were finally replaced with stainless tanks that better filled the available space. The bottling line was replaced with a new Krones filler and Krones labeler that do in four days what used to take the old line six. Advertising costs have been pared to about $2 a barrel, just about enough to pay for the brewery's fishing promotions and calendars.

The Pick: Straub is a good mainstream lager, and out here in Straub country, it turns over so fast that it's always fresh. If you're on the tour and are offered a bottle right off the line, take it. This is the freshest beer you may ever get, fresher even than most beer from a brewpub. It's eye-opening.

Why does Straub face the happy problem of meeting high demand? Dan Straub gives beers like Samuel Adams some of the credit. "Up until about 1988, things were steady," he explained. "Then the micro craze started and drew people's attention to brands other than the nationals." At the same time, they saw that many small businesses had closed or been swallowed up by much larger concerns. "People noticed that all the local bakeries were gone," said Dan. "I guess they decided they didn't want to lose the breweries, too.

"We've got an excellent beer, and that helped too!" Dan hastened to add. Straub has always been free of additives, and the label proudly says that no syrup, sugar, or salt is added. It's all barley malt, shaved corn, and hops. The beer also has been marked with a bottling date since 1989. Budweiser's vaunted born-on date is no new revelation to the people in St. Marys; Straub's been doing it for sixteen years.

The Straubs are content to stay small. It's the German ideal—sell the beer within the smell of the brewery. They sell 60 percent of their beer right in the town of St. Marys, and 25 percent of their sales is draft, more than twice the national average.

Speaking of draft, I promised to tell you about the Eternal Tap. Anyone of age is welcome to walk into the brewery, up the stairs to the keg washing room, and over to the Eternal Tap to pour a beer. Free. All the brewery asks is that you limit yourself to two beers (for the ever-present legal reasons) and that you remember to wash your glass. Things like the Eternal Tap make Straub a rare and priceless gem, a brewery with one foot firmly in an older, simpler time.

Opened: 1872.
Owners: The Straub family.
Brewer: Thomas Straub.
System: 160-barrel Vendome brewhouse, 35,000 barrels annual capacity.
Production: 34,000 barrels estimated in 2004.

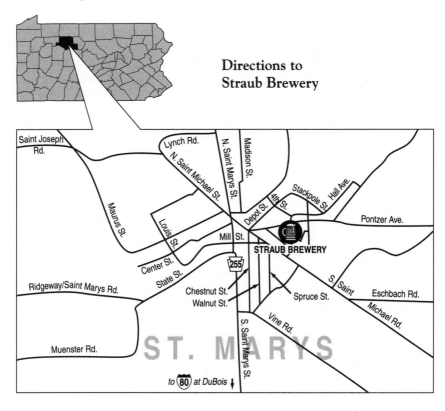

Directions to Straub Brewery

Tours: Monday through Friday, 9 A.M. to noon; please call in advance. Gift shop and Eternal Tap open Monday through Friday, 9 A.M. to 4 P.M.; the Tap is also open Saturday, 9 A.M. to 1 P.M.

Take-out beer: Straub has a store in front of the brewery where you can get cases and kegs. Home delivery is available in the local area.

Special considerations: Children under twelve are not allowed on the tour, and the tour is not handicapped-accessible. Closed-toe shoes are required.

Parking: Off-street lot.

Lodging in the area: Old Charm B&B, 444 Brussells Street, 814-834-9429; Towne House Inn, 138 Center Street, 814-781-1556; Comfort Inn, 976 South Street, 814-834-2030; Bavarian Inn Motel, 33 South St. Marys Street, 814-834-2161.

Area attractions: The biggest attraction in Elk County outside of Straub is Pennsylvania's only elk herd. The free-ranging herd of 350 to 400 animals is most often seen near the St. Marys airport or in the Benezette area. Elk bugling can be heard in September. The other major attraction is the ***Allegheny National Forest*** (814-723-5150), where you can boat, canoe, camp, cross-country ski, snowmobile, hike, fish, hunt, and picnic. A special part of the national forest is **Hearts Content Scenic Area,** a rare stand of virgin old-growth Pennsylvania forest west of Sheffield; be prepared for miles of well-graded dirt roads to get there. Visit **The Winery at Wilcox** (814-929-5598) if you need a change of pace from beer. Bradford is the home of Zippo lighters and Case knives, two extremely sturdy and attractive pieces of American technology. The **Zippo/Case Visitor Center** has a variety of exhibits and a store (1932 Zippo Drive, 888-442-1932).

Other area beer sites: You can get a good German meal and the best beer selection around at the **Bavarian Inn**'s restaurant and bar at 33 South St. Marys Street (814-834-2161). Dan Straub recommends **Dino's Place** (233 Market Street, 814-834-6770) and **Genevro's** (901 South St. Mary's Street, 814-834-4968). Who am I to argue? I spend all my time in St. Mary's hanging around the Eternal Tap!

The Lion Brewery

700 North Pennsylvania Avenue,
Wilkes-Barre, PA 18705
570-823-8801
www.lionbrewery.com

Wilkes-Barre, Pennsylvania

A relative newcomer among Pennsylvania regional brewers, The Lion Brewery of Wilkes-Barre was founded in 1901 as the Luzerne County Brewery. The Lion outlasted local rival Stegmaier, swallowing up its labels and those of Esslinger and Bartel's, two other local brewers. By the early 1980s, The Lion, with its 390-barrel brewhouse, was still brewing its own Liebotschaner Cream Ale and some American premium lagers but was best known among beer geeks for the licorice-hinted, bottom-fermented Stegmaier Porter.

Lee Holland, a grand old man who's been in American brewing for years and has done publicity work for The Lion, credits former owner Bill Smulowitz with the brewery's survival. "The brewery had to make money to survive, so whatever new idea came around, Bill gave it a try." Bill said yes to some weird stuff, like cherry-flavored Red Baron (named for the local minor league ball team) and an oat-bran lager for health-obsessed beer drinkers. The brewery pioneered malt-based coolers with the briefly popular Calvin Coolers. They also made the first clearmalt years before Zima and Bacardi Silver came along, the bizarre, gin-flavored Sting Ray. Such obscure and short-lived beers are the stuff of beer dinner lectures.

Oddest, yet most successful, was malta soda. Dark, sweet, and malt-based, malta is popular in Hispanic and Caribbean markets. It is not fermented, but must be made at a facility where it can be brewed, briefly aged, bottled, and pasteurized.

The Lion started contract brewing, too. Familiar names from the past fifteen years, like Neuweiler's, Trupert, Hope Lager, Nude Beer, Tun Tavern, Red Bell, and others, came through The Lion, and the brewery continues to take new brands. They did an Oktoberfest beer recently for Cincinnati-based Christian Moerlein that was superb and have even brewed some Pabst Blue Ribbon to help that brand keep up with surging demand.

Beers brewed: Year-round: Stegmaier Gold Medal Beer, Liebotschaner Cream Ale (GABF Gold, 1994, 1995, 1999), Stegmaier Porter, Stegmaier 1857 Lager (GABF Gold, 1994), Gibbons Beer, Lionshead Beer, Lionshead Malt Liquor, Bartels Beer. Pocono line: Pocono Pilsner (GABF Gold, 1999), Lager, Pale Ale, Black & Tan. Seasonals: Brewery Hill Caramel Porter. The Lion also makes a very good root beer and makes beers under contract for a variety of labels.

Between contract brewing, malta and other sodas, and their own brands, The Lion squeaked by. Smulowitz finally got tired and sold the business to an investment consortium, Quincy Partners, which in 1993 pumped new money and spirit into the brewery. Improvements to the plant were made, including the purchase of a new malt mill and a state-of-the-art lagering cellar from the old Val Blatz Brewery. New emphasis on quality control and standard procedures paid off early: The Lion scored a double gold at the Great American Beer Fest in 1994 with Liebotschaner Cream Ale and Stegmaier 1857, an American premium lager. Stegmaier Porter has become an honest, top-fermenting porter, with a resultant boost in character that is a pleasant surprise to beer snobs.

The brewery also started a new line with a more craft-brewed approach: the Pocono beers, originally called Brewery Hill. This line started with the smooth Black & Tan, and other beers have been added: a Saaz-hopped Pocono Lager; brightly aromatic Pale Ale; the smooth, rich Brewery Hill Caramel Porter; and the newest, Pocono Pilsner. There is also a Brewery Hill root beer. The Smulowitz traditions still hang in there, as The Lion continues to experiment with some odd malt-based coolers: a Cosmopolitan-like malternative, a "hard" root beer, and a Long Island Iced Tea.

The Lion Brewery • 13

Things continue to improve for The Lion. Brewery management bought the brewery from Quincy Partners in 1999, taking it private, away from the worries of shareholder relations. Brewmaster Leo Orlandini and the brewery were noted as Medium-sized Brewmaster and Brewery of the Year by the GABF in 1999. Pocono Pilsner scored a GABF Gold in 1999, and the Liebotschaner received its third gold medal. Even after a recent expansion, the brewery is running at more than 90 percent of capacity, still making malta and other sodas, and their own brands are growing. Beer accounts for a little over 20 percent of production, and that figure is increasing. "We're not surviving, we're not doing okay," Leo Orlandini told me the last time I visited, "we're doing great!"

The Pick: Because of the wide range of beers brewed at The Lion, I've got two picks. Pocono Pale Ale is spankingly crisp and bitter, a great fridge-filler beer, particularly for the price range. Liebotschaner Cream Ale took the Great American Beer Festival Gold for cream ales in 1994, 1995, and 1999. It's authentic, one of the best examples you'll find of this mild yet distinctive American style.

Opened: 1901 (Stegmaier Brewery, later absorbed by The Lion, opened in 1857).
Owner: Private investors.
Brewers: Brewery operations director, Leo Orlandini; head brewer, Brandon Greenwood.
System: 390-barrel Pfaudler brewhouse, 500,000 barrels annual capacity.
Production: 480,000 barrels in 2003 (including soda).
Tours: Saturday at 1 P.M. (please call ahead for reservations); not given in winter months. The Lion tour is not handicapped-accessible.
Take-out beer: Kegs (with both the Hoff-Stevens "two-prong" and Sankey "ball" types) available Monday through Friday, 8:30 A.M. to 4 P.M.
Parking: Free on-site parking available.
Lodging in the area: Best Western East Mountain Inn, 2400 East End Boulevard, 570-822-1011; Red Roof Inn, intersection of Routes 115 and 315, 570-829-6422; Bischwind B&B in Bear Creek, on Route 115, three miles south of the Pennsylvania Turnpike, 570-472-3820.
Area attractions: *The River Commons* (570-825-1701) is a park along the Susquehanna in the center of Wilkes-Barre. This was the site of numerous skirmishes during the all-but-forgotten Yankee-Pennamite Wars, fought over land rights by Pennsylvania and Connecticut between 1769 and 1785. Historic markers dot the commons. The *Japanese Double Blossom* garden in the park is a colorful display of

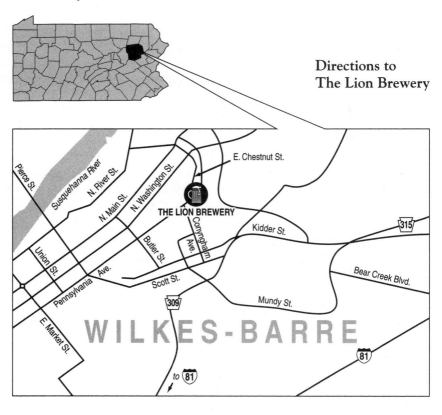

**Directions to
The Lion Brewery**

Japanese cherry trees, begonias, geraniums, and petunias. Feeling sporting? **The Wachovia Arena** (255 Highland Park Boulevard, 570-970-6700, www.wachoviaarena.com) is the home of the Wilkes-Barre Scranton Penguins (AHL) and the Wilkes-Barre Scranton Pioneers (AFL), and hosts concerts and other events as well.

Call the Luzerne County Tourist Promotion Agency (888-905-2872) or the Greater Wilkes-Barre Chamber of Commerce (570-823-2101) for more suggestions.

Other area beer sites: *Elmer Sudds* (475 East Northampton Street, 570-825-5286) is Wilkes-Barre's original beer bar. They've got some amazing beers that you will not believe you're finding at this corner bar. ***Cooper's Seafood House*** (Washington Avenue and Pine Street, Scranton, 570-346-6883) is a nationally ranked seafood restaurant with an outstanding beer selection . . . and wildly nautical architecture. It was one of the first beer bars in the area. ***Cooper's on the Waterfront*** (304 Kennedy Boulevard, Pittston, 570-654-6883), son of Cooper's Seafood House, is a comfortably plush restaurant with a very good beer list. We got a great recommendation from Leo one time: **Dukey's Café** (785 North Pennsylvania Avenue, 570-270-6718) is just down the street and has fresh-as-a-daisy Stegmaier and some really good bar food. It's not the dive it once was . . . but we still stop there. For the book, Leo also suggested the **Waterfront Bar and Grill** (670 North River Street, 570-270-6565) and the **Arena Bar and Grill** (533 Scott Street, 570-970-8903).

D. G. Yuengling and Son

**Fifth and Mahantongo Streets, Pottsville, PA 17901
(Production brewery—no tours available—
is at 310 Mill Creek Avenue, Pottsville, PA 17901)
Brewery phone: 570-622-4141
Tour information: 570-628-4890
www.yuengling.com**

Andrew Jackson was inviting all his friends to the White House when David Yuengling started brewing at his Eagle Brewery in Pottsville in 1829. The brewery burned later that year, and the new brewery opened up in 1830 on the slope of Sharps Mountain at Fifth and Mahantongo Streets. Brewing has been going on there ever since, making D. G. Yuengling and Son America's oldest brewery. The brewery is in its fifth generation of family ownership, and the sixth generation is settling nicely into the harness.

Those of you with an interest in American history may be thinking, "Did they brew during Prohibition?" Under the leadership of Frank Yuengling, who ran the brewery from 1899 through 1961, Yuengling made it through the Noble Experiment in pretty good shape. They started a dairy (Yuengling ice cream was made until 1986), opened large dance halls in Philadelphia and New York, and yes, they brewed. Yuengling invested in an expensive vacuum distillation process that made it possi-

Beers brewed: Yuengling Premium, Lord Chesterfield Ale, Dark Brewed Porter (GABF Bronze, 1987), Yuengling Traditional Lager, Light Lager, Yuengling Light, Yuengling Black & Tan (packaged blend of Porter and Premium).

ble to brew Juvo, the best-tasting near beer in Schuylkill County. Juvo outsold competitors by a large margin.

The Pick: I prefer a do-it-you self black and tan mixed from Porter and Lord Chesterfield Ale. The Chet is Yuengling's hoppiest beer and cuts through the Porter more sharply than the Premium. Get a big mug and a few bottles of each beer, and find the ratio you prefer.

When Prohibition was repealed, Yuengling was sitting pretty. The dairy business provided a fleet of refrigerated trucks and a steady cash flow, the successful near-beer business meant they had retained almost all their trained workers, and the dance halls had made them a lot of friends in big markets. On the day of Repeal, Frank turned off the vacuum distillation machine and sent a truckload of Yuengling's new Winner beer to FDR at the White House. Happy days were here again.

They didn't last forever. By the 1970s, the brewery was in trouble, operating from payroll to payroll some months as national megabrewers pushed hard to level all markets. In the end, two things saved the brewery: The dogged loyalty of Schuylkill County beer drinkers made for a steady demand that sustained the brewery on a week-to-week basis, and the American Bicentennial in 1976 raised interest in American history and made the brewery's status as America's oldest a bankable quality. There was a slow rise in sales from 1976 through the 1980s.

In 1985, when Dick Yuengling Jr. bought the brewery from his father—the traditional Yuengling family way of gaining control of the business—he felt continued pressure from the national breweries threatening to throttle his business. He also saw the rising interest in non-mainstream beer and thought there might be a way to tap that market. "I was not going to be the last Yuengling to own the brewery!" he told me once.

Dick already had one of the most varied lineups of any regional brewer. Besides the mainstream Yuengling Premium, there were the dark, roasty Celebrated Pottsville Porter and the hoppy Lord Chesterfield Ale. Dick and brewmaster Ray Norbert added Yuengling Light—"because we had to," Dick explained, "and it's a good light beer"—and Yuengling Traditional Lager, an amber-colored, somewhat more robust lager. He also pushed the brewery's history and non-national underdog appeal. A key player, David Casinelli, was hired to head sales and marketing efforts. Yuengling started to appear in Philadelphia markets.

At first it was the Yuengling Black & Tan, a premixed blend of porter and premium. People in Schuylkill and Berks Counties had been mixing Yuengling porter with premium or Lord Chesterfield for years to create a custom-made black and tan. When the NorthEast Taproom in Reading had the brewery make up premixed barrels of half porter, half

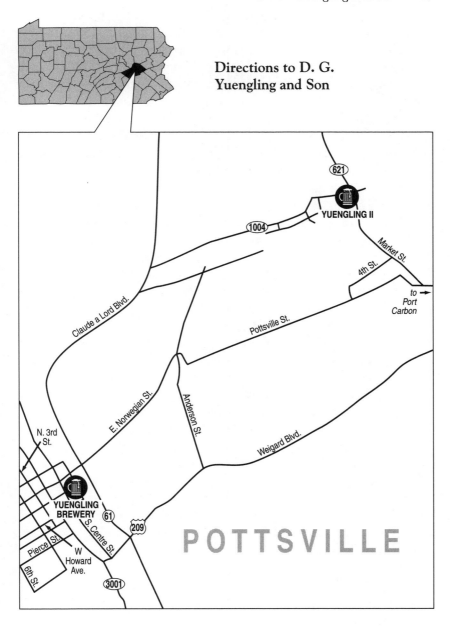

**Directions to D. G.
Yuengling and Son**

Lord Chesterfield, and sold a lot of it, the brewers saw they had a winner. They switched the mix to porter and premium, put it in a snazzy
16-ounce can, and released it on the market. "Got any Black & Tan?"
became the question every beer distributor in eastern Pennsylvania
hated to hear.

But it was Dick's next project, the Lager—a little darker, a little more flavorful, and a lot less national—that really blew the doors off the brewery. Yuengling Lager taps cropped up everywhere in southeastern Pennsylvania. The brewery went to high-gravity brewing for the first time, they put in their first expansion in decades, they went to seven days a week and two shifts . . . and they still couldn't keep up.

After years of soul-searching, Dick made the decision to build a second brewery to meet the apparently unending demand for Yuengling. The new brewery is sited about a mile away in an industrial park by a rail line—something they'd have loved to have at the original brewery—and has come online with a capacity of 1.1 million barrels.

Shortly after making that decision, he took an even bigger plunge. Stroh Brewing, trundling toward dissolution, had shut down a 1.5-million-barrel-capacity brewery in Tampa, Florida. Dick and his staff flew down and looked it over. They weighed the still-growing demand for Yuengling and all the untouched markets on the borders of Pennsylvania against the time until the new Pottsville brewery came online. A big ready-to-run brewery would solve a lot of problems, so they bought it. They hired back most of the laid-off Stroh workers—which involved working with a union for the first time in the brewery's history—and were brewing Yuengling in a few months, while work on the new brewery in Pennsylvania continued on schedule and under budget.

With all this capacity, will Yuengling cheapen the beer, sell out, lose the character that has made them an endearing success story? Fear not, loyal fans. Yuengling is committed to being a regional brewery and has no national aspirations, nor do they intend to close the original historic brewery. When I took my twenty-sixth Yuengling tour (I took my first one in 1986), the canning line was running, lager was in the brewkettle, the gift shop was busy, and a fresh keg of porter was on draft in the taproom. Success looks good on the oldest brewery in America. It appears Dick won't be the last of the Yuenglings after all.

Opened: 1829. St. Clair brewery opened August 2001.
Owner: Richard L. Yuengling Jr.; chief operating officer, David A. Casinelli.
Brewers: Pottsville/St. Clair director of brewing, Mike Brennan; Tampa director of brewing, John Houseman; brewers, James Buehler, Jennifer Yuengling-Franquet.
System: 450-barrel Enerfab brewhouse, 600,000 barrels annual capacity. (The Tampa brewery has a capacity of 1,500,000 barrels. St. Clair facility has a capacity of 1,100,000 barrels.)

Production: 1,331,878 barrels in 2003.

Tours: Monday through Friday, 10 A.M. and 1:30 P.M.; Saturday from April to December, 11 A.M., noon, and 1 P.M. This is without a doubt one of the best brewery tours in the country. Others may be more polished or more intimate, but few take you right down onto the floor of a hard-working, sizable brewery. Tour includes two complimentary beers in the uniquely handsome brewery taproom. Gift shop open Monday through Friday, 9 A.M. to 4 P.M. You can also tour the Tampa brewery (11111 North Thirtieth Street, Tampa, FL, 813-972-8529).

Take-out beer: None available.

Extras: The only special event at Yuengling is an unofficial one: the First Day of Beer Season. In upstate Pennsylvania, deer hunting is almost a religion, and most public schools have declared the Monday after Thanksgiving—the opening of deer season—a day off, since most of the male students and teachers, and a few females, don't show up anyway. Some nonhunting teachers from Reading began coming out for a brewery tour that day, and the event has grown—but not too much. After all, it is deer season!

Special considerations: Kids will enjoy Posty's birch beer in the taproom. This locally made soda is traditional and delicious, and it's a good choice for designated drivers, too. Wearing closed-toe shoes is required on the tour, which is not handicapped-accessible.

Parking: On-street parking. Don't use the church lot on the far side of the street, or you will be ticketed or towed.

Lodging in the area: Quality Hotel, 100 South Center Street, 570-622-4600; River Inn, Route 61, south of Pottsville, 570-385-2407; The Stone House B&B, 16 Dock Street, Schuylkill Haven, 570-385-2115.

Area attractions: Go on up Mahantongo Street from the Yuengling brewery to the *Yuengling Mansion* (570-622-2788), the family's restored Victorian-era home, for a short but interesting self-guided tour. Then hit the road for other attractions. Jim Thorpe, Pennsylvania, named for the famous American Indian athlete, has a restored Victorian-era downtown, with shops and taverns, that's great for an afternoon stroll. You'll also find an extensive model train layout (41 Susquehanna Street, 570-325-2248) and whitewater rafting expeditions (*Pocono Whitewater Rafting,* 800-944-8392). Tour coal baron *Asa Parker's Victorian mansion* (570-325-3229), which is on the hill overlooking downtown. Son Harry's adjacent mansion is open as a B&B (570-325-8566). For the more outdoorsy types, the *Hawk Mountain Sanctuary* (east of Drehersville on Hawk Mountain Road,

610-756-6961) is located at the convergence of the autumn migration routes of numerous raptors. The fall months offer unparalleled views of hundreds of hawks, eagles, and other birds of prey.

Other area beer sites: *The Brass Tap* (112 East Norwegian Street, 570-622-9155) is the brewery's unofficial tied house in Pottsville, a place where the Yuenglings taste as fresh as at the brewery. *Hubert's Inn* (570-385-3613) has good, hearty Pennsylvania hotel food and a nice carved wood backbar. You'll find it on the left side of Route 183 coming into Cressona from Pottsville. *The Kempton Hotel* (610-756-6588), across from the feed mill in Kempton, is a real find. Three ceiling murals painted by talented local artists depict Kempton history, U.S. history, and the life of Christ. The snappy bartenders serve brilliantly fresh Yuengling and good regional food.

Ales and Lagers

If you're going to go to the breweries in this book, you'll have to know how to talk shop with the bartenders and tour guides and not embarrass yourself on the tour. First off, beer is any fermented beverage made from malted barley, usually with an addition of hops. The two main types of beer are ales and lagers.

What's the difference between the two? It's quite simple: two different yeasts. These have a number of small differences, the most important of which is that the optimum temperature for fermentation and aging is higher for ale yeasts (in the 60s F) than for lager yeasts (in the 40s F). That's more than just a thermostat setting. The warmer operating temperature of ale yeast encourages a faster, more vigorous fermentation that creates aromatic compounds known as phenols and esters. These can give ale-fermented beers aromas such as melon, banana, raisin, clove, and vanilla. (I call these aromas "alefruit.")

On the other hand, the cooler lager fermentation produces a very clean aroma and flavor palette. Lagers generally have purer malt and hops characteristics. A lager brewer will tell you that there's nowhere to hide when you make lager beer; the unadorned nature of the beer makes flaws stand out immediately.

I like to think of the two yeasts in terms of jungles and pine forests. Warm ale fermentations are like lush jungles—exotic arrays of flavors, splendid in their diversity. By comparison, cold lager fermentations are more like northern pine forests—intense, focused, and pure.

Among small brewers in America, ale brewers outnumber lager brewers by more than ten to one. Given that lagers are by far the most popular beers in the world, how did this come to be? Tom Pastorius of Penn Brewing put it quite simply: "More ale is being made because it's cheaper, easier, and more flexible." Hard words, perhaps, but the facts bear them out.

After lagers are fermented, they undergo an extended aging period of at least three weeks at low temperatures. The cooling and the tank time required add energy costs and decrease turnover. In the same amount of time, it would be possible to put twice as much ale through those tanks. Add the energy and labor costs of the more complicated

21

decoction brewing process used for lagers, and you wind up with a product that costs substantially more to brew than ales but has to be priced the same. No wonder there are more ale brewers!

When it comes to lager, Pennsylvania has been blessed with some real pros. The five surviving regional brewers are all about lagers, but we also have one of the greatest concentrations of small lager brewers in the country. Stoudt's was built on lagers, Victory makes excellent classic examples, and Penn founded their business squarely on their pilsner, dark, and gold lagers. Lancaster and Legacy both make great pilsners, Erie brews their Presque Isle Pilsner, and even little Bube's proudly brews a lager in tribute to their heritage. By any measure, these breweries include some of the very best lager brewers in the country. How did we get so lucky?

In a word, ethnicity. It's no coincidence that the areas of the United States where old brewers survived and new lager brewers sprang up are those that welcomed vast numbers of German, Scandinavian, and Eastern European immigrants. Where those lager lovers settled—Pennsylvania, upstate New York, Wisconsin, and Minnesota—is where lager brewing thrives today.

American beer enthusiasts are slowly coming around to micro-brewed lagers. Carol Stoudt attributed their hesitation to a megabrew backlash: "People who have had nothing but bland lagers for years want the extremes: heavy-handed hops, fruit beers, even smoked beers. As their palates become more sophisticated, they'll come around to appreciate the subtleties of a good lager beer." If you haven't had some of Pennsylvania's fine fresh lager beers, be sure to put one or more of these brewers on your list. Put a little sophistication on your palate!

Philadelphia

W. C. Fields wrote his own tongue-in-cheek epitaph: "On the whole, I'd rather be in Philadelphia." Well, me too, W. C. When my wife and I moved to Bucks County in 1991, we mostly stayed out of Philadelphia. What with the city's poor financial condition, the lingering air of disaster from the MOVE battle in which the city bombed one of its own neighborhoods, and the One Meridian Plaza skyscraper fire less than two months after we got there, there didn't seem to be any good reasons to go.

I've learned differently, and I have Ed Rendell to thank. The vibrancy that was missing for years is back, thanks largely to Fast Eddie. When he took office as mayor in 1992, the former district attorney began a whirlwind of action reminiscent of FDR's 100 Days. His landslide reelection gave the city's seal of approval to his work. After two terms, the baton was passed to longtime Philly politician John Street just as the last long-standing remnants of the skyscraper fire were finally cleared away. Rendell has gone on to become governor of Pennsylvania (the first Philadelphia mayor to do so since 1914), but his stamp remains on the city.

Rendell was well known as an avid fan of Philly's major contribution to American fare, the cheesesteak. Local papers printed plenty of photos showing his big happy mouth wrapped around these hot, greasy beauties. Check out some classics at Pat's Steaks or Gino's, right across from each other at Ninth and Passayunk. Another well-known politician, Bill Clinton, stood between the two places during a rally, alternately munching a cheese steak each—safe from politics and not a bad lunch! The city's other staple, the soft pretzel, is available all over and should be eaten with a good squirt of yellow mustard.

Philadelphia is one of the great restaurant centers of the United States. Proprietor-chef Georges Perrier's Le Bec Fin (1523 Walnut Street) is one of the best restaurants anywhere in the United States, and the prix fixe lunch is a major bargain. You'll find all kinds of food in the city. There's authentically *ausgezeichnet*—excellent—German cooking at the Blüe Ox Brauhaus (7980 Oxford Avenue in Northeast Philly), wonderful Persian cuisine at Roya (1823 Sansom Street), and even stylish Malaysian food at Penang (117 North Tenth Street). You can also sample American Colonial fare from the city's past at City Tavern, a restored historic site with a good restaurant and costumed waitstaff (138 South Second Street).

But for the beer lover, Philadelphia has three treasures, restaurants devoted to Belgian beer. **Bridgid's** (726 North Twenty-fourth Street, near the art museum) is a small, warmly welcoming bistro. It has an impressive cellar of vintage beers, draft beers, and a very reasonably priced menu of delicious entrées and desserts. **Eulogy** (136 Chestnut Street), a relative newcomer in Old City, caught on fast with a good menu and beer list right out of the gate. Finally, **Monk's Café** (264 South Sixteenth Street) is one of the very best beer bars in America, with a bunch of Belgian taps (including their own Belgian-brewed Monk's Sour Ale) and a ridiculous stack of bottled Belgian beers aging in the cellar. The must-have dishes are mussels steamed in Belgian beers such as Rodenbach or *gueuze* lambic, served with *frites* and delicious French rolls, and steak marinated in Trappist ale. Get on the mailing list for Monk's fabulous, extreme monthly beer dinners; beers make their American debut, sometimes their world debut, at these dinners, usually attended by the brewers in question.

But you didn't come to Philadelphia just to drink beer and eat! This is the heart of American independence, home of the Liberty Bell and Benjamin Franklin, and the birthplace of the Declaration of Independence and the Constitution. At **Independence National Historical Park** (215-597-8974), visit Carpenter's Hall, Congress Hall, Independence Hall, Franklin Court, and the Liberty Bell Pavilion. The huge new **National Constitution Center** (in the block between Arch and Race Streets and Fifth and Sixth Streets, 866-917-1787) has interactive exhibits and Signers Hall, with lifesize statues of the founding fathers for photo opportunities. The **Betsy Ross House** (239 Arch Street) has been restored as a working-class house of the Colonial period. **Christ Church** (Second and Church Streets) contains William Penn's baptismal font and was the church of fifteen Declaration signers. Benjamin Franklin and four other signers are buried in the Christ Church burial ground at Fifth and Arch Streets.

Other famous people lived in Philadelphia as well. The peripatetic Edgar Allan Poe lived at 532 North Seventh Street for a year. You can tour the house, and a library and audiovisual program are next door. Louisa May Alcott was born in Germantown; visit the **Germantown Historical Society**'s museum (5501 Germantown Avenue). At the **National Shrine of St. John Neumann** (Fifth and Girard Streets), the saint's remains can be viewed in a glass casket under the main altar.

Philadelphia also has a number of fine museums. The **Philadelphia Museum of Art** (215-763-8100), at the end of the Benjamin Franklin Parkway, houses one of the world's best collections. And yes, that's where Sylvester Stallone did his dance in *Rocky*. Just down the parkway is the **Franklin Institute Science Museum,** with an extensive display of hands-on science exhibits. You could easily spend a day in these two museums, but I would also send you down to the river to see the **Independence Seaport Museum** (Penn's Landing, 215-925-5439). You can visit this museum of Philadelphia's maritime heritage and crawl around the **USS Becuna,** a World War II–era submarine, and the **USS Olympia,** Admiral Dewey's flagship from the Spanish-American War.

Philadelphia hosts a number of annual events, starting on January 1 with the **Mummers Parade,** a unique folk-art festival put on by associations similar to the Mardi Gras "crews" in New Orleans. The elaborate feathered outfits and string bands (mostly banjos and saxophones) are impossible to describe concisely. Go, freeze, enjoy. The **Philadelphia Flower Show** draws flower fanciers to the Convention Center in early March. Later in the month, **The Book and The Cook Festival** brings chefs and cookbook authors from around the world for a week of fantastic food events, including a mass tutored tasting by beer writer Michael Jackson. May brings the **Dad Vail Regatta** on the Schuylkill, a happy, exciting mob scene.

There's so much more. Call the Philadelphia Convention and Visitor Center (800-537-7676) and ask for the full package of travel information. You'll have a great time. And don't forget the cheesesteaks!

More and more great beer bars have spread across the city, and you wouldn't want to miss any of them. Likewise, it's easier to have all the attractions and lodging suggestions in one list. So for this edition, I have decided to consolidate **Lodging, Area attractions,** and **Other area beer sites** sections for Philadelphia. My thanks to Rich Pawlak and Jack Curtin for their suggestions (and sometimes persistent nagging) on Philadelphia bars.

Lodging in the area: Holiday Inn City Line, 4100 Presidential Boule-
vard, 215-477-0200; Comfort Inn, 100 North Christopher Columbus
Boulevard, 215-627-7900; Holiday Inn Independence Mall, 400
Arch Street, 800-THE-BELL; Penn's View Inn (a historic hotel in a
building dating from 1828), 14 North Front Street, 215-922-7600;
Abigail Adams B&B, 1208 Walnut Street, 215-546-7336; The Belle-
vue (if you want to shoot the works, this is the place to do it), Broad
Street between Walnut Street and Locust Street, 215-893-1776;
Chestnut Hill Hotel, 8229 Germantown Avenue, 215-242-5905.

Area attractions: Independence Mall and all the historic buildings and
exhibits are described in the introduction to this section. If you're
looking for some "real Philly," head down to the open-air **Ninth
Street Market,** also called the Italian Market, which runs south
from the 700 block of Ninth Street. The market is open Monday
through Saturday mornings, starting around 8 A.M. You can find
clothing, meat, great Italian cheeses, cookware, olives, pastries,
fresh fish, and produce—but don't touch the produce; it's a market
tradition that the seller picks it for you. **South Street** is Philly's
answer to Greenwich Village. Take some time to walk around and
shop, then maybe stop over at the **Dark Horse** (215-928-9307) for
its great single malt and tap beer selection, or **Bridget Foy's** (215-
922-1813), an excellent place to sip a cool beer and people-watch.
Both are on Headhouse Square at Second and South.

If you're at the big, beautiful fountain at Logan Circle on the
Benjamin Franklin Parkway, it's only a ten-minute walk to the
Philadelphia Museum of Art (Twenty-sixth Street on the Parkway,
215-763-8100), exhibiting the artwork of Renoir, Monet, Cezanne,
Van Gogh, Rubens, and many others; the **Franklin Institute Sci-
ence Museum** (Twentieth Street and Benjamin Franklin Parkway,
215-448-1200); the **Please Touch Museum** (210 North Twenty-
first Street, 215-963-0667), the very popular children's science
museum; and the **Rodin Museum** (Benjamin Franklin Parkway and
Twenty-second Street, 215-763-8100), with the largest collection of
Rodin originals outside of Paris. You're also not far from one of
Philadelphia's odder museums, the **Mütter Museum** (19 South
Twenty-second Street, 215-563-3737) of the College of Physicians
of Philadelphia, with its displays of disease, genetic oddities, and
medical grotesqueries. It's as unsettling as it sounds; use your judg-
ment about visiting! Following the Benjamin Franklin Parkway past
the art museum will lead you into **Fairmount Park,** Philly's
immense greenway. There you'll find **Boathouse Row,** the Victorian

boathouses of the city's sculling teams, decorated with strung lights that sparkle across the Schuylkill. Also in the park are the restored Fairmount homes (215-684-7922), including **Strawberry Mansion,** the largest of the homes, and **Cedar Grove,** an eighteenth-century Quaker farmhouse. If you go straight across the Schuylkill on Girard Avenue, you will see the signs for the **Philadelphia Zoo** (3400 Girard Avenue, 215-243-1100), which features a children's zoo, a newly rebuilt primate house, and a captive balloon for sightseeing.

In the heart of the city stands **City Hall** (215-686-2840), unmistakable with its 37-foot statue of William Penn on the top. You can tour this impressive "hollow square" building for free; ninety-minute tours leave at 12:30 P.M. on weekdays, and there are tower tours every fifteen minutes. You can also walk down to the **Reading Terminal Market** at Twelfth and Filbert Streets, the other of Philadelphia's great markets, a bit touristy but no less real for that, and studded with great little restaurants that cook with the fresh food from the market. If you want something a bit more exotic, Philly's **Chinatown** wraps around the Convention Center north of the market.

Main Street, Manayunk, is a very happening strip of shops, bars, and restaurants, pleasant to stop in or stroll along, and Manayunk Brewing is right on it. Just wander on down Main Street, shopping, eating, and drinking as you go. **Rails to Trails** goes right past the back of the brewpub on its way from the Art Museum all the way out to Valley Forge National Historical Park. Call 215-985-9393 for information on the trail; punch up www.dcnr.state.pa.us/rails/index for an excellent guide to all of the state's rail-trails.

Other area beer sites:

Northeast Philadelphia. The **Grey Lodge Pub** (6235 Frankford Avenue, 215-624-2969) is still the only real beer bar in Northeast Philly. Its pleasantly eccentric owner, Scoats, has taken the G-Lodge from a somewhat run-down boozer to a destination bar that recently had a 360-degree photo of its elaborate tile-mosaic men's room in the *Philadelphia Inquirer.* The G-Lodge has a constantly changing tap menu, cask ale every day, and a bottle collection that ranges from 40s of Old Milwaukee to 750s of high-end lambics (as well as an excellent whisky selection picked out by yours truly). But what put the Grey Lodge on the map is Friday the Firkinteenth, a cask ale festival that occurs every Friday the thirteenth, when Scoats puts up to fifteen casks of locally brewed real ale up on the bar, and the place just goes mad for six hours. It's all about great beer in a comfortable, completely unpretentious neighborhood bar setting. The **Blüe Ox**

Brauhaus (7980 Oxford Avenue, 215-728-9440) serves seriously authentic and delicious German and Swiss food, matching it with great German tap beers and a nice assortment of bottles. Ray Swerdlow's *Six Pack Store* (7015 Roosevelt Boulevard, 215-338-6384) is one of the few bottle shops in town and has a great selection of the big East European lagers I love; they recently added three taps for growler sales.

Northern Liberties. You can easily walk to six good bars in this hot neighborhood. Start in the southwest corner at *Abbaye* (Third and Fairmount Streets, 215-940-1222), which is kind of a combination of Bridgid's, Monk's Café, and Standard Tap. The taps are quite good, and usually have something out of the ordinary, and the food is outstanding; this is where we went to celebrate my wife's promotion and my signing the deal on this book. Walk north one block on North Third to . . . *North Third* (801 North Third Street, 215-413-3666). If the weather's pleasant, you'll want to eat out on the sidewalk, with the trees and the torches and all. Inside, it's very arty, and the beer's well chosen, with good taps and a solid Belgian bottle selection. The food's great and the vibe's cool. If you need to walk off that dinner, head up to Poplar Street and hang a left, passing through increasingly gentrified residential neighborhoods to the rough, ready, and beer-hip *Ministry of Information* (447 Poplar Street, 215-925-0999), where it's loud and loose. If you're looking for another of Philly's best, take a right on Poplar instead and walk down to *Standard Tap* (at the corner of Poplar and North Second Streets, 215-238-0630). If you look down American Street as you walk down Poplar, you'll see the old Ortlieb brewery, also the site of the former *Poor Henry*'s brewpub and what is thought to be the site of the first lager brewery in America. You'll find only local and regional draft beers at Standard Tap (plus a full bar); partner William Reed's kind of a gearhead when it comes to draft beer systems, and this is probably the best draft system in the city. The food is fully up to the quality of the beer; try the fried smelts with a glass of Sly Fox O'Reilly's Stout while you're sitting out on the upstairs deck on a cool evening. From here you can walk down to Brown and take a left to the *Druid's Keep* (149 Brown Street, 215-413-0455), a secluded, rough gem of a corner neighborhood taproom with good beers on tap and in bottle, and a small bar where you can settle in to enjoy them. The Keep is a great place to slip off to when things get a little crazy at Standard Tap. Walk back to Second, turn left, and **700** (700 North Second Street, 215-413-3181) is only a block away, with a very select assortment of great bottled beers and usually at least one rare beer on tap as well. This is not your usual geek bar; anyone might be drinking good beer here, and there's a good selection of offbeat liquor as well.

Old City. **The Plough and the Stars** (123 Chestnut Street, 215-733-0300) is an upscale Irish pub with delicious food and just the beers you'd expect, plus a nice assortment of Irish whiskeys. **Eulogy** (136 Chestnut Street) was described earlier (see page 24). **Sugar Mom's Church Street Lounge** (225 Church Street, well back from the alley and downstairs, 215-925-8219) has slipped a bit from its former glory, but you'll still find a good tap array and some surprising bottles at this subterranean saloon. The **Khyber Pass** has reopened at 56 South Second Street (215-238-5888), one of the city's oldest bars and a longtime friend of good beer, with a backbar that dates from the 1876 Centennial Exposition in Philadelphia. **City Tavern** (138 South Second Street, 215-413-1443) is a meticulously re-created historic site with a good restaurant and costumed waitstaff serving good beer (including two special brews from Yards that re-create Colonial-era recipes) and excellent food, but be prepared to pay for it. Sly Fox brewer Brian O'Reilly put in a word for the **Race Street Café** (208 Race Street, 215-574-0296), and what I've heard indicates he's probably right; it's on my list to visit.

Fairmount/Art Museum. Park once (likely in the big lot at Twenty-third Street and Fairmount Avenue) and visit all these places: **Bridgid's** (726 North Twenty-fourth Street) was described earlier (see page 24). **London Grill** (2301 Fairmount Avenue, 215-978-4545) is famous for its bar menu; it's a bit more upscale, but still quite beer-friendly. **Rembrandt's** (741 North Twenty-third Street, 215-763-2228) is similar to the London Grill, but cozier, much more intimate; the beer selection's not huge, but it's adequate. **Bishop's Collar** (2349 Fairmount Avenue, 215-765-1616) is laid-back and well beered, with an old marble floor and a rotating tap selection. **Jack's Firehouse** (2128 Fairmont Avenue, 215-232-9000) is in here not because it's a very cool bar in an old firehouse, or because of Jack McDaniels's great grilled menu, but because it has the best selection of bourbon in town (and some pretty good beers for a chaser).

Center City. **McGillin's Old Ale House** (1310 Drury Lane, 215-735-4515) is Philly's oldest bar, open and owned by the same family since 1861, a great place to have a beer with a buddy or your spouse, and they have some really good stuff on tap. Just down the alley is a great German bar and restaurant, **Ludwig's Garten** (1315 Sansom Street, 215-985-1525), where lagers rule: more than twenty-five taps of gorgeously German beer and tons of German bottles. **McGlinchey's** (259 South Fifteen Street, 215-735-1259) may not look like much— one big room dominated by a big U-shaped bar, and with pretty plain hand-lettered signs—but the people are real, and it has the cheapest prices for good beers in town. When you stop to visit **Nodding Head,** make a little left at the foot of the stairs and get some fresh shellfish and stout at the **Sansom Street Oyster House** (1516 Sansom Street, 215-567-7683), a Philadelphia institution . . . without the inertia and poor service that often go with that classification. And don't miss the bars belonging to the godfathers of Nodding Head. **Fergie's** (1214 Sansom Street, 215-928-8118) is the bar where Fergus Carey himself runs a square house and pulls one of the finest jars of Guinness in the city (and an excellent Yards ESA as well). Fergie is partnered in **Monk's Café** (264 South Sixteenth Street, 215-545-7005) with the beer genius and Burgundian bon vivant Tom Peters, a man who has brought much incredibly good beer to Philadelphia. Go see what Monk's has on tap today, and eat some mussels! It's one of America's foremost beer bars. One of the better Irish pubs in the city, a favorite of my *Malt Advocate* publisher, **The Black Sheep** (247 South Seventeenth Street, 215-545-9473) is just around the block; stop in for a jar of Guinness. Probably the best bottle shop in the area is **The Foodery** (Tenth and Pine Streets, 215-928-1111), with hundreds of different bottles, including some fairly rare and vintage stuff. That's "vintage," not "old"; these beers are aged on purpose, like wines. Bring your wallet and go crazy.

Rittenhouse Square Area. A new place, **Tria** (123 South Eighteenth Street, 215-972-8742), is centered around three "fermentables": beer, wine, and cheese. Neat idea, and beer definitely does not take a backseat to either of the other two. Bring your wallet and prepare to enjoy yourself. There are two Irish pubs, the **Irish Bards** (215-569-9585) and the **Irish Pub** (215-568-5603), practically side by side at Twentieth and Walnut Streets. Take your pick. The Bards probably has a better jar of Guinness, but the Pub's food seems better to me.

Manayunk. Dawson Street Pub (100 Dawson Street, 215-482-5677), tucked way back along the tracks, is one of the city's great unknown bars but is definitely worth hunting for, with cask ale on every day and a deep bottle selection. Try the vegetarian chili. The **Flat Rock Saloon** (4301 Main Street, 215-483-3722) has Manayunk's biggest bottled beer selection.

Other Neighborhoods. McMenamin's Tavern (7170 Germantown Avenue, Mount Airy, 215-247-9920) is a great neighborhood bar with taps you won't find elsewhere in the city, a talented chef, and a very friendly bunch of regulars. **Ten Stone** (Twenty-first and South Streets, 215-735-9939) gets a really European look and feel from thick walls and deep-set windows, but there are plenty of American craft beers on tap and even more in bottles. It's a varied crowd and everyone's friendly—an instantly comfortable place. You could be on your way to the Italian Market when you stop at **For Pete's Sake** (900 South Front Street, 215-462-2230), a friendly corner bar with an Irish feel and a full array of Irish whiskeys, all the way up to the phenomenal Redbreast, but also with plenty of beer surprises, like draft Chimay White. **O'Neal's Pub** (611 South Third Street, 215-574-9495) is giving good beer a serious try; why not give them a try? William Reed and Paul Kimport's second project is **Johnny Brenda's** (1201 Frankford Avenue, 215-739-9684), a real dive bar that has been turned into . . . a great dive bar, with clean floors and great beer and a Mediterranean menu that has proved incredibly popular. The **White Dog Café** (3420 Sansom Street, 215-386-9224) was one of the city's first bars to serve good beer, and it still has good beer, well-made food, and a commitment to liberal causes and education that is admirable in a restaurant and bar.

Nodding Head Brewery and Restaurant

**1516 Sansom Street, upstairs,
Philadelphia, PA 19102
215-569-9525**

The buzz was on in Philly's beer culture for months after the Samuel Adams Brew House quietly closed in May 1999. Tom Peters and Fergus Carey, owners of Monk's Café, were going to buy it and open a brewpub, but it didn't happen, Tom and Fergie didn't say a word, and the buzz chased itself till it wore out. Then suddenly the word was out: Nodding Head.

Owners Curt Decker and Barbara Thomas (Tom Peters's wife) ripped out the old extract brewhouse and put in a specially designed, very compact JV NorthWest brewhouse. Large parts of the engineering were done by brewer Brandon Greenwood. Brandon had brewed in Philadelphia at Red Bell and at Yards, and he has a strong technical background with a degree from Herriot-Watt, a famed Scottish brewing school. Now he had a brewery of his own, and the curiosity about what he would do was intense.

So was the disappointment when those first beers came out at an opening that may have been somewhat rushed; they were largely undistinguished. Greenwood is, as always, painfully honest about them. "We opened with the first three beers I made at this brewery," he recalled. "Was I happy? No. Was it necessary? Yes. Was it a good thing to do, in retrospect? No. But by the end of that first year, I had a pretty good idea of what our customers really wanted."

It turned out that what his customers wanted was tasty session beers, stuff that had real flavor to it, but low enough in alcohol that they could have three. That suited Greenwood and Decker just fine. "I am taken with low-gravity brewing," Greenwood said. "It's harder, but who'd have thought I'd have to make seven batches of Berliner Weisse in a summer? And it makes sense, too. If I'm selling 9 percent beer, how many of those can a 115-pound woman drink? How many will she buy?"

These low-alcohol session beers are not, however, usually the beers that get the geeks going. Decker sees that as a problem and Nodding Head as the solution. "The beers that get the attention from everyone, from guys like you, are the big psycho beers," he said. "That's not good. We're trying to hold the line here. I want to bring the Yuengling Lager drinkers in and say, 'Taste this,' and hear them say 'Wow!'" He laughed. "And I only need about 1 percent of them!"

He's getting them. Nodding Head is firmly committed to being a brewpub of and for Center City. "Most of the people in here are city dwellers, and most of them are not beer geeks," Greenwood said. The brewery was running at near capacity at the time, and he and Decker were both pleased. Nodding Head is not about trying to shock your

Beers brewed: Year-round: Grog (GABF Gold, 2002; RAF Silver, 2003), 700 Level Ale. Seasonals: Ich Bin Ein Berliner Weisse (GABF Silver, 2003, 2004), BPA, 3C Double IPA, Monkey Knife Fight, 60 Shilling (GABF Silver, 2003), Chocolate Stout, Sledwrecker Winter Ale, Pilsner (GABF Bronze, 2002), Abbey Normal.

The Pick: Grog does it for me. This is the quintessential session beer, and the fruits of Brandon's obsession: tasty stuff that you can keep drinking and still make a political argument that will at least befuddle your opponent, if not convince him. Great pub beer.

**Directions to Nodding Head
Brewery and Restaurant**

taste buds; it's about well-made, drinkable beer that people like to stay and drink a few pints—a very British model, in some ways.

They have some British-style beers, too, like the popular (and medal-draped) Grog and the 60 Shilling Ale that current brewer Gordon Grubb came up with when he was Greenwood's assistant. But that's not all, by any means. There's the aforementioned Ich Bin Ein Berliner Weisse, the popular 700 Level Ale (a tribute to the cheap seats at the now-demolished Veterans Stadium), the innovative and intriguing Monkey Knife Fight lemongrass-spiced lager, and Greenwood's bow to the geeks, the crushing 3C Double IPA.

Decker is slowly, carefully looking for just the right location for another Nodding Head. "We don't need to open a second place," explains Decker. "If possible, if the neighborhood and the space allow it, we'd like to open a production brewery with a taproom. We're curious; we want to see if we can sell our beer on the street. Selling it in a brewpub is a controlled situation. But how will it sell in a bar, when they can drink your beer or Victory or Yards? It's something we want to find out, a little bit of an ego thing; we want to satisfy ourselves."

The slow, deliberate pace of the search eventually led Greenwood to accept an offer when The Lion approached him with the brewmaster job. Grubb has slipped right into his shoes, and not much has changed in the brewery.

If you were wondering, Nodding Head, which sounds so very British-pub-like, is actually very American; it's a reference to the bobble-head dolls that you see everywhere these days. An assortment is building at the bar, and anyone who donates one that's new to the collection gets a free pint. Get a pint of Grog or Monkey Knife Fight one way or another and you'll be doing some head-nodding yourself: Yes, yes, yes, I'll have another. Sounds like a session to me.

Opened: December 1999.
Owners: Curt Decker, Barbara Thomas.
Brewer: Gordon Grubb.
System: 7-barrel JV NorthWest brewhouse, 750 barrels annual capacity.
Production: 650 barrels in 2003.
Brewpub hours: 11 A.M. to 2 A.M. daily.
Tours: By appointment.
Take-out beer: Not available.
Food: Expect anything from game dishes to a full vegan section in the menu. The selections range all the way from salads and sandwiches to full-bore entrées. Call about the weekend brunch.
Extras: Full liquor license. Live music for special occasions (call for schedule). Dartboards.
Special considerations: Kids welcome. There is a cigar-smoking area. Vegetarian meals available.
Parking: On-street parking is dicey at best. There is a parking garage across the street (Fifteenth and Sansom Streets); expect to pay Center City rates.

Yards Brewing Company

**2439 Amber Street (in the rear, on Martha Street),
Philadelphia, PA 19128
215-482-9109
www.yardsbrewing.com**

Yards Brewing Company is a classic microbrewery story. Two friends, Tom Kehoe and Jon Bovit, started homebrewing together at Western Maryland University and discovered a knack and a love for it. They thought about brewing, then they considered what they were in college for . . . and the next thing you know they're working in a tiny brewhouse tucked into a tiny, back-alley space and going to beer festivals to get their name out there.

That is when I met Jon and Tom, back in 1995, when I was starting out as a beer writer. I was wandering through a fest, writing notes, when a cloud of East Kent Goldings hops aroma enveloped my head and drew me into the Yards booth. WOW! How did they do that? Turns out, they put a little cloth bag full of Goldings—a hops pocket—into each keg. This extra little step (which is a pain in the neck when it comes to cleaning kegs) keeps the beer dry-hopped right up to the moment each pint is dispensed. It's traditional but labor-intensive.

That respect for tradition, regardless of the effort required, characterizes Yards brewing. Their first non-British beer was a saison, a Belgian farmhouse ale with odd fermentation requirements. Yards is one of the foremost Pennsylvania brewers of "real ale," cask-conditioned ales that must be racked into special kegs and cellared at the serving tavern until it is ready to serve (and Tom went out to the bars to make sure they were doing it right). The Love Stout is brewed with whole oysters (fresh from the Italian Market, about 125 per batch), not because of the brine or the meat, but because English brewers used to boil oyster shells in the beer for the calcium salts. It's hard work, but it's paying off.

Beer geeks caught on to Yards first and spread the word. Customers found the ESA (Extra Special

Beers brewed: Year-round: Yards ESA (Extra Special Ale), Philadelphia Pale Ale, India Pale Ale, General Washington's Tavern Porter, Thomas Jefferson's Tavern Ale. Seasonals: Old Bartholomew, Saison, PYNK, Love Stout, Trubbel de Yards.

Ale) surprisingly approachable, and many had their first beer from a handpump because of it. The Saison became a very popular local summer beer. Yards quickly maxed out the brewing capacity of its site and moved into new digs in the back of a Pennsylvania Liquor Control Board warehouse in Manayunk. Brewing sometimes makes for strange bedfellows.

That lasted for a while, longer than the original partnership. Bovit left the company, and Tom took on new partners, Bill Barton and his wife, Nancy. After adding a bottling line and a few new beers, they needed space again, and this time Bill was determined to have a space they owned. That space turned out to be a former brewery in the Kensington neighborhood, the old Weisbrod and Hess Brewery—"The Oriental Brewery," as it was known.

They now have a big 25-barrel brewkettle, though it's still insulated with firebrick ("Things just weren't right without the bricks," Kehoe said)

The Pick: I love all these beers. The ESA has been one of my favorites from the first day I tasted it. It is a beautiful example of how a beer can be very hoppy without being overwhelmingly bitter. The hop aroma is outstanding and Brit to the core, the slippery fullness of the malt body is sensually delighting, and the unabashed fruitiness of the yeast is enough to make you laugh out loud with pleasure. A day spent with friends eating good food and drinking this beer will be one you remember for years. And that Philly Pale Ale . . . WHOAAA!!!

and heated by direct gas fire. A new bottling line gives much better quality in the bottling. The building was somewhat decrepit looking at first but has cleaned up nicely; like all old breweries, it was built solid as a rock. There is a huge hall and tasting room on the second floor that hosts a variety of events throughout the year, including the annual Valentine's Day oyster feast, when the oysters from the Love Stout are shucked and eaten—funny how an oyster tastes after boiling for an hour in dark stout wort.

ESA is still the brewery's signature beer, but Yards has taken a few swings at a "mass-market" beer. Mass-market for Yards, that is. The first was Brawler, a well-hopped bitter meant to be dispensed on nitrogen. It didn't translate too well. The next was Premium, a crisp ale with lager hops that was then retuned as a British-style "ordinary bitter." It just wasn't extraordinary. Then came Philadelphia Pale Ale, but it was a bit heavy for a mass-market beer.

It was the latest tweak to Philadelphia Pale Ale that was a shocker. They lightened it up by substituting some pilsner malt for the classic English malt, and threw in some spicy American hops. I'm not kidding, for a month serious Philadelphia beer lovers greeted each other like this: "Hey! Have you tried—" "The new Philly Pale?" Both together: "WHOAAA!!!" I remember the first pint I had, at the Standard Tap. There were five beers on tap that I'd been waiting to try, but I had the

Directions to Yards Brewing Company

Philly Pale first and just stuck with it. I didn't want to drink anything else. Yards has got a serious winner on their hands.

But some things haven't changed. Yards still uses open fermenters, still does cask ale, still does the big St. Bart's barleywine every winter. Best of all, Tom Kehoe still gets out to the bars where the beer is served, making sure it's properly served and that people understand what they're drinking.

Opened: March 1995.
Owners: Tom Kehoe, Bill Barton.
Brewers: Josh Irvine, Joe Beddia, Tom Kehoe.
System: 25-barrel brewhouse (designed by Kehoe, locally fabricated), 9,000 barrels annual capacity.
Production: 6,000 barrels estimated in 2004.
Tours: Fridays by appointment, noon to 4 P.M.; Saturdays, noon to 3 P.M. You're advised to call ahead.
Take-out beer: Kegs (call for availability), cases.
Special considerations: Kids welcome. Handicapped-accessible. Dog-friendly.
Parking: Plenty of off-street parking.

Red Bell Brewing Company

**1 Wachovia Center,
Broad and Pattison Streets,
Philadelphia, PA 19148
215-235-2460**

Red Bell has had a tempestuous history. At the beginning, in 1993, Red Bell splashed I-95 with billboards to jump-start its brand. The beer, however, contract-brewed at The Lion, was a little too much for the mainstream beer drinker, yet way too little for the beer geek. There were also some small production problems with the beer. As a result, Red Bell lost a lot of the free goodwill that a new brewery usually gets from the local market. It certainly didn't help when company president

Jim Bell admitted in an interview with the local press that he didn't really like beer and preferred grape juice.

Red Bell opened their brewery at Thirty-first and Jefferson, in the old F. A. Poth brewery, a casualty of Prohibition. This would be Red Bell's best shot at success. They had a state-of-the-art small brewery, a string of talented brewers (Nodding Head's Brandon Greenwood and Iron Hill's Bob Barrar both brewed here), and plenty of cash. Red Bell edged up toward 10,000 barrels a year in sales.

The brewpub opened in what was then the Core States Center, later to be the unfortunately named First Union Center, and now the Wachovia Center. It was a high-profile launch—one of the few press conferences I've actually attended—and we sampled the chili and the roast beef sandwiches that made up most of the menu. The brewpub would be open for business during "appropriate" events at the center—i.e., *not* during Disney on Ice, when little Jenny must not see Daddy and Mommy drinking Black Cherry Stout. The pub is popular during those appropriate events; I was at a Wings lacrosse game at the center and saw the drinkers four-deep around the bar.

What wasn't made clear at the time was that the 10-barrel Newlands system at the brewpub was not really meant to supply the pub's entire needs; that would be supplemented by kegged beer from the mother ship at Thirty-first and Jefferson. This was a plan that would have repercussions that continue to this day.

At about the same time, Red Bell was in a deal with a major local investor to open a Red Bell brewpub in October 1998 in the Reading Terminal Headhouse building at Twelfth and Filbert Streets, by the Convention Center and across the street from the Terminal Market. It was a killer location, and it would have provided a huge cash flow for the brewery. Again, the brewpub was deliberately "underbreweried" with a 10-barrel Newlands system and designed to be supplemented by kegged beer from the big production brewery.

The deal went sour just short of opening. I still remember Red Bell head brewer Jim Cancro telling me "Lew, this place is so ready to open that the salt and pepper shakers are on the tables." The brewpub wouldn't open for another eight months, and when it did, it opened not under the Red Bell name, but as the second Dock Street brewpub (third, actually, but that story is in *Virginia, Maryland, and Delaware Breweries*).

Beers brewed: Year-round: Philadelphia Lager, Philadelphia Light, Philadelphia Irish Amber, Black & Tan. Red Bell line: Apocalypse Now IPA, Hefe-Weizen, American Pale Ale, Black Cherry Stout. Some beer brewed under contract at Matt Brewing in Utica, New York.

The Pick: Red Bell's Black Cherry Stout is the rare combination of a good stout and a tasty fruit beer.

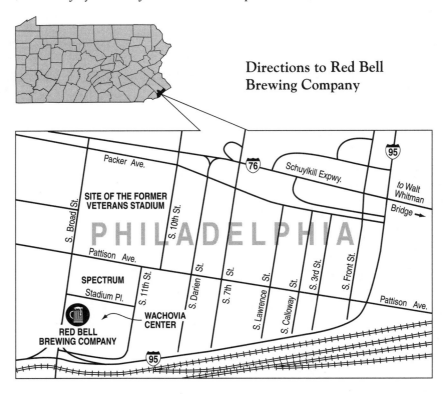

Directions to Red Bell Brewing Company

The local investor had decided to pull support from Red Bell, reportedly because of personality clashes with Jim Bell.

Jim Bell fought that in court, spent a ton of money on an attempt to merge with Pittsburgh Brewing and go public, and spent money on studies of a possible brewpub in State College, a project that was always "about to open" but was never more than a vacant lot. He tried to create an IPO to take Red Bell public on its own and released ridiculously optimistic figures that were then retracted two weeks later. And the company built a "brewpub" in Manayunk that would eventually open as a bar, but again, I was told it was about to start brewing . . . at least four times.

Before that happened, there was a stockholder revolt and Jim Bell was kicked out of the company. The general consensus among the beerfolk in Philly was that if Bell had spent his legal fees on actually building brewpubs, or simply brewing beer at the breweries he had, the company probably would have been a success. Meanwhile, just to complete the sad and somewhat pathetic tale, the Manayunk brewpub finally did produce two batches of their own beer . . . and closed a week after they went on tap.

But the tale's not quite complete. What about the brewpub at the Wachovia Center, the one this entry is purportedly about? It soldiered on through the whole mess, first supplemented by beer from the big brewery (which has been scrapped and sold off), then by beer brewed under contract at Matt, in Utica, New York. They still sell a bunch of beer (during appropriate events), they still sell roast beef sandwiches (with some of the most piercing, killer-good horseradish I've ever had), and they're still called Red Bell. As I wrote this, they were between brewers, but a new guy was being trained to take over.

What can we take from this story (which is still only part of a monstrously involved story that continues in the Independence Brew Pub entry)? It reminds me of pioneer English microbrewer Peter Austin's four rules for brewers: 1. Keep the brewery clean. 2. Buy the best ingredients. 3. Boil the copper. 4. Pray to God.

I don't see a fifth rule about "Go to court and sue everyone in sight" in there. Keep the focus on the beer, and whatever money will come, will come.

Opened: August 1996.
Owner: Corporation.
Brewer: Between brewers at time of publication.
System: 10-barrel Newlands brewhouse, 800 barrels annual capacity.
Production: 350 barrels in 2003.
Hours: Open only during appropriate events, so don't expect to get a beer during Disney on Ice. Call for schedule.
Tours: None.
Take-out beer: Not available.
Food: The brewpub has a limited menu: really good roast beef sandwiches and chili.
Special considerations: Kids welcome. Handicapped-accessible.
Parking: There's plenty of pay parking at the Wachovia Center.

Independence Brew Pub

1150 Filbert Street, Philadelphia, PA 19107
215-922-4292
www.independencebrewpub.com

Struggle through the traffic to Center City, down I-95 or the Schuylkill Expressway, or take SEPTA and work on their schedule. If you drove, find parking in one of the nearby lots without having to sign away your firstborn (it can be done, if you know how; see the tips below). Weave your way through the throngs of tourists and conventiongoers, maybe slip into the Reading Terminal Market for a quick fried oyster sandwich at Pearl's to brace you after that fight. Scramble across Filbert Street ahead of the kamikaze taxis, and push into Independence Brew Pub. Elbow your way through the crowd of twenty-something regulars to the bar, and bawl out your order for a glass of Oatmeal Stout. Sigh with relief when it arrives, take a big sip of Tim Roberts's finest, and watch all that nasty stuff you just went through vanish into a mist of beer enjoyment (not the fried oyster sandwiches, though; they're delicious).

Independence is a very busy place most times, particularly during lunch, happy hour, and late nights. If you're looking for a smart, fashionable brewpub in the city, this is it. It's conveniently placed for Center City denizens, it's a great alternative to the Hard Rock Café if today just isn't a day when you feel like "loving all, serving all" (or being marketed to within an inch of your credit limit), and the staff is not afraid to serve Guinness and light beers as well as their own. Why should they be? They are already selling quite literally every drop of beer Tim Roberts can brew; the guest beers don't seem to harm house sales at all.

There's a story behind why they're selling as much as Tim can brew. You've already read part of it in the Red Bell listing (see page 39): how the brewpub was deliberately equipped with a brewhouse too small to provide enough beer for the pub's capacity, and how it was supposed to be a Red Bell brewpub. If you haven't read that yet, go read it now, because it's time for . . . (*cue the Paul Harvey soundbite*) the *rest* of the story.

Beers brewed: Year-round: Kölsch, Red Ale, India Pale Ale, Oatmeal Stout. Seasonal: Winter Warmer, Scotch Ale, Imperial Stout, Belgian Single, Summer Ale, American Pale Ale, Ocktoberfest, Cream Ale, Double IPA.

If you didn't know, there was a Dock Street brewpub at Eighteenth and Cherry Streets (see The Boneyard for its fate, page 247). It was originally owned by the same folks who owned the Dock Street bottled beer brands, but they sold it, with the agreement that the new owners could continue to use the Dock Street name. At some point, they also got out of the beer business by licensing the Dock Street bottled brands to Poor Henry's (see The Boneyard for *their* fate, page 248).

The Pick: Oatmeal Stout does it for me. Tim's is creamy, opaque, and smooth, and it has just enough bite to be refreshing. You'll definitely want to get a full pint.

When Red Bell's money man decided to part company with Red Bell, a deal was struck with the new owners at the Dock Street brewpub to run the place. Supposedly, this was at least partly because the city (which has an interest in the building) required that any brewpub in the building have the name of an existing Philadelphia brewery. So they ginned up a snazzy 1930s Raymond Loewy–looking train logo to go with the Terminal location and opened it as Dock Street II.

There was some hassle over their brewing license at first (possibly instigated by disgruntled parties), but then brewing began and things looked great. The real trouble broke out when the former Dock Street bottle owner cried foul: He'd only signed to allow *one* Dock Street brewpub to use the name. But wait! Henry Ortlieb at Poor Henry's stepped in to say that he had the licensed rights to the Dock Street name, and they could use it if they sold the beer.

While the lawyers argued, life went on and beer got brewed at a feverish pace, because there was no support from the huge Red Bell brewery. Then Poor Henry's collapsed; the Dock Street claims consequently gained new strength, and the brewpub owners wanted out. But things took a truly odd turn as a deal was struck to allow the new owners to use the name and brands of the defunct Independence Brewing (see The Boneyard on page 247, you know the drill by now). Independence Brew Pub was born, and anticlimactically, the problems went away.

All but one: Tim's brewhouse still can't keep up. "I've got the expansion all planned out," he told me. "We just need to make the decision to do it." I have to hope they make the decision soon. This is a great space for a brewpub, fully rivaling the big Capitol City and Gordon-Biersch beer temples in Washington, D.C. There are acres of tables, a huge bar, a big game room, and plenty of standing room. The Filbert Street entrance isn't much to look at, but the Market Street side is a beautiful expanse of marble floors and glass walls, a dream of a railroad station.

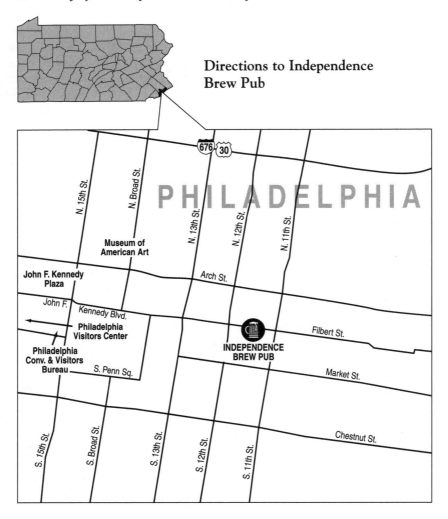

Directions to Independence Brew Pub

How's the beer that Tim can't make enough of? Excellent, and largely underrated, from what I've seen. Tim makes a variety of good beers, including a massive Double IPA that's right up there with best of this new breed. The food has gone from good to better; the last meal I had there was both delicious and adventurous.

The story, then, is interesting but, except for a few ghosts, like the name and the brewhouse, largely in the past. Belly up to the bar, boys, and show the twenty-somethings how it's done.

Opened: July 2000.
Owners: Private investors.
Brewer: Tim Roberts.
System: 10-barrel Newlands brewhouse, 1,000 barrels annual capacity.

Production: 1,000 barrels in 2003.

Brewpub hours: Monday through Saturday, 11:30 A.M. to 2 A.M.; Sunday 11:30 A.M. to midnight.

Tours: By appointment.

Take-out beer: Six-packs of other beers available; growlers should be available in near future.

Food: If you're at the bar between 4 and 7, Monday through Friday, you can order shrimp, wings, baked brie, and other goodies on the $3 bar menu, a steal. A full list of sandwiches is available (make mine the Pittsburgh Pork), as is a classic chop house menu: New York strip au poivre, surf and turf, twin tenderloins, Swordfish Oscar, lump crab cakes. That kind of food calls for Double IPA.

Extras: Twenty-seven TVs (plus big screen), darts, pool tables, live music (call for schedule).

Special considerations: Kids welcome. Handicapped-accessible. Vegetarian meals available.

Parking: The Convention Center Garage is only $7 after 5 P.M., $5 all day on Sundays—a steal in Center City.

Manayunk Brewing Company

4120 Main Street, Philadelphia, PA 19127
215-482-8220
www.manayunkbrewery.com

Manayunk has lost a bit of its gleam to neighborhoods like Northern Liberties, but it is still one of Philadelphia's hippest areas. Fashionable beaneries and trendy boutiques line Main Street, drinking decks overhang the canal, and parking is almost unavailable. Manayunk is the old Lenape Indian word for "The Place Where We Go to Drink," so it practically screams for a brewpub called Manayunk Brewing Company. That's what developer Harry Renner thought, and he had just the spot for it.

The space—originally a water-powered woolen mill, the Krook's Mill of the house beer by that name—works beautifully, with its original brick walls, seating for more than four hundred, and an operating, in-floor scale that has become a favorite conversation spot. But this isn't just a brewpub, it's a complex, with a patio bar and an upper deck overlooking the Schuylkill and the canal. The bar, in classic brewpub style, is backed with glass to expose the good-looking 15-barrel Bohemian brewhouse. Back at the far end of the dining room is the Rotisserie, a casual dining area that's all about meat. There's also a sushi bar and a stone pizza oven. They've got it all, baby.

Manayunk's been through some tough times and endured trials that might have closed other breweries. The brewery was slammed by Hurricane Floyd in 1999, with the tanks in the brewhouse floating loose, ripping glycol cooling systems out of the wall; it took five weeks of nonstop work to get the brewery back online. Harry's father was murdered at the brewpub two years later, a robbery gone bad. Then Harry himself died after complications from surgery in 2004. His family, however, decided that the brewpub should stay open, which is probably exactly what Harry would have wanted.

Larry Horwitz had taken over brewing duties when Jim Brennan quit (Jim's currently at Flying Fish in Cherry Hill, New Jersey) and did some wild things, including an authentic "stone beer," a beer brewed with the addition of white-hot rocks, an ancient method of brewing that produces a smoky, caramelized flavor. Then Horwitz got the head brewer job at Iron Hill, North Wales (see page 65), . . . just about the time Harry Renner died.

With Horwitz's help, the Renner family found and hired Chris Firey, a hotshot young brewer who was learning the ropes out at Victory. He's come in and shaken things up, and he looks to be making a name for himself. The beers are changing, and people are coming to the brewpub for the beers as well as the nightlife once again.

Manayunk has been through a lot—a lot of water over the dam. And it is *still* a good place to spend an evening, to end an evening, or to while away a weekend afternoon. Come on down—it's The Place Where We Go to Drink!

Beers brewed: Year-round: Bohemian Blonde, Philadelphia Porter, Manayunk Lager, Schuylkill Punch, Krook's Mill American Pale Ale. Seasonals: Grand Cru, Call IPA . . . so far. The seasonals are under changes for now. Expect anything, though. Chris is fearless, and Manayunk has a tradition of lots of different beers going all the way back to Tom Cizauskas, the first brewer here.

The Pick: Chris's Call IPA was one hot pint of beer when I had it, a beer that wakes up your whole mouth. Don't be afraid to try anything here; that Victory training has stood Chris in good stead.

Opened: October 1996.
Owner: The Renner family.
Brewers: Head brewer, Chris Firey; Steve Zweir; Billy Young.
System: 15-barrel Bohemian brewhouse, 2,800 barrels annual capacity.

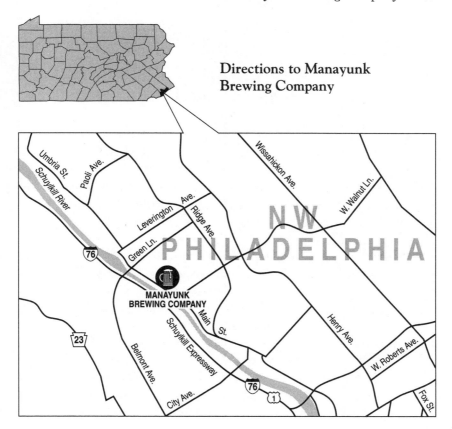

Directions to Manayunk
Brewing Company

Production: 1,600 barrels in 2008.

Brewpub hours: Monday through Thursday, 11 A.M. to midnight; Friday and Saturday, 11 A.M. to 2 A.M.; Sunday, 10:30 A.M. to 11 P.M.

Tours: By appointment.

Take-out beer: Growlers.

Food: The menu at Manayunk varies as months pass, and it maintains a high level of quality and innovation . . . but the grilled meatloaf and mahogany wings have righteously stayed on there since opening day. Find them and love them.

Extras: Live music (call for schedule). Happy hour Monday through Friday, 5 P.M. to 7 P.M. Sunday, jazz brunch from 10:30 A.M. to 2:30 P.M. Extensive outdoor seating in good weather.

Special considerations: Kids welcome. Handicapped-accessible. Cigars allowed and are for sale at the bar. Vegetarian meals available.

Parking: On the street and at some small lots, but can be a bear on weekends. The brewpub has valet parking service Wednesday through Sunday during evening hours. In the summer months, there is a boardwalk from the Lock Street parking lot down to the outside bar.

Micros, Brewpubs, and Craft Brewers

My son Thomas sometimes accompanies me on brewery tours. Much to my delight, he's fascinated by words and what they mean and how people use them. I've explained to him that much of what people say is said because they don't want to say something more blunt or honest. Code words, euphemisms, and evasions are part of our everyday speech. Here's a little secret of the beer world: *Microbrewery* is just another code word.

When the new brewing movement started in America in the 1970s, no one knew what to call these little breweries. "Brewery pub," "boutique brewery," and "microbrewery" were all used. By the early 1980s, two words had settled into general use: *microbrewery* and *brewpub*. At the time, the industry's pundits defined a brewpub as a brewery that sold most of its beer in an in-house taproom. They defined a microbrewery as a brewery that produced less than 15,000 barrels a year. These terms gained legal recognition in some states, as deals were struck to allow the new businesses to start up and as tax rates were determined. The federal government acknowledged the special nature of small breweries in the early 1990s, granting a substantial tax break to those with an annual production under 50,000 barrels.

Eventually the industry itself came up with a whole set of labels. "Brewpub" continued to be used for breweries that sold the large majority of their beer on-premises by the glass. "Microbrewery" was for packaging breweries whose production was less than 50,000 barrels. "Regional" brewery applied to smaller breweries established before 1970 that did not distribute to all of America. Nationally distributing giants like Anheuser-Busch, Miller, Coors, and Stroh were dubbed "national brewers" or "megabrewers."

But the growth of some successful micobreweries has made even 50,000 barrels an uncomfortable fit. Boston Beer Company, the contract brewery responsible for the Samuel Adams line of beers, sells around 1 million barrels a year, and Sierra Nevada Brewing Company, an early microbrewery that produces all its own beer, is pushing 600,000 barrels. Clearly these are no longer *micro*breweries, yet their beer is exactly the same as it was. "Microbrewery" has a cachet that most microbrewers don't want to surrender. What to call them?

Some propose the blanket term "craft brewery." This implies that the beer is somehow crafted rather than produced in a factory. Craft breweries are different, the brewers explain, because the beer is made in single batches, not in several that are then combined in one huge tank or blended after fermentation to ensure consistency.

Putting a label on a brewery these days is not as easy as putting a label on a bottle. For example, what do you call a place like The Lion, a regional brewery that brews mainstream lagers but also brews the small, all-malt line of Pocono beers? Penn Brewing has a beautiful brewery pub and bottles beer brewed in-house, but it also has its Penn Pilsner brewed on contract. What about Porterhouse, which always has their own four beers and four other beers from the brewery down the road? These breweries aren't readily pigeonholed.

The fact is, microbrewery has always been a code word, and so has craft brewery. They both mean the same thing. They describe a brewery that makes beer in an authentic manner—using ingredients and techniques appropriate to a given style of beer or brewing—and that brews beers other than mainstream American-style lager. What do I think such places should be called? How about *breweries*?

The distinctions are really all nonsense. Brewery size has nothing to do with the quality of a beer. Guinness Stout, the beer to which most microbrewers hopefully compare their own dry stouts, is brewed by a globe-girdling gargantuan of a brewer. Blending is likewise a nonissue. It goes on at microbreweries across the country.

In this book, I have bowed to convention and called Pennsylvania's Old Guard breweries *regionals*, and used the words *brewpub, microbrewery,* and *craft brewery*. Brewpub is the best of these terms. A brewery where beer is taken directly from the conditioning tanks to serving tanks and sold from a tap on-premises truly deserves a unique name. But if I had my way, the others would all be called simply breweries. To differentiate a brewery based on the kind of beer it makes seems to be missing the point. Categorizing them by size penalizes the ones that succeed and outgrow the class. Call them breweries, and then let the beer do the talking.

FROM HORSE COUNTRY
TO THE DELAWARE
Southeastern Pennsylvania

Southeastern Pennsylvania is often called "the five-county area." This includes Philadelphia, Bucks, Montgomery, Chester, and Delaware Counties. If you take out Philadelphia County, the remaining counties are considered the suburbs of Philadelphia, even though they reach almost to Bethlehem in the north and well into Amish farm country in the west.

Of course, there are suburbs and there are suburbs. Bucks County has cookie-cuttered Levittown, and Montgomery County has the gritty streets of Norristown. The tightly packed streets of Upper Darby blend Delaware County right into Philadelphia, and Chester County's Coatesville is like a little bit of Rust Belt. These are border counties, where farmers and financiers coexist in the gently rolling countryside.

The well-known Main Line area stretches out through Montgomery, Delaware, and Chester Counties. This is a wealthy strip of beautiful old homes, boutiques, and Mercedes-Benz dealerships along what used to be the Main Line of the Pennsylvania Railroad, now the SEPTA commuter rail line. Out here, tucked away among the big homes, you'll find the controversial Barnes Foundation, where one of the world's great art collections is *still* trying to work out its future . . . seven years after I first wrote those words in the first edition of *Pennsylvania Breweries*.

There is a substantial presence of the arts in the suburbs. Chadds Ford on Brandywine Creek is home to the Wyeths and the Brandywine River Museum. On the northeast edge of the five-county area is New Hope, a well-known artists' colony and haven for alternative lifestyles on the Delaware River. Chadds Ford and New Hope used to be BYOB

51

territory for the beer traveler, but McKenzie Brew House and Triumph have changed that!

Not far from New Hope is Doylestown, where James Michener lived and endowed an excellent art museum. You'll also find the Mercer Museum and the Moravian Pottery and Tile Works, the lifework of Dr. Henry Mercer, an enthusiast of American folk art and craftsmanship. His mansion, Fonthill—a concrete castle—is a unique example of free-form architecture filled with artwork and memorabilia that Mercer collected.

Valley Forge National Historical Park is here in the suburbs, with miles of trails and reconstructions of the cramped huts where the Continental Army spent the harsh winter of 1777. In Bucks County, at Washington Crossing Historic Park, there's an annual reenactment of General Washington's famous Christmas crossing of the Delaware. You can get a dramatic overview of the area from Bowman's Hill Tower, a 110-foot tower atop the hill used by Continental Army lookouts.

The area is dotted with Revolutionary War battle sites. Brandywine Battlefield near Chadds Ford is where Washington was defeated by the British in 1777. Historical markers note little skirmishes like the battle of the Crooked Billet Inn in Warminster and a set-to that supposedly occurred in the alleys of my own little town of Newtown.

Chester County is horse country. The area's biggest equestrian event, the annual Devon Horse Show, is where the cream of the county show off their horses—and themselves!

If all this sounds a bit upper-crust, it can be. Although the suburbs have plenty of working stiffs and average joes and janes, you can't help noticing that this is a very wealthy area. Big $500,000 homes are commonplace, luxury cars clog the narrow roads, and you can't throw a rock without clocking a doctor or lawyer. So don't throw any rocks around. Just relax, see the sights, and stop someplace nice for a beer.

There are a lot more places to stop for a beer out here these days, too. The Philadelphia suburbs continue to be the hot spot in Pennsylvania, with twice as many breweries as any other area. Three have closed since the last edition, but there are six new ones, including an expansion by Sly Fox and a jump across the river from Princeton by Triumph. Philly continues to rule on beer bars, but even there the suburbs are catching on. It's a good time for a beer lover to live in the counties.

Triumph New Hope

400 Union Square Drive, New Hope, PA 18938
215-862-8300
www.triumphbrew.com

I've lost one of my best lines. "The best place to go for a beer in New Hope," I'd tell people when they'd ask where to find a good beer in this artsy little town on the Delaware, "is Lambertville." New Hope has lots of good restaurants and a number of popular bars, but the beer selections they offer range from predictable to pathetic. You were best off to walk across the bridge to Lambertville, New Jersey, to someplace like River Station.

But Triumph New Hope has made a liar out of me, and I couldn't be happier. Well, yes, I could. The brewpub up by the New Hope and Ivyland Railroad station was *supposed* to be in my hometown of Newtown, and having a brewpub within walking distance would have made me deliriously happy. But a coalition of Quakers and homeowners, convinced that a brewpub would "turn Newtown into another New Hope," browbeat the town council into putting so many restrictions on the proposed site that Triumph decided against locating here and went off to New Hope. Maybe the Quakers gave them the idea.

In any case, it was a good one. The pub's caught on in this tourist town, helped by a canny level of involvement in festivals (they recently hosted a Slow Food event) and community activities. That's how you get noticed in New Hope: You have to *be there*. Triumph caught on quickly, and no surprise: Partner Brian Fitting is the president of the town Chamber of Commerce.

I talked about the pub with brewer Patrick Jones and Triumph "executive brewer" Jay Misson. Misson goes way back in craft brewing, and while writing *New York Breweries*, I'd come across his name a number of times as a mentor to current brewers. Misson was trained under Stefan Muhs at Vernon Valley, where Muhs was running an early brewpub at

Beers brewed: Year-round: Honey Wheat, Bengal Gold IPA, Amber Ale. Seasonals: Octoberfest, Kellerbier (GABF Gold, 2004), Helles, Dunkles, Blonde Doppelbock, Bock, Roggenbock, Rauchbier, Snakebite, Imperial Stout, Double Amber, Jewish Rye, Oatmeal Stout, Coffee & Cream Stout, Irish Dry Stout, and probably more to come.

the Action Park water park. It was old school all the way. "We were putting out half-liter swingtops of unfiltered, organic-ingredient lagers, brewed to strict Reinheitsgebot standards," Misson recalled.

He learned a lot about lager brewing and almost inevitably wound up at Gordon-Biersch, the national chain of lager brewpubs. That's where he met Jones: Misson trained him at the Miami Gordon-Biersch. It didn't take him long to lure Jones up here once he got the job with Triumph.

Can we expect a lot more lagers from Triumph? Sounds that way; when I asked the brewers about

The Pick: Patrick hadn't really had a chance to get any lagers on yet, but I know they'll be good, especially th Blonde Doppelbock. In the meantime, the Double Ambe pretty near knocked me out with its huge, sweet body, enough esters to swim in, ar wads of hops. "It's 100 per-cent Cascades. More like 15 percent Cascades," Jay joke

upcoming beers, a long string of lagers was the first thing I got. That suits this area (and this beer drinker) to a tee; this is lager country, and people up here won't know what hit them when they taste good, fresh, clean lager beers.

The Triumph folks are not afraid to try new things, though. The hot technique in brewing right now is to age big beers in bourbon barrels; Weyerbacher Heresy, for example. Jones and Misson figured to do something a little different. They aged some of their Snakebite—a half-cider, half-beer mix—in a barrel used by Laird's for applejack. Laird's is a New Jersey distiller, the country's oldest, that made applejack for the troops of the Continental Army. The Snakebite that came out of the barrel rocked me back on my heels—phenomenal stuff with a big, boozy wood and vanilla character to it, pressed by Eve right out of the Apples from the Tree of the Knowledge of Good and Evil: Here, Adam, try it; you'll see God.

After they stopped laughing at the look on my face, we took a look around the pub. If you've been to Triumph in Princeton, the New Hope pub is similar in design, though not as strikingly narrow or high. It has lots of exposed brick; high ceilings straight up to a second level; a raised, exposed brewhouse; and a distinctly uncluttered look that the warm brick and wood keep from being stark.

The menu is a bit exotic, and delicious, with real vegetarian choices and innovative appetizers. But the bar menu will be familiar to any brewpub regular, and the trademark house-cut fresh potato chips, served in a big paper cone, are great greasy beer food.

You don't have to go to Lambertville to get a good beer in New Hope anymore—though it's still a gorgeous walk across the bridge right down the hill from Triumph. You could even take a growler along and bring New Hope's good beer to Lambertville.

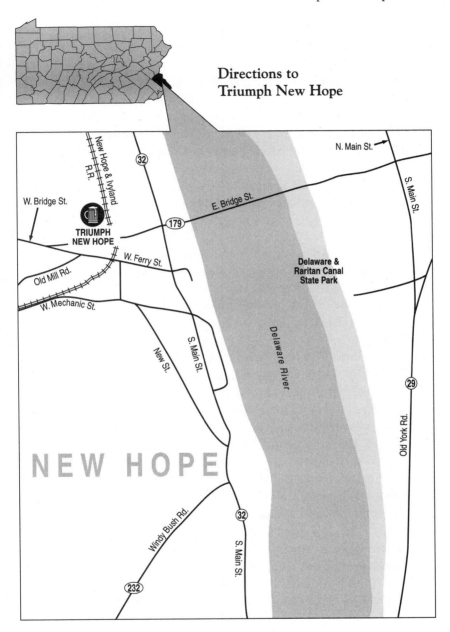

Directions to Triumph New Hope

Opened: May 2003.
Owners: Adam and Brian Fitting, Adam Rechnitz.
Brewers: Patrick Jones; Jay Mission.
System: 12-barrel Newlands brewhouse, 2,000 barrels annual capacity.
Production: 1,000 barrels in 2004 (estimated).

Brewpub hours: Thursday through Saturday, 11:30 A.M. to 1 A.M.; Sunday through Wednesday, 11:30 A.M. to midnight.

Tours: By appointment.

Take-out beer: Growlers; call ahead for kegs.

Food: Triumph has a sophisticated menu, with appetizers like coconut curry mussels, ahi tuna carpaccio, and panzanella salad, and main dishes of orange vodka-cured salmon and lamb chops . . . but they also have their cone of fries, fresh-cut chips, crab tater tots, and a variety of sandwiches on the bar menu. There is also an exceptional variety of vegetarian dishes: vegan paella (saffron jasmine rice with artichoke hearts, roasted tomatoes and peppers, and garbanzos), farfalle rustica, and portabella bisque.

Extras: Live music or a DJ every Friday and Saturday, karaoke Thursday; call or check website for schedule.

Special considerations: Kids are welcome. Handicapped-accessible. Vegetarian meals available.

Parking: Reasonable pay lot is a deal in New Hope.

Lodging in the area: See entry for Porterhouse Restaurant and Brewery (page 59).

Area attractions: You can see (and hear) the **New Hope and Ivyland Railroad** (32 West Bridge Street, 215-862-2332, www.newhoperailroad.com) right out back. Their steam and antique diesel engines will take you on a ride on this historic short-line railroad; the dinner trains and fall foliage runs are very popular. There is a station at Lahaska, too; you can ride the train from Triumph to Porterhouse. The town of New Hope is one of the most popular strolling and shopping towns in southeastern Pennsylvania, with shops galore, restaurants from deli to haute cuisine, and some of the best people-watching around. Lambertville, just across the Delaware River, is noted for its large number of antique shops; you can't go two blocks without hitting one. Also see Porterhouse listing on pages 59–60.

Other area beer sites: Triumph's other brewpub is in Princeton, New Jersey (138 Nassau Street, 609-924-7855), not too far away, where brewer Tom Stephenson takes a more ale-brewed slant on things and the architecture is, if anything, even more striking than in New Hope. Also see Porterhouse listing (page 60) for more bars.

Porterhouse Restaurant and Brewery

5775 Lower York Road, Lahaska, PA 18931
215-794-9373
www.porterhousepub.com

Porterhouse Restaurant and Brewery is new, but it's in the building of the old Buckingham Mountain brewpub in Lahaska. If you have bad memories of the often-infected beer at Buckingham, new owners, a new approach, a new brewer, and new beers have completely changed the place.

"We had a lot of work to do," partner Lisa Fricke, who manages the brewpub, told me. "It was filthy, and there was no equipment at the bar, not even shelves for glasses. We tore up the carpet and cleaned before laying new carpet. We did major renovations." They removed the four serving tanks behind the bar, opening up an intimate dining area and expanding the bar, redoing the surface in a distinctive quarry tile. The upstairs was converted to an upscale dining room.

Get the picture: This is not Buckingham Mountain at all. We won't talk about that again.

Fricke and her two partners, chefs Clay Hull and Chris McDonald, had years of experience in the restaurant business. They bought a brewpub only because the timing and the price were a great match. "We had few options on the brewery," Fricke said. "It was too difficult to remove, and we didn't know enough about brewing to know if we were hiring a good brewer. So we approached River Horse."

River Horse is an established brewery in Lambertville, New Jersey, just across the Delaware River. Coincidentally, they had just had a proposal for a brewpub in New Hope fall through, so they were ready for the idea. It was an interesting deal that was eventually worked out. The River Horse owners are not owners or partners in Porterhouse. They were to supply four tap beers and brewer Matt Howard, who would brew four other beers in the Porterhouse brewery. That's how it was originally, but eventually Matt Howard

Beers brewed: Year-round: Special Ale, Lager, Harvest Ale, Porter. Seasonals: McHenery's Stout, Blonde, Tripel Horse, Summer Ale, Oktoberfest, Winter Ale, Maibock.

proved such a good fit with Porterhouse that he was hired full-time as a brewer and to work the front of the house.

"We still brew under the River Horse name," explained Fricke. "It works out well for everyone. We promote each other, and we sell the six-packs of bottled River Horse beer here."

They made out well on their choice of brewer. Matt Howard is a pleasant fanatic who keeps the brewery so spotless that if you hadn't ever seen him brewing, you might think nothing was happening there. It shows in his beers. It was a complete delight to sample beers in this building and have them all be clean as fresh-fallen snow. Get some Tripel Horse, a Porterhouse seasonal favorite with its orangy, sweet-tart fullness.

Still, given the background of Fricke and her two partners (who are excellent chefs and very nice guys, by the way), it's not surprising that they concentrate mostly on the menu. See the list of entrées, the pastas with salmon or pan-flashed vegetables, the macadamia-encrusted red snapper, breast of duck with dried cherry chutney, and inevitably, a massive Porterhouse steak. Even the pub menu gets the treatment, with a praline chicken salad sandwich, an andouille and spinach frittata, and a smoked duck breast quesadilla. Not the usual fare at all; this is a restaurant cleverly disguised as a brewpub.

The upstairs dining room gives a view across a conservancy-protected farm to the southern ridge, a beautiful slice of rural Bucks County. You can walk to the shops of Peddler's Village, and the famous Rice's Flea Market is only 2 miles away, if you need to persuade some companions to come out for a visit. Once they get here and see the menu and taste the beer, it may be hard to get them to leave.

The Pick: The Harvest Ale was light but still tasted rich, with a definite chocolate note. Eye-openingly good; a real stand-out.

Opened: April 2002.
Owners: Lisa Fricke, Clay Hull, Chris McDonald.
Brewer: Matt Howard.
System: 10-barrel Pub Brewing System brewhouse, 700 barrels annual capacity.
Production: 150 barrels in 2003.
Brewpub hours: Tuesday through Sunday, 11:30 A.M. to midnight.
Tours: By appointment.
Take-out beer: Growlers and six-packs of River Horse beers.
Food: A carefully prepared high-end set of alluring appetizers and innovative entrées with an emphasis on steaks and seafood parallels a more pubby menu of burgers and pasta.

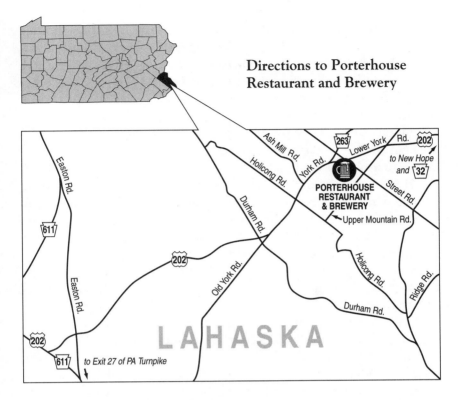

Directions to Porterhouse Restaurant and Brewery

Extras: Full liquor license. Mug club.

Special considerations: Cigars not allowed. Kids welcome. Handicapped-accessible. Vegetarian meals available.

Parking: Plenty of off-street parking available.

Lodging in the area: Golden Plough Inn, Route 202 and Street Road, 215-794-4004; Red Roof Oxford Valley, I-95 and Oxford Valley Road, 215-750-6200.

Area attractions: Next-door *Peddler's Village* is a 42-acre complex of shops and boutiques, a favorite shopping destination for the area. Another favorite, about two miles from the brewery, is *Rice's Market* (215-297-5993), a long-running (since the 1920s) flea market open year-round on Tuesdays, rain, snow, or shine, and on Saturdays from March to December. Lahaska also has *Carousel World,* a carousel museum with a working carousel available for rides. *Buckingham Valley Vineyards* (215-794-7188) is just 3 miles south of Buckingham on Route 413 (the intersection is west of the brewpub on Route 202) and has a self-guided tour and a tasting room. East of Lahaska on Route 202 is New Hope on the Delaware River, home of the *Bucks County Playhouse* (215-862-2041) and an amazing plethora of shops and restaurants. New Hope is a favorite strolling spot; parking can be tough. **Washington Crossing Historic Park** (215-493-4076) is just downstream from New Hope by way of a pleasant drive along the river. In warm weather, **Sesame Place** (215-752-7070) is very attractive for young children. Big Bird's theme park (which is owned—surprise!—by Anheuser-Busch) is only fifteen minutes south of Lahaska in Oxford Valley; it was recently rated the fourth-best kids' park in the world.

Other area beer sites: Head west 3 miles on Route 202 to the Route 413 intersection and you'll find two good beer places. The **Heart of Oak** taproom (215-794-7784) is tucked under Baci's restaurant, and you'll find a very English menu (chicken and leek pie, bangers and mash, Scotch eggs) with some very English taps. Right across the street is the **Candlewyck Lounge** (215-794-8233), a beef and ale restaurant that also has a good deli with a bottle shop. The bottle shop has an excellent selection of Belgian, German, and local beers at pretty good prices. You've probably been drinking the beer; why not take a tour of the **River Horse Brewery** at 80 Lambert Lane in Lambertville (609-397-7776)? It's just a walk across the bridge from New Hope. **Mesquito Grill** (128 West State Street, Doylestown, 215-230-RIBS) is a neat little pair of bars, one smoking, one non-smoking, connected to a larger dining space. They have a great set of taps, but the taps are almost secondary to the knockout bottle selection, an absolutely uncompromising list that's also available for takeout. The nonsmoking bar also has satellite sports (i.e., British football) on a plasma TV. **Isaac Newton's** (215-860-5100), my local bar, has seventeen outstanding taps, including at least two Belgian and two nitro, and an outstanding bottle selection. Find it off the town parking lot in the middle of Newtown.

Crabby Larry's Brewpub, Steak, and Crab House

237 West Butler Avenue, Chalfont, PA 18914
215-822-8788
www.crabbylarrys.com

I like brewpubs. Big brewpubs, little brewpubs, brick brewpubs, wooden brewpubs. A brewpub with beers for me and for you, a brewpub that smokes a mean barbecue. A brewpub that wins a big shiny medal, a brewpub that throws funky stuff in the kettle. Brewpubs serving steaks on a white tablecloth, brewpubs serving soups of fresh veggies and broth. A brewpub for pizza, served on a big dish; or a fine brewpub market, stuffed full of fresh fish! I like brewpubs.

It seems like only yesterday I was reading Margaret Wise Brown's *The Friendly Book* to my children. I always liked how many different kinds of things there were to like. Brewpub owners seem largely to have forgotten that. They tend to fall into a rut, with the same general "concept," the same general menu: artichoke and spinach dip, some kind of encrusted salmon, wings, quesadillas, pizza . . . There are exceptions, to be sure, but I've never seen one quite as out of the ordinary as Crabby Larry's.

Crabby Larry's is a seafood market, and it operated for ten years under the name of Jones Family Seafood. Then Larry Jones took over, added a restaurant to serve up the fish and seafood in dinners, and renamed it Crabby Larry's. Larry seemed pleasant enough to me, so I'm assuming the nickname refers to the big steamed "beautiful swimmers" he serves up . . . but you never know.

Next, Larry got the idea to stick a little brewery in his seafood market, which in Pennsylvania meant that he could then offer his house-brewed beers and Pennsylvania wines by the glass—not a bad deal for a lot less than the price of a liquor license. So he got himself a little 2.5-barrel electrically heated brewkettle from North American Brew Systems, a bunch of malt extract, and hooked up with Owen Hutchins, the former brewer at the General Lafayette Inn. Owen, a long-time homebrewer who really wanted to brew but

Beers brewed: Year-round: Golden Ale, Calico Jack Amber. Seasonals: Lite Ale, Irish Stout, German Wheat, American Wheat, Pale Ale.

needed to make some money too, saw an opportunity to keep his hand in while holding down a full-time nonbrewing job.

He's still homebrewing, kind of. "We buy our extracts, malts, and hops at Keystone Homebrew in Montgomeryville," he said. "It's cheaper! The prices are better from the big outfits, but with the amounts we're buying, we get killed on the transport fees."

The Pick: The German Wheat had the telltale notes of clove, banana, and apple that any hefe fan knows means this is the real deal. Maybe not the best with fish—I'd probably go with the Pale Ale for that—but it made a great after–Crab Bread drink.

The homebrew touches don't stop there. When it's time to make a batch of beer, Owen puts cheesecloth bags full of cracked specialty grains in what he calls his "homebrewer's mash tun," a 54-quart picnic cooler full of hot water, and makes a kind of malt tea. "I let them steep while the kettle comes to a boil," he told me, "then drain it right into the kettle. When the beer's done, we put it right in the kegs. We don't filter—I wouldn't know where to put a filter in here! It's okay with me; I'm a big fan of simplicity."

So is Larry, evidently, because he's a hands-off owner. "He lets me go," said Owen. "He doesn't second-guess me." That's why you'll find a slightly larger range of beers here than at most extract brewpubs: Besides the standard golden and amber ales, you may see a stout or a hefeweizen, and there are some very nice fruit extracts to put in the beer, if you'd like, black cherry for the stout, raspberry for the American Wheat.

I know what you're thinking: all very nice, but it's an extract brewery. Is the beer any good? To be honest, the first time I went up, it wasn't. I told Owen, and he agreed that there were problems and said he was working on them. The main source of the problem, oddly enough, given his earlier statement, was a filter. An in-line water filter had been installed years before the brewery was put in, and then forgotten. The cartridge hadn't been changed in three years or more. No surprise that the beer was affected!

Once that was fixed, the beer took a definite turn for the better. The last time I was up, I had a glass of Calico Jack Amber that was malty, chewy, and clean as a whistle. There was a slight mineral taste to the lighter beers, but that same taste is in the water you'll get with your meal.

Oh yes, don't forget your meal. Open up your multipage menu, and you'll see that this is undisputedly, unabashedly a seafood restaurant. There are a few nice steaks on there, sure, but there's a whole separate section just for the different grilled fish offered. Seafood appetizers, seafood soups, seafood casseroles, seafood pasta—the backdoor of this place must be the favorite hangout for every cat within 3 miles. I got the Crab Bread, a *boulle* sliced open, stuffed with lump crabmeat, doused

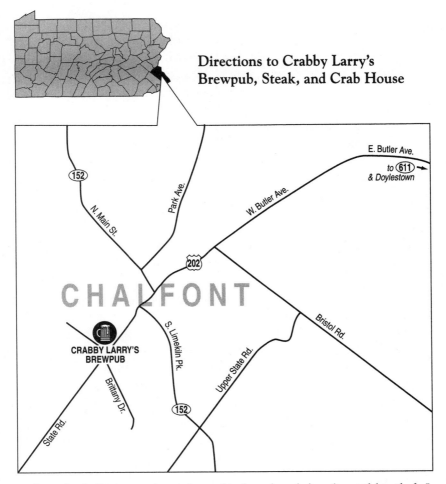

Directions to Crabby Larry's Brewpub, Steak, and Crab House

with melted cheese and a rich, garlic-laced crab broth, and broiled. It was sloppy but delicious. I recently made a trip up to Chalfont just to get another one. And you can always pick up some fresh seafood to take home.

Do you like brewpubs? All kinds of brewpubs? If you like fish, too, I've got just the place for you, tucked away in a little shopping plaza in Chalfont . . .

Opened: November 2001.
Owners: "Crabby" Larry Jones.
Brewer: Owen Hutchins.
System: 2.5-barrel North American Brewing Systems extract brewhouse, 250 barrels annual capacity.
Production: 50 barrels in 2003.

Brewpub hours: Tuesday through Thursday, seafood market open noon to 9 P.M., kitchen opens at 4:30 P.M.; Friday, market open 10 A.M. to 10 P.M., kitchen opens at 4:30 P.M.; Saturday, market open 10 A.M. to 10 P.M., kitchen opens at 3:30 P.M.; closed Sunday and Monday.

Tours: The brewery's right there in front of you at the bar; if Owen's there, ask him a question.

Take-out beer: Not available.

Food: Fish, shellfish, and combination platters of both, in plain and fancy dishes. Some steaks, but this place is all about fish.

Extras: Seafood market has fresh fish, salads, and sauces for take-out.

Special considerations: Children are welcome. Handicapped-accessible. Vegetarian options are limited. Crabby Larry's is nonsmoking.

Parking: Large, free, on-site lot.

Lodging in the area: Pine Tree Farm B&B, 2155 Lower State Road, Doylestown, 215-348-0632; Chalfont Motor Lodge, 413 West Butler Avenue, 215-822-2532.

Area attractions: Doylestown has a cluster of interesting and different museums, all related to Henry Chapman Mercer, a local Renaissance man. *The Mercer Museum* (Pine and Ashland Streets, 215-345-0210) is a five-floor wander through the implements of a variety of preindustrial trades, from tinsmithing to whaling, whole parts of our culture that no longer exist. Mercer put his ideas to work at the *Moravian Pottery and Tile Works* (130 West Swamp Road, 215-345-6722), where a group of artisans created decorative and mosaic tiles. There are tours and a serious gift shop; many area homes have accents of Moravian Tile Works tiles.

The *Peace Valley Winery* is in Chalfont (159 Beaver Valley Road, 215-249-9058), if you feel like a change of palate. *Delaware Valley College* (700 East Butler Avenue, Doylestown, 215-345-1500) has a strong program in agricultural studies, food science, dairy science, and agribusiness, and proves it with its farm market, where students sell produce, eggs, cheese, milk, honey, and salad dressings.

Other area beer sites: See Porterhouse Restaurant and Brewery (page 60) for suggestions.

Iron Hill Brewery and Restaurant, North Wales

1460 Bethlehem Pike, Shoppes at English Village,
North Wales, PA 19454
267-708-BREW
www.ironhillbrewery.com

IROΠ HILL
BREWERY & RESTAURAΠT

Iron Hill is one of the most successful small brewpub chains in the country. I have nothing to back up that statement: no numbers, no comparisons, no spreadsheets, nothing. I don't care, I'm sticking with it, because I know what I see. I see five busy brewpubs that all look terrific. They're all filled with bright, energetic staff that show more energy and customer-service savvy than you find most places these days. The food is excellent, fresh, and innovative without being outlandish. The brewers are proud, happy, technically proficient, and imbued with an honest camaraderie. And the beer—my heavens, the beer is just fantastic. That is success. You can't be doing that well, with so many happy people, and not be making it.

How many happy people? I was talking to Mark Edelson about that on a chilly January morning in 2004. I remember it was chilly because we were at Iron Hill in North Wales, watching the Iron Hill brewing staff manhandle (and womanhandle) the new brewhouse, kettle, mash tun, and tanks into the uncompleted building, with future North Wales brewer Larry Horwitz, a man of many talents, running the forklift.

"You know," Mark confided to me, "I have to think to remember everyone's name now. We're working with a payroll of almost five hundred people these days." But I looked at that team of brew-

Beers brewed: Year-round: Iron Hill Light Lager, Raspberry Wheat, Lodestone Lager (GABF Gold, 1997; GABF Bronze, 2000), Anvil Ale, Ironbound Ale, Pig Iron Porter (GABF Bronze, 2002; RAF Silver, 2002, 2003). Seasonals: Altbier, Barleywine, Belgian White, Bohemian Pils, Bourbon-Aged Russian Imperial Stout (GABF Bronze, 2004), Dry Stout, ESB, Hefeweizen, Imperial IPA, India Pale Ale, Lambic de Hill (GABF Gold, 2003), Maibock (GABF Bronze, 2000; GABF Gold, 1999), Munich Dunkel (GABF Bronze, 2003), Nut Brown Ale, Oatmeal Stout, Oktoberfest, Old Ale, Russian Imperial Stout (GABF Gold, 2003), Saison (GABF Bronze, 2003), Tripel (GABF Bronze, 2002), Vienna (GABF Bronze, 1999), Wee Heavy (GABF Bronze, 1998, 2001), Oud Bruin, Doppelbock, Weizenbock. (Note: The medals were won at brewpubs within the group, not necessarily at this particular pub.)

ers, every one of whom had honestly volunteered to come out and shove a couple tons of steel around, and saw people who were happy with their work. The same crew shows up at events like Friday the Firkinteenth and parties together. Size may have its pitfalls, but Edelson and Finn and Davies are neatly skirting them so far.

The Pick: I've come to like it only recently, but Anvil Ale has been getting more and more of my attention. It's a pale ale that's firmly hopped with East Kent Goldings, a very spicy hop without the citrus cut that many American brewers treasure. Larry's emphasized the earthy, nutty character of this classically English ale. Good show!

What about North Wales and Larry Horwitz in particular, though? The pub has familiar Iron Hill elements: dark red-brown wood interior, an open kitchen, hollow square bar, and the cast-iron "barley bird" decoration. It's divided into four bays—two high-ceilinged dining rooms, the bar, and the brewery—with connecting passages at each end. The menu is identical to that at the other Iron Hills, with all items prepared from scratch ingredients. Every location has a chef, not just cooks, and all the chefs get together with regional chef David Anderson to set the menu.

The brewers from each Iron Hill get together to work on the regular beers—Iron Hill Light Lager, Raspberry Wheat, Lodestone Lager, Anvil Ale, Ironbound Ale, and Pig Iron Porter—and to discuss their plans for specials. They all have their favorites that they're encouraged to develop: Media's Bob Barrar likes big beers, Belgian types in particular; West Chester's Chris LaPierre has a weakness for "bug beers," inoculated with souring bacteria; and Larry Horwitz is a lager lover. I sampled his Vienna when I stopped in, and it was beautiful: very malty, a deep amber color, Oktoberfest the way it used to be.

The chefs and the brewers meet together, too, and go over pairing suggestions with upcoming beers. They also spend a lot of time and money on server training, Larry told me. "There are two hours of beer training for each new server."

He called a relatively new server over and asked her to run a sampler for me. She not only tapped and arranged the beers expertly and without pause, but she also gave me brief, accurate descriptions of each one that went well beyond the "this is our pale ale, it's hoppy; this is our stout, it's black" you'll get many places. Best of all, she did it without an air of imposition or recitation; there was a real feeling that she knew what she was saying and understood it. "Every one of our servers can do that," Larry said proudly.

What about servers that don't like beer? I asked; it drives me crazy when I run into servers trying to sell me beer who have no idea what it tastes like because they don't drink it. What are they doing working at

Directions to Iron Hill Brewery and Restaurant, North Wales

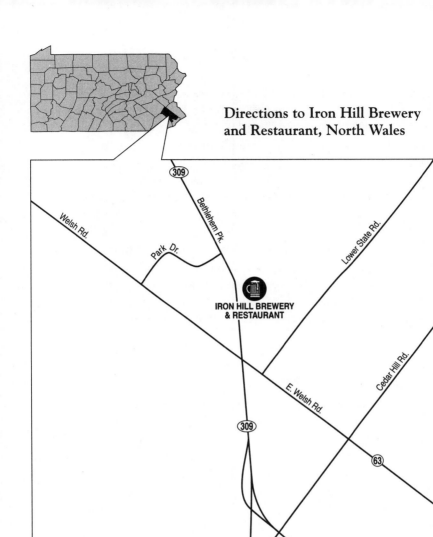

a brewpub? "They don't work here," Larry said. "That was one of the first questions Mark asked me: 'Do you like beer?' Is this an interview? He was serious!" Larry laughed out loud. Then he dragged me back into the cold room and tapped up a sample of barleywine. Larry likes beer.

He likes working at Iron Hill, too. "These guys are great; they're really serious about beer, and they let me make anything I want as long as I make the regulars," Larry said. "And it's always brand-new equipment, always top-of-the-line malts and hops, and never cutting any corners on the process." Larry beamed with pleasure. "I *love* this place!"

I like drinking at a place with a happy brewer. I like drinking at a place where I know everyone really likes beer. I like drinking at a place where the staff knows their beers well enough to explain them to my mother. I like drinking at Iron Hill, North Wales, because Larry Horwitz—like Edelson, Finn, and Davies—likes beer. It makes a difference.

Opened: March 2004.

Owners: Mark Edelson, Kevin Finn, Kevin Davies.

Brewer: Larry Horwitz.

System: 10-hectoliter Specific Mechanical brewhouse, 1000 barrels annual capacity.

Production: 820 barrels in 2004 (estimated).

Brewpub hours: Monday and Tuesday, 11:30 A.M. to 12:30 A.M.; Wednesday through Saturday, 11:30 A.M. to 1:30 A.M.; Sunday, 11 A.M. to 11:30 P.M.

Tours: Upon request.

Take-out beer: Growlers.

Food: See Iron Hill, West Chester (page 89).

Extras: North Wales, like the other Iron Hills, has a regular weekly schedule of specials: Fat Tuesday, a Creole-style prix fixe dinner; Thursday, seafood, and Quizzo night, with special prices on pitchers; and Sunday, brunch and a special prime rib dinner.

Special considerations: Kids welcome. Handicapped-accessible. Vegetarian meals available. Cigars allowed at the bar.

Parking: Large on-site free lot.

Lodging in the area: Joseph Ambler Inn, 1005 Horsham Road, 215-362-7500; Residence Inn, 1110 Bethlehem Pike, 267-468-0111; Comfort Inn, 678 Bethlehem Pike, Montgomeryville, 215-361-3600.

Area attractions: See Porterhouse (page 60) and Crabby Larry's (page 64).

Other area beer sites: The *Drafting Room* (900 North Bethlehem Pike, Spring House, 215-646-6116) has a solid, often exciting draft selection and good bottles as well. Well worth a stop.

General Lafayette Inn

**646 Germantown Pike,
Lafayette Hill, PA 19444
610-941-0600
www.generallafayetteinn.com**

Brittingham's Irish Pub, just two doors down Germantown Pike from the General Lafayette Inn, is a great place to go for a good jar of Guinness. Brittingham's is in a building that predates the American Revolution, built in 1744.

Big deal, 1744. The Brittingham is the new kid on the block. The General Lafayette was built in 1732 and has been a tavern, hotel, or restaurant nearly the whole time. The age of the building is evident in the small rooms and low doorways in the older parts, and the uneven, originally hand-dug basement that makes life interesting for brewer Christopher Leonard.

Make that brewer-*owner* Chris Leonard. After founder Mike Mc-Glynn died in 2003, Chris put together the finances and in 2004 became the owner of the General Lafayette. He once told me the reason he brewed: "I thought I'd do something for a living that I'd really do for free: play guitar, play ice hockey, or brew." I asked him now, would you run the place for free?

"No," was his quick response. "For a while I would, but I'd hire someone and I'd be brewing. It's a matter of getting good people you can trust. Get the system in place, and train them up. Hopefully I can manage people well enough. The rewards are so much greater."

He's earned that. Chris took a cut in pay to come to the General Lafayette from the Hops Bistro in San Diego back in 1999. "I didn't want the job," he said. "It wasn't as much money, but the challenge was great. We got a mill, improved the grist hydra-

Beers brewed: Year-round: Raspberry Mead Ale, Germantown Blonde, Sunset Red Ale, Pacific Pale Ale. Seasonals: Union Jack ESB, English Mild, Belgian Dubbel, Winter Warmer, Barley Wine, Imperial Stout, Belgian Wit, Trippel, Loch Ness Monster Scotch Ale, IPA, Bavarian Hefeweizen, Weizenbock, Irish Stout, Oatmeal Stout, Chocolate Thunder Porter, Wunderbar Pils, Oktoberfest, I'll Be Bock, Lafayette's Bière de Framboises, Alt Who Goes There?, and more . . .

tion, put venting on the kettle. The mill paid for itself in a year in savings over premilled malt."

The freshness of just-milled malt is important to Chris. "I love malt," he said. "It's much more interesting and complex than just hopping something. When I hop a beer, I'm looking for hop flavor, not just bitterness." But he knows the geeks. "I try to juggle beer types as much as possible, but when in doubt, it's IPA. It always flies."

If you want to know what kind of brewer Chris Leonard really is, listen to this DeNiro-esque statement of the lengths he's willing to go to for accuracy: "When you take the beer out of here," he told me, "it tastes really different. There's no dark lighting, no smoke. I've thought about taking up smoking just to get an angle on what beer tastes like to a smoker, to make a smoker's beer." Hey, Raging Bull, take it easy there. You take up smoking for one beer, you won't taste any of the others.

Don't worry. The beer at this often underrated brewpub is still excellent, still interesting, still top-notch and innovative. "The beer's a draw," Chris affirmed. "More people come just for the beer than for any other single thing. You've got to compete with the beer bars. Your beer's got to be *good*, and you've got to have variety . . . or they'll go to the beer bar." It's great to hear a brewpub owner talk so positively about beer, as a draw rather than as a gimmick or a waste of floor space.

But then, Chris Leonard isn't just an owner. He's an owner-*brewer*. So you'll find innovative ideas at the General Lafayette that revolve around the brewing. Last year it was a mead festival, with as many commercially brewed meads as he could get together, along with several versions of his braggot, a beer-mead mix (and Chris's aged braggot was the clear winner of that taste-off, for my money: a graceful heavyweight, like butterscotch-tinged whisky). This year it was a multiple-course beer and cheese pairing, done with great care and fanfare.

The more I learn about brewing and the brewing industry, the more I come to realize that it isn't better malt, hops, water, or yeast that make better beer. What it really takes is the will to make great beer. Chris has that will, and he's willing to do it for free. Is it any wonder that I think he consistently makes some of the best beer in the area?

The Pick: I'll take the Union Jack ESB. This style confuses some people, because the name, Extra Special Bitter, make it sound like a very hoppy, bitter beer. It shouldn't be, and this one isn't. It's one of the best-balanced examples of an ESB I've had, with good hop character and good malt character in union.

Opened: January 1997.
Owners: Christopher Leonard, William Leonard.
Brewer: Christopher Leonard.

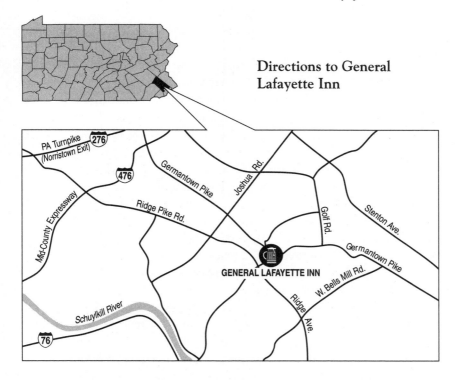

Directions to General Lafayette Inn

System: 7-barrel DME brewhouse, 900 barrels annual capacity.

Production: 600 barrels in 2003.

Brewpub hours: Monday through Saturday, 11:30 A.M. to 2 A.M.; Sunday, 10 A.M. (for brunch) to 2 A.M.

Tours: By appointment or by request as possible.

Take-out beer: Growlers, half kegs, 5.2-gallon minikegs.

Food: American regional and continental, with a strong emphasis on locally farmed and organic foods. The brewpub follows the Slow Food movement (and so should you!), representing U.S. craft brewers at the Terra Madre conference in Turin, Italy.

Extras: The inn has a pool table and darts. There's live music Thursday through Saturday nights, and open mike night on Wednesday.

Special considerations: Kids welcome (special menu). Handicapped access to first floor. Cigars permitted in main bar and sold at the bar (a new air-handling system has significantly reduced the smoke in the bar area). Vegetarian meals available.

Parking: Large off-street lot.

Lodging in the area: You can stay right at the inn—a separate building in the rear has five-bedrooms and 4-bathrooms and is quiet and secluded; call for details. Chestnut Hill Hotel, 8229 Germantown

Pike, 215-242-5905; The Inn at King of Prussia, 127 Gulph Road, King of Prussia, 800-528-1234.

Area attractions: You're not far from Valley Forge National Historical Park, described in the introduction to this section. At Plymouth Meeting Mall, right off Germantown Pike, on the other side of the turnpike, you'll find plenty of good shopping. But the best attraction when you're at the General Lafayette is Germantown Avenue itself. Drive toward Philadelphia and watch the neighborhoods change. When you get to Mount Airy, make a stop at McMenamin's, then turn right down the hill and pick up Lincoln Drive. Check out the huge houses before you drive into Fairmount Park. You can easily spend an hour sightseeing and shopping.

Other area beer sites: *Brittingham's Irish Pub* (next door, 610-828-7351) is actually a pretty good place on its own, with an excellent jar of Guinness and a great Irish breakfast on weekends. *McMenamin's Tavern* (7170 Germantown Avenue, Mount Airy, 215-247-9920) is a great neighborhood bar with a beer selection that doesn't mimic every other beer bar in town, surprisingly adventurous food (and dynamite wings), and P. J. McMenamin, one terrific guy. One of the area's original multitaps, *Flanigan's Boathouse* (113 Fayette Street, Conshohocken, 215-828-BOAT), goes through a lot of beer, so you can count on the freshness. *Lucky Dog Saloon* (417 Germantown Pike, 610-941-4652) gets the nod from Chris. Also see the suggestions at John Harvard's, Wayne (page 86).

Sly Fox Brewhouse and Eatery

**Route 113, Pikeland Village,
Phoenixville, PA 19460
610-935-4540
www.slyfoxbeer.com**

Things have changed completely at the Sly Fox. A new logo, a new menu from a new chef, new beers, a great new tap system, a new outdoor dining area, new events, new attitude—and much of it is thanks to their new brewer, who used to be at New Road over in Collegeville: Brian O'Reilly.

O'Reilly was dropped at New Road by owners too foolish to realize what a draw they had in his excellent beers (their inevitable closure followed less than a year later—just deserts). Beer aficionados in the area were concerned that he would leave the area—he's from New Hampshire and still visits regularly—but O'Reilly took a line brewer job at Victory and kept his contacts open.

Luckily for him—and us—one of those contacts put O'Reilly in touch with the Giannopoulos family at Sly Fox, and after some negotiations, he joined them in March 2002. It was a good move for everyone, because the family realized that not only had they hooked up with a great brewer, but O'Reilly had a head for promotion and a gift for energizing the staff as well. He organized an annual goat race to launch his Maibock, and employees not only went along with it, they even entered goats in the race!

He energized the customers, too. Sly Fox has one of the most beer-savvy groups of regulars I've ever seen in a brewpub, with wide-ranging tastes and happy enthusiasm. Anything Sly Fox does, they're right there with it, including O'Reilly's latest idea: nine new and different IPAs for each of the nine months leading up to the brewery's ninth anniversary in December 2004 (he plans a ten-month repeat in 2005, of course). They show up and kick a keg of O'Reilly's huge Belgian-style ale, Incubus, on the first Friday of every month. They even go to O'Reilly's house parties, and he goes to theirs.

Don't be worried that you won't fit in, though. The Sly Fox has become a destination brewpub, one that's right up there with Victory and Stoudt's on the lists of visiting beer geeks. They've heard about this brewpub that serves great beers from all along the beer spectrum—lagers to ales to a great bunch of Belgian-type specialties—and they are welcomed just like family. So grab a beer at the bar (there are usually seven or eight to choose from), maybe a cask-conditioned ale, and look around.

Though the brewpub sits in a shopping center, it does not lack character or charm. The central staircase gives it a homey feel, as if

Beers brewed: Year-round: O'Reilly's Stout, Incubus (one keg tapped every first Friday of the month). Seasonals: Abbey Xtra, Black Raspberry Wheat, Burns' Scottish Ale, Christmas Ale, Dunkel Weisse, C-quest Dubbel, French Creek Helles (GABF Bronze, 2002), Gang Aft Agley Scotch Ale, Gold Rush Lager, Ichor (bottle only), Instigator Doppelbock, Jake's ESB, Keller Pils, Oktoberfest, Odyssey Double IPA, Pete's Peerless Ale, Phoenix Pale Ale, Pikeland Pils (GABF Bronze, 2003), Pughtown Porter, Renard D'or, Robbie Summer Scottish Ale, Royal Weisse, Rt. 113 IPA, Saison Vos, Sly Fox Dark Lager, St. Charles Pilsner, Weird Beard Maibock (2004), White Horse Wit, and nine different Anniversary IPAs. These beers are mostly not so much seasonal as on when Brian feels like it.

Grandma decided to build a brewery in her home (we should all be so lucky). You can relax at the bar and eye those tanks, or take a table and sink your teeth into some great food. "It's not the Taj Mahal," says manager Pete Giannopoulos, "but it's comfortable." Yes, it is.

Not content to limit themselves to regular beer events, the family took on a Burns Night dinner, where diners are invited to mount the stairs to the landing and recite (or simply read) a Robbie Burns poem of their choice to the adoring (and loud) crowd; better than the first year, when we had to climb up on the bar! Then the haggis is piped in, the ode is recited by a be-kilted local Scots enthusiast, and we all set to. To O'Reilly's surprise, the kitchen has run out of haggis every year, despite ordering more each time. Might have something to do with the presence of his Aft Gang Agley Scotch Ale.

The Pick: Gang Aft Agley makes me do just that, and it's great tonsil oil for getting limbered up for declaiming or Burns Night. It's multilayered, malt-heavy, and luscious. I'd also advise you to get the Keller Pils if it's available; too few brewpubs offer an unfiltered pilsner, and I think it's just the best way to drink this style. It's alive, vibrant, and charged with hop spirit.

The new Sly Fox that has opened up the road in Royersford is quite different: a bigger space, with a bigger brewery that will put Sly Fox beers in many more area bars. O'Reilly's looking forward to being able to change the character of the original Sly Fox again, creating a more intimate feel, with cask-conditioned ales on all the time. "It's not going to be the same," he said. "You can get your Fox Fix at either place, but if you want to taste everything, you'll have to visit both."

It won't be a hardship, I can assure you. Ever since I found out that I can be at Sly Fox in less than an hour by slipping through the beautifully winding roads of Valley Forge National Historical Park, I've taken my share of time on the patio, sipping tall, cool glasses of Royal Weisse, and I've sunk a few pints inside when the cold winds blow. It's not just the great beer, good food, or energized service that brings me back. It's the sociable feel of the Sly Fox, the "never a stranger" vibe that folds you in. Come take a look; you're sure to be welcome.

Opened: December 1995.
Owners: The Giannopoulos family.
Brewers: Head brewer, Brian O'Reilly; Tim Ohst.
System: 15-barrel Pub Brewing System brewhouse, 1,200 barrels annual capacity.
Production: 870 barrels in 2003.
Brewpub hours: Monday through Thursday, 11:30 A.M. to midnight; Friday and Saturday, 11:30 A.M. to 1 A.M.; Sunday, noon to 10 P.M.

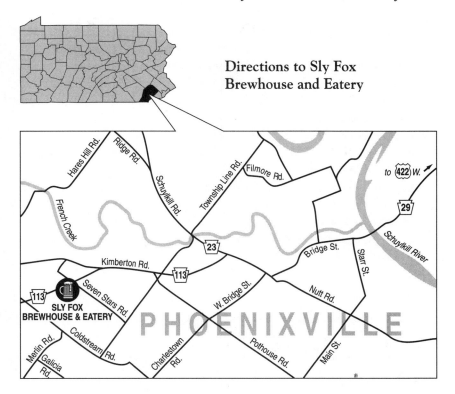

Directions to Sly Fox Brewhouse and Eatery

Tours: Upon request.

Take-out beer: Growlers, bottles of Incubus, kegs.

Food: Sly Fox's menu not only has *all* the standards—wings, smoked salmon, Thai skewers, burgers, pulled pork, crab cakes, fish and chips, pasta primavera—but it's also got *more:* an appetizer of fresh mozzarella, basil, bruschetta, and smoked sausage; a classic Cuban sandwich; gyros; Blue Corn Southern Fried Chicken Salad; steak au poivre, and Seafood Pasta fra diablo. There are some real choices on this menu. Bravo!

Extras: Sly Fox has no liquor license, but it has an excellent selection of Pennsylvania wines.

Special considerations: Kids welcome. Handicapped-accessible. Cigars allowed. Vegetarian meals available.

Parking: Plenty of free parking in off-street lot.

Lodging in the area: Comfort Inn, 99 Robinson Street, Pottstown, 610-326-5000; Exton Comfort Inn, Routes 113 and 100, Lionville, 610-524-8811; Holiday Inn, Routes 113 and 100, Lionville, 610-363-1100.

Area attractions: You're not far from **Valley Forge National Historical Park** (described in the introduction to this section), down Route

422. **French Creek State Park,** which is west on Route 23, then north on Route 345, has camping, swimming, boating, fishing, 32 miles of hiking trails, and 15 miles of cross-country skiing trails. The park is also the location of the **Hopewell Furnace National Historic Site** (215-582-8773), a reconstructed anthracite iron furnace and ironmaking village.

Other area beer sites: *The Epicurean* (Route 113 and Township Line Road, 610-933-1336), a very nice restaurant with six good taps and a wide bottle selection, also has a six-pack store that sells bottles to go. See and be seen with one of the great beers at the **Drafting Room** (635 North Route 113, Exton, 610-363-0521), where things have been kicked up several notches. The Drafting Room has become one of the hottest beer spots in the five-county area; there's a very good whisky selection, too.

Sly Fox Brewery and Pub

314 Lewis Road, Royersford Plaza,
Royersford, PA 19468
610-948-8088
www.slyfoxbeer.com

I was standing on the back steps at Royersford with brewer Brian O'Reilly while work was going on behind us: the plumbing, steam-fitting, drywall hanging, and painting necessary to get this new brewery-pub open by October 2004. We were looking at stores and homes and lots of trees, off in the direction of the Limerick nuclear plant. "Why here?" I asked him. "The closest town of any size is Pottstown, isn't it?"

"This is all growing out here," O'Reilly replied, taking a bite of a delicious Cuban sandwich we'd split for lunch (from the new menu at the original Sly Fox, and you should get one). "It's one of the fastest-growing areas in the state. We'll have plenty of traffic through here." He's probably right; this guy does his homework.

Beers brewed: Same as the Sly Fox, Phoenixville, list on page 73 for now. Expect some new, limited-release beers here, however.

That's why I have no fear at all about putting this entry in the book before Sly Fox Royersford has even opened. O'Reilly and the Giannopoulos family have a pretty good track record at this point.

What's the deal at this new Fox? Bigger. A bigger dining area, a game room that doubles as a banquet room, a bigger bar with a cozy fireplace, and a much, much bigger brewery. "We're at 10,000 barrels annual capacity with these tanks," O'Reilly told me, a number that's more than six times the barrelage that Sly Fox did at its Phoenixville location.

The Pick: I'm sure they'll have O'Reilly's Stout here, and I'm eating my words—it's great. I once told Brian I thought it was too dry, and he's never let me forget it, every time he sees me drinking it. Which is often.

There's room for more tanks, too, and a bottling line that's going to be set up "in Phase II," O'Reilly said with a wry grin. If that sounds like plans for a production brewery, give yourself a pat on the back; it is. The folks at the Fox figure to grow quite a bit in the next few years, propelled by O'Reilly's great beers and his seemingly magical ability to sell area bar owners on the idea of planting a foxtail tap in their lineup. Up till now, that's mostly been about promoting the brewpub. Now they're moving into the new territory of promoting a brand.

It's not just taps, either; figure on more specialty bottles from Sly Fox once this new brewery gets up and running smoothly. Brian's huge Belgian-style Ichor, already a big hit at the brewpub in 750-millileter bottles, will join other beers in that format; I hope one of those is the delicious Renard d'Or, a Belgian-type strong ale that has aged beautifully. Will we see 12-ounce bottles in cases around southeastern Pennsylvania? O'Reilly's mum about that, probably because he hopes to sell quite a bit of draft beer.

Meanwhile, folks out this way will find it much easier to get their "Fox Fix," as O'Reilly puts it. That keeps the movement moving, keeps the brewpub front pushing into new territory. With the loss of Ortlieb's at Sunnybrook, this area needed a brewpub, and now it's got a great one. The location, just off the Route 422 expressway, will make this an easy destination for lots of people once the word's out. We'll have plenty of traffic through here. At least, that's what I hear.

Opened: October 2004.
Owners: The Giannopoulos family.
Brewers: Head brewer, Brian O'Reilly; Tim Ohst.
System: 20-barrel Beraplan brewhouse, 10,000 barrels annual capacity.
Production: 4,500 barrels in 2005 (estimated).
Brewpub hours: Sunday through Wednesday, 11:30 A.M. to 1 A.M.; Thursday through Saturday, 11:30 A.M. to 2 A.M.

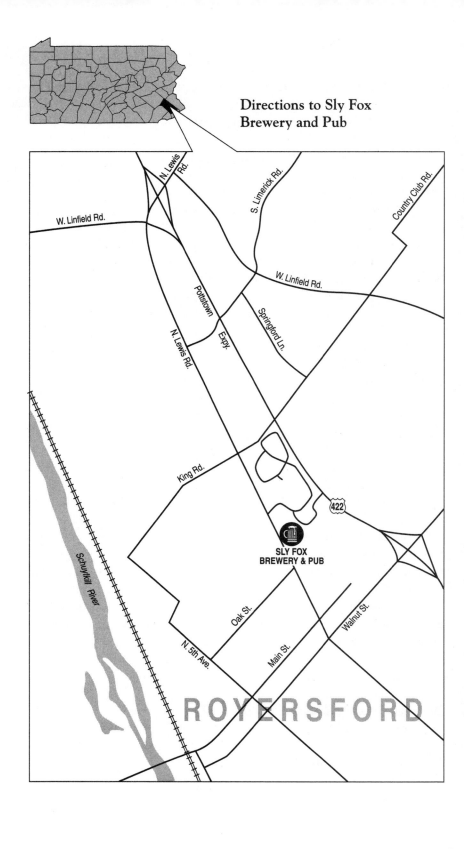

Directions to Sly Fox Brewery and Pub

Tours: Upon request, subject to brewer availability.

Take-out beer: Growlers, specialty 750 ml bottles, six-packs, call ahead for kegs.

Food: Similar to the Phoenixville Sly Fox, but with some different items. Stop by both places; you won't be bored.

Extras: Full liquor license. Private dining room. Large game room with pool tables, darts, video games, and a full-size shuffleboard table. And I think it's safe to say that there will be some events unique to this venue.

Special considerations: Kids welcome. Handicapped-accessible. Vegetarian meals available.

Parking: Large on-site lot.

Lodging in the area: Shearer Elegance B&B, 154 Main Street, Linfield, 610-495-7429; Days Inn Pottstown, 29 High Street, 610-970-1101; Holiday Inn Express, 1600 Industrial Highway, 610-327-3300.

Area attractions: *Pottsgrove Manor* (100 West King Street, Pottstown, 610-326-4014) is the restored 1752 home of John Potts, ironmaster, merchant, and founder of Pottstown. It is a typical eighteenth-century Philadelphia merchant's home, built of sandstone in the Georgian style. See the Sly Fox, Phoenixville, attractions (pages 75–76) as well.

Other area beer sites: *Ortino's* (800 Main Street, Schwenksville, 610-287-8333) and *Northside* (1355 North Gravel Pike, Zieglersville, 610-287-7272), both owned by the Ortino family, are really coming along on the whole good beer idea. Farther out, the friendly *Douglassville Hotel* (Route 422 East, Douglassville, 610-385-2585) serves huge dinners and has a hefty beer list. Nearby, you'll find the *Yellow House Hotel* (intersection of Routes 562 and 662, Yellow House, 610-689-9410), a great example of how a hotel bar can keep abreast of the times and not lose its charm.

Rock Bottom, King of Prussia

**160 North Gulph Road, The Plaza
at King of Prussia (beside Sears),
King of Prussia, PA 19406
610-230-2739
www.rockbottom.com**

GOOD FRIENDS. GREAT FOOD. GREAT BEER.

There's something that irks me a bit about beer geeks. Rock Bottom often gets very little credit from the geekerie, usually something about "It's a chain," or "The beers are all bland brewpub beers," or "They're full of yuppies." All I can figure is that these guys haven't actually spent much time in a Rock Bottom.

When I think of Rock Bottom, I think of Van Hafig, who used to be at the Arlington, Virginia, Rock Bottom and is now wowing the beer-savvy people of Portland, Oregon; and Geoff Lively, a genius with cask ales who I hope is chained to a long-term contract at the Bethesda Rock Bottom. In my experience, Rock Bottom brewpubs are places with bright, technically skilled brewers who like to stretch things as much as they can.

This Rock Bottom is a little bit different from the rest, but only a little. It was a brewpub before it was a Rock Bottom brewpub, part of the Boston-based brew moon chain. The space is mostly the same, though the decor has changed completely. There was a lot of carryover in personnel as well: The brewer, Jon Thomas, stayed on through the change, and so did some of the kitchen and service staff.

Thomas may not be a multiple-medal winner like Hafig and Lively, but he's no slouch, either. I had a tripel he made in 2003 that was phenomenal, and the beers I had when I stopped in for the official book visit were plenty impressive. What particularly grabbed me was his "required" light beer, the Lumpy Dog Light Lager. My notes read: "Nice and clean, tasty. I'd not only drink this, I might even order it!" I don't believe I've ever said that about a light beer in a brewpub.

While we're busting stereotypes about chain brewpubs, let's bust some about mall brewpubs as

Beers brewed: Year-round: Lumpy Dog Light Lager, Munich Gold Export, North Star Amber, Double Barrel I[Seasonals: Ben Politz Porte[Czar's Nightmare Imperial Stout, Scotch Ale, Czech M[Pilsner, Prussia's Pride ESB[Hefeweizen, Porter, O'Kiefe Irish Stout.

well. Rock Bottom is in the big King of Prussia mall complex, one of the biggest malls on the East Coast. But I hear the same damning, faint praise all the time, about this brewpub and others that are in malls: "Well, it's not a bad place, for a mall brewpub." Eh? Check this scenario: I'm in the mall, or I'm in the mall parking lot. It looks like a mall, or a parking lot. Now . . . I walk into the brewpub. It looks like a brewpub. What makes it a mall brewpub, *except for its location?* The mall part is all outside! If you don't want to look out the entrance at the mall, then turn your seat around.

The Pick: I'm not sure who Ben Politz is, but the porter Jon named for him was really excellent, a big gutsy porter with plenty of dark roasted malt character, hops—all that good porter stuff. A porter that stands up and fights back.

The Rock Bottom in Arlington, Virginia; Stewart's in Bear, Delaware; Malt River in Latham, New York; a number of John Harvard's—they're *all* in malls. If I took you in and sat you down at the bar, how would you know you were in a mall? What does "mall brewpub" mean, anyway? You have to go to a mall to get there? That's got nothing to do with what the place is like. This is like the people who complain that a brewpub is swarmed by "yuppies" (there's an outdated term for you), or that it's "too full." Sounds like Yogi Berra's classic "Nobody goes there anymore, it's too crowded" line to me.

Rock Bottom at King of Prussia is popular because it's a solid oasis of good beer in a fairly bland wasteland. Okay, and because they do dollar drafts on Thursdays. But most of it is that Rock Bottom does a great job of providing good beer and good food with great service in a setting that's easy to get to: I can be at the bar ordering a cold Double Barrel IPA within five minutes of getting off Route 202. They have the Rock Bottom Mug Club, which is a ridiculously good deal—because it's *free*. You're going to raise a fuss because it's in a mall?

Well, whatever. All I know is that if you turn up your nose at Rock Bottom, King of Prussia, because it's a chain or because it's in a mall, you're missing a good brewpub. Think about it a bit, then stop in and have one of Jon's beers. You can e-mail me to thank me.

Opened: January 2001.
Owner: Rock Bottom Restaurants.
Brewer: Jon Thomas.
System: 15-barrel Pub Brewing System brewhouse, 1,500 barrels annual capacity.
Production: 1,350 barrels in 2004.
Hours: Monday through Thursday, 11:30 A.M. to midnight; Friday and Saturday, 11:30 A.M. to 2 A.M.; Sunday, 11:30 A.M. to 11 P.M.

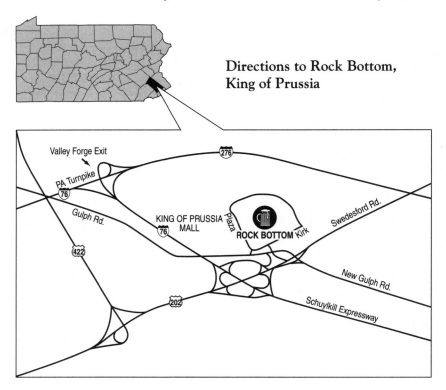

Directions to Rock Bottom, King of Prussia

Tours: Monday through Friday, subject to brewer availability.

Take-out beer: Growlers.

Food: Rock Bottom's menu really has a bit of everything, and every-thing I've ever had has been delicious. I particularly like the home-style favorites, like chicken-fried chicken, alder-smoked salmon, jambalaya, and barbecue ribs. Don't miss the white cheddar pota-toes, a Rock Bottom signature side.

Extras: Full liquor license.

Special considerations: Handicapped-accessible. Vegetarian meals avail-able. Kids welcome.

Parking: Lots of free mall parking.

Lodging in the area: McIntosh Inn, 260 North Gulph Road, 610-768-9500; Holiday Inn, 260 Mall Boulevard, 610-265-7500; Fairfield by Marriott, 258 Mall Boulevard, 610-337-0700.

Area attractions: Hey, the ***Plaza and the Court at King of Prussia*** together constitute one of the biggest malls in the country, what do you want? If "shop till you drop" doesn't thrill you, ***Valley Forge National Historical Park*** is just across the road; check out the Val-ley Forge Visitors Bureau website, www.valleyforge.org, to get all the stuff to do there and in the surrounding area. And all the excitement of Philadelphia is just a hop, skip, and a half-hour traffic jam away down the Schuylkill Expressway.

Other area beer sites: I haven't had a lot of luck right around here, except for **Michael's Deli** (610-265-3265), north about a mile on Route 202, tucked in a little plaza across from the Hilton, behind Kinko's. Michael's is a really good deli, with overstuffed sandwiches and a great assortment of single-bottle beers to choose from for lunch. You can also pick some up for takeout. If you find something you like and you want more, take a left on Route 202 down to the next light, take a right on Henderson, and go down about half a mile to find **Kunda Beverage** (610-265-3113) on your right. Kunda is a major wholesaler that also has a retail store, and they really know beer. You'll have to buy by the case, but just think of all the money you're saving!

Valley Forge Brewing Company

267 East Swedesford Road, Wayne, PA 19087
610-687-8700
www.vfbc.com

It took a long time for Valley Forge Brewing Company to get any respect around Philadelphia. I can think of several reasons. It was one of the first brewpubs to open in the Philadelphia suburbs, and there's a very strong city prejudice. It's located in an old movie theater in a shopping center, not in an old historic building or fancily designed urban space. The brewpub has always been popular with a young crowd that seems mostly interested in pounding down the pints on the weekend. But I think the big reason was the covered bridge.

There is a covered bridge inside the restaurant, a visual non sequitur in a brewpub where darts, pool, and big-screen ESPN are taken quite seriously. The bridge was made out of heavy oak timbers by an Amish carpenter from Morgantown.

Beers brewed: Year-round: King's Gold Ale, Red Coat Ale, Peach Wheat, Regiment Pale Ale, George's Porter. Brewer's specials: Irish Stout, Drunken Monkey.

The covered bridge doesn't actually bridge anything. It's just a semiprivate dining space with a somewhat more romantic air to it as a result of the electric candle lighting and lower ceiling. It's kind of odd, and a bit jarring, but the pub's in an old movie theater; it needs every possible distraction to help you forget that.

The Pick: Easy call. The George's Porter has been my favorite since my first visit to Valley Forge. It's rich, dark, and chewy, with a slight hint of chocolate and coffee.

Valley Forge Brewing (with the bridge) was originally built by the Biles brothers, David and Greg. They ran it, and David brewed the beer part of the time, and even opened a second Valley Forge, though that was doomed by traffic patterns and closed. They had a good run, but they eventually got tired and looked for a buyer. They found the Pattons and the Franiaks in 2003, and the brewpub changed hands in August. David stayed on and taught Michael Patton to brew, and Tracy Patton is an accountant with restaurant experience.

I talked to Tracy when I stopped in. "I wanted a business with Mike," she said, "and opportunity knocked. It's been good. Our main worry was brewing the beer, but Dave took the time to teach Mike. They've really been great."

Brewed by Dave before, then by Mike, and now by brewer Ryan Michael, Valley Forge has some beers that drink well by the pint, real session beers like the King's Gold Ale and Red Coat Ale. The well-known Peach Wheat is still light, still almost fuzzy in its freshness, and never a bit cloying. Any of these would work for an afternoon of watching sports, playing darts, and checking out the other people along the bar.

That's the kind of brewpub this is. There are no pretensions to some higher worshipful purpose of beer. This is a place for fun, where the emphasis is on the people drinking the beer, not the beer itself. Once you've visited, it makes a lot of sense. I'm still not sure about the bridge.

Opened: May 1995.
Owners: Michael and Tracy Patton; Ken and Kelli Franiak.
Brewer: Ryan Michael.
System: 10-barrel Specific Mechanical brewhouse, 1,400 barrels annual capacity.
Production: 800 barrels in 2004 (estimated).
Brewpub hours: Sunday, noon to 11 P.M.; Monday through Thursday, 11 A.M. to midnight; Friday and Saturday, 11 A.M. to 1 A.M.
Tours: Any afternoon except Sunday.
Take-out beer: Growlers; kegs (available with prior notice).

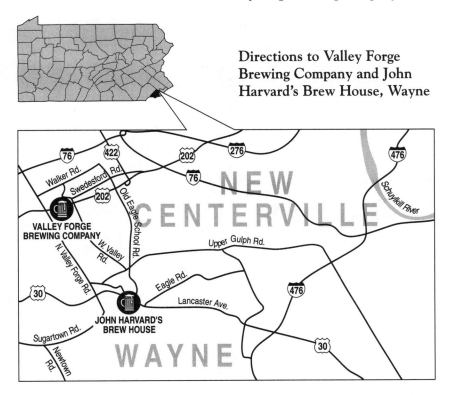

Directions to Valley Forge Brewing Company and John Harvard's Brew House, Wayne

Food: Full menu includes sandwiches, salads, steaks, seafood, pasta, and daily specials.

Extras: VFBC has one of the longest bars in Pennsylvania, pool tables, British dartboards, and a game room. Several TVs including two wide-screen make VFBC a great spot for watching sporting events.

Special considerations: Kids welcome. Handicapped-accessible. Vegetarian meals available.

Parking: Free off-street parking in shopping-center lot.

Lodging in the area: Courtyard by Marriott, 1100 Drummers Lane, Wayne, 610-687-6700; Comfort Inn, 550 West DeKalb Road, King of Prussia, 610-962-0700; The Inn at King of Prussia, 127 Gulph Road, King of Prussia, 800-528-1234.

Area attractions: See the introduction to this section (page 52) for a description of nearby Valley Forge National Historical Park. If you want to work off your lunch, try indoor rock climbing at *Philadelphia Rock Gym,* in the 422 Business Center (610-666-7673).

Other area beer sites: The multitap *Boat House* (16 Great Valley Parkway, Great Valley Corporate Center, Malvern, 610-251-0207) has good food, but drink at the bar, not at the tables—trust me. *The*

Flying Pig Saloon (121 East King Street, Malvern, 610-578-9208) has a bottle selection that's definitely worth your time and ten rotating taps of the good stuff. See more bar suggestions at the Victory entry (page 101).

John Harvard's Brew House, Wayne

**629 West Lancaster Avenue,
Wayne, PA 19087
610-687-6565
www.johnharvards.com**

John Harvard's Brew Houses have invaded Pennsylvania! The time must have seemed right, because we got three in less than a year. We're not alone. There's another just across the border in Wilmington, another out on Long Island, and more in New England. Grenville Byford and Gary Gut started the first Brew House on Harvard Square in Cambridge, Massachusetts, in 1992, and the idea has proven to have some serious legs.

The idea is embodied in the company slogan: "Honest food, real beer." The corporate history tells the tale of the young John Harvard watching William Shakespeare brew beer in Southwark, England. We are told that Shakespeare wrote, in addition to his plays and sonnets, a book of brewing recipes that John Harvard brought with him to America in 1637. The book was found in 1992 and is claimed as inspiration for the brewpub's beers. You can decide for yourself how "honest and real" the story is.

Don't doubt the sincerity of the slogan, though. The menu is innovative and eclectic, with a number of regional influences. The desserts are excessive, just the way you want them. A few local specialties may show up, but the food varies little from pub to pub.

The pubs have very similar brewing equipment with which they brew the same core beers. Each location has a handpump for serving cask-

Beers brewed: Year-round: All-American Light Lager, John Harvard's Pale Ale, Nut Brown Ale, a rotating fruit-wheat beer, and either a porter or stout. Seasonals: Manchester Alt, Loch Lanier Scottish Ale, Georgia Smoke Beer (GABF Silver, 1999), Winter Strong Ale, Bock, Mai-Bock, Hefe-Weizen, Pilsner, Ocktoberfest, Harvest Spice Ale.

conditioned versions of some of the beers. The Brew Houses exchange recipes and information with each other and with head brewer Tim Morse, a practice the brewers find very helpful. If a brewer runs into a problem, chances are someone else has had the same problem and can offer a solution, or at least some ideas. Brewers can also formulate some of their own beers, and they are encouraged to tweak the core beers toward local tastes.

The Pick: Choosing John Harvard's Pale Ale is the right thing to do. The hops and malt are in balance—a distinctively East Coast concept. This is the beer I'd send to brewers in the Pacific Northwest and say to them, "When you get tired of overhopping your beer, try making something like this."

Even the decor is similar. The three Pennsylvania pubs all have dark wood paneling. The brewhouse is visible from the dining area. There are illustrated panels of the John Harvard/Shakespeare story. It's not obtrusive, just similar enough to be familiar.

Hardly anyone outside the world of beer geeks seems to be bothered by this "McBrewpub" phenomenon. In fact, the two eastern John Harvard's Brew Houses were named Best of Philadelphia, Best Brewpubs, by *Philadelphia Magazine* in 1997. The Brew Houses I've been to always seem to be at least half full of happy customers who often come up to the brewmaster and compliment him on the beer.

People had speculated that the relatively small John Harvard's chain was ripe for takeover by one of the larger brewpub chains like Rock Bottom or Gordon Biersch, which have several plum locations and a good track record. But a white knight named Boston Culinary Group came along, bought the group, and . . . did almost nothing to it. They know a good thing when they see it. You may even see the chain start growing again; brewpub chains seem to be the wave of the future.

I must confess that when I try to work up a good head of righteous beer geek indignation over this chain brewpub idea, it never lasts longer than half a pint of whatever beer is best at the local Brew House. Would restaurant critics hate McDonald's so much if they served exciting, healthier fare with more flavors than just fat, sugar, and salt? It's a deep philosophical problem, and I intend to ponder it the next time I'm at one of the Brew Houses, probably over a pint of Scottish Ale.

The Wayne Brew House is in a big, comfortably rambling place with a great location right on the Main Line. It has become very popular with local office workers, to the point where every neighboring parking lot has signs up specifically warning John Harvard's customers away; that's notoriety for you! Head brewer Brian McConnell has the formulation duties here, as well as at the Springfield John Harvard's (see page 92) and the Wilmington pub (see *Virginia, Maryland, and Delaware Breweries*). That may sound like a man who's stretched thin, but Brian's up to it.

Opened: February 1997.

Owner: Boston Culinary Group.

Brewer: Brian McConnell; John Rehm.

System: 15-barrel Pub Brewing System brewhouse, 3,000 barrels annual capacity.

Production: 600 barrels in 2004 (estimated).

Brewpub hours: Seven days a week, 11:30 A.M. to 1:30 A.M.

Tours: During lunch through dinner hours, subject to brewer availability.

Take-out beer: Growlers.

Food: The John Harvard's menu features upscale pub fare, including chicken pot pie, Aztec Chicken Salad, and calamari, plus some local specials.

Extras: Full liquor license.

Special considerations: Kids welcome. Handicapped-accessible. Cigars allowed. Vegetarian meals available.

Parking: Large on-premises lot; free valet service in the evenings.

Lodging in the area: Radnor Hotel, 591 East Lancaster Avenue, Radnor, 610-688-5800; Courtyard by Marriott, 762 West Lancaster Avenue, 610-687-6633; Wayne Hotel, 139 East Lancaster Avenue, 610-687-5000.

Area attractions: King of Prussia has some massive shopping malls, where you'll find the only Nordstrom's in the area. There is also plenty of shopping in the sometimes pricey stores along Route 30 through Wayne and Radnor. In May, the **Devon Horse Show** is the place to rub elbows with the horsey set. See the introduction to this section (page 52) for a description of nearby **Valley Forge National Historical Park.**

Other area beer sites: *Gullifty's* (1149 Lancaster Avenue, Rosemont, 610-525-1851) is a classy place with a beautiful bar, a very well-chosen bottle selection, and good taps to boot. Brian recommends **Casey's Ale House** (543 Lancaster Avenue, Berwyn, 610-644-5086) and **Cunningham's Court** (31 Front Street, West Conshohocken, 610-834-8085). That's the "court" of Billy Cunningham, and even a sportsophobe like me knows who that former player and coach of the 76ers is. Surprise: There is a bunch of Sixers memorabilia, but there is also some pretty decent beer here. Who knew?

I'd also send you to **The Beer Yard,** behind the Starbuck's at 218 East Lancaster Avenue (610-688-3431). Matt Guyer has built up a great selection of case beer and the best selection of microkegs you'll find in the state; he also knows one heck of a lot about beer. Check out the website www.beeryard.com regularly for fresh Philly-area beer news. Matt also recommends **Landis's,** a pretty good little bottleshop/deli just down Lancaster Avenue (118 West Lancaster Avenue, 610-688-5895).

Iron Hill Brewery and Restaurant, West Chester

High and Gay Streets, West Chester, PA 19380
610-738-9600
www.ironhillbrewery.com

This is a big place. There's a good-size bar, a big dining room, and more dining nooks tucked in here and there. But big as it is, Iron Hill fills it. Iron Hill was the "Brewpub of Dreams" in West Chester; the partners built it, and people came in droves. The biggest problem Iron Hill had in its first six months of business was making enough beer to meet demand. I remember stopping by in December 1998 and finding only one of the brewery's own beers on tap. People drank them right out of beer.

What a problem to have! That's all taken care of now, with new tanks in place, and everyone's happy. Even with the experience partners Mark Edelson, Kevin Finn, and Kevin Davies had from operating their first Iron Hill brewpub in Newark, Delaware, they just weren't ready for the terrific thirst they found in West Chester.

That first Iron Hill has been a smashing success, winning popular opinion polls for best restaurant, best brewpub, and best place to look at women (and they say geeks are only interested in beer!). Though the West Chester pub isn't an exact copy, most of the good bits have been carried over. The dark wood decor is in place, looking elegant and established. The menu is similar, with well-executed pub food and adventurous yet solid dinner entrées. The service is attentive and friendly, just as it always is in Newark.

As if you needed to ask, yes, the beer is the same. Although the partners have always said that Iron Hill is a restaurant first and a brewpub second, you'd never know it from the quality of the brewing.

When you're as concerned about the total quality of your establishment as these guys are, nothing really comes second.

The beer is not just good, it's outstanding, as you can see from the GABF medals listed. Iron Hill does ales that are superb and has been putting some in cask to serve as "real ale" to the connoisseurs. They also have made a commitment to brewing lagers, and not just Yuengling-clone cash-in lager, either. They regularly brew a malty-dry Munich helles-style lager and add heftier seasonals.

West Chester is growing rapidly, and the town's restaurant scene is growing along with it. Iron Hill is at the forefront, both as restaurant and brewpub. Stop in for a beer or two, and take a look around town as well.

Opened: September 1998.

Owners: Mark Edelson, Kevin Finn, Kevin Davies.

Brewer: Chris LaPierre.

System: 10-hectoliter Specific Mechanical brewhouse, 1,600 barrels annual capacity.

Production: 1,250 barrels in 2004.

Brewpub hours: Monday and Tuesday, 11:30 A.M. to 12:30 A.M.; Wednesday through Saturday, 11:30 A.M. to 1:30 A.M.; Sunday, 11 A.M. to 11:30 P.M.

Tours: Upon request.

Take-out beer: Growlers.

Food: "Regional American fare" doesn't do justice to this toothsome menu, ranging from well-executed pub fare to the saffron-infused Brewmaster's Mussels and daily salmon specials. Sundays are special, with a popular, laid-back brunch and a prime rib special for dinner. Save room: Iron Hill's desserts are phenomenal.

Extras: Full liquor license. Pool tables, outdoor dining in season, live music Thursdays and Fridays (call for schedule). Like the other Iron Hills, this one has a regular weekly schedule of specials: Fat Tuesday, a Creole-style prix fixe dinner; Thursday, seafood; and Sunday, brunch

Beers brewed: Year-round: Iron Hill Light Lager, Raspberry Wheat, Lodestone Lager (GABF Gold, 1997; GABF Bronze, 2000), Anvil Ale Ironbound Ale, Pig Iron Porter (GABF Bronze, 2002; RAF Silver, 2002, 2003). Seasonals: Altbier, Barleywine, Belgian White, Bohemian Pils, Bourbon-aged Russian Imperial Stout (GABF Bronze, 2004), Dry Stout, ESB, Hefeweizen, Imperial IPA, India Pale Ale, Lambic de Hill (GABF Gold, 2003), Maibock (GABF Bronze 2000; GABF Gold, 1999), Munich Dunkel (GABF Bronze 2003), Nut Brown Ale, Oatmeal Stout, Oktoberfest, Old Ale, Russian Imperial Stout (GABF Gold, 2003), Saison (GABF Bronze, 2003), Tripel (GABF Bronze, 2002, 2004), Vienna (GABF Bronze, 1999), Wee Heavy (GABF Bronze, 1998, 2001), Oud Bruin, Doppelbock, Weizenbock. (*Note:* The medals were won at brewpubs within the group, not necessarily at this particular pub.)

The Pick: The Lambic de Hill was fabulous, deeply deserving the GABF Gold. It had all the puckery, funky character of a lambic, plus a creaminess from the relatively young oak barrel it was aged in (lambics are typically aged in well-used barrels and don't pick up much wood character). Not for everyone, but for the right person, it's a winner.

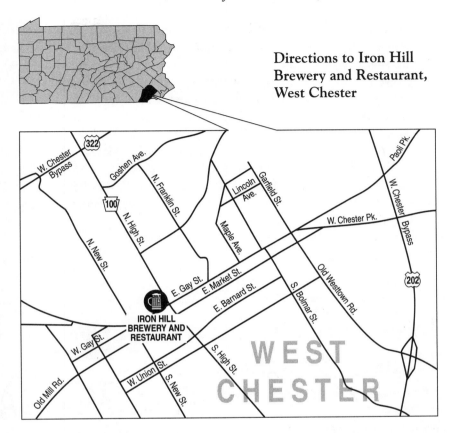

Directions to Iron Hill Brewery and Restaurant, West Chester

and a special prime rib dinner. Iron Hill, West Chester, also has Throwdown Thursdays, featuring a 10 P.M. happy hour with drinks and bar food specials and a DJ, and Featured Fridays, with a 5 P.M. to 7 P.M. happy hour offering martini and pint specials.

Special considerations: Kids welcome. Handicapped-accessible. Vegetarian meals available. Cigars allowed at the bar.

Parking: On-street metered parking can be tight, but there is a garage at Chestnut and Walnut Streets; Iron Hill will validate tickets.

Lodging in the area: Abbey Green Motor Lodge, 1036 Wilmington Pike, 610-692-3310; Beechwood Motel, 1310 Wilmington Pike, 610-399-0970; Holiday Inn West Chester, 610-692-1900.

Area attractions: Fly over to the ***American Helicopter Museum*** (1220 American Boulevard, 610-436-9600) and check out the vintage rotary-wing aircraft and museum exhibits. Nearby is ***Longwood Gardens*** (800-737-5500 or 610-388-1000), the former country estate of Pierre Du Pont and one of the most impressive horticultural displays in the United States. The conservatory building and 3.5 acres of greenhouses allow year-round displays of bounteous flowering plants. The gardens have three sets of impressive fountains. Reservations are suggested for seasonal shows. This is also mushroom country; growers in Kennett Square and Avondale supply most of the country's mushrooms. The **Phillips Mushroom Museum** (909 East Baltimore Pike, Kennett Square, 610-388-6082) provides an interesting look at this edible fungus. Not far away are the Brandywine area attractions, including **Brandywine Battlefield Park** (Routes 1 and 100) and the **Brandywine River Museum** (610-388-2700), which houses artwork by the Wyeths. The Brandywine River offers a beautiful, serene canoe trip; paddle your own or check into the canoe rental services in the area.

Other area beer sites: See Victory listing on page 101.

John Harvard's Brew House, Springfield

1001 Baltimore Pike, Springfield, 19064
610-544-4440
www.johnharvards.com

For the John Harvard's story, see the entry for John Harvard's Brew House, Wayne, on page 86.

The Springfield Brew House is in a strip mall, but it's a nice one, anchored by a Borders bookstore and located across the street from Springfield Mall. That's perfect positioning for holing up while friends or significant others go shopping!

Brewer Brian McConnell is mixing up the taps a lot, offering a wide variety of beers. I recently tried his winter beer, St. Nick's Red, and found it a real tongue-spanker of an IPA with a refreshingly big hop flavor. He also knows what to do with malt, as witnessed by his Imperial Stout, a warm and gentle giant. And just because every brewpub

Beers brewed: Year-round: All-American Light Lager, John Harvard's Pale Ale or American Amber Ale, Nut Brown Ale or Loch Lanier Scottish Ale, a rotating fruit-wheat beer, and something from the porter/stout/schwarzbier category. Seasonals: Rotate as Brian decides what to make throughout the year.

needs a lighter beer, he does a clean, malty, pint-worthy Munich Helles. Something for everyone!

Opened: June 1997.

Owner: Boston Culinary Group.

Brewer: Brian McConnell; Pete Heneks, assistant brewer.

System: 15-barrel Pub Brewing System brewhouse, 2,000 barrels annual capacity.

Production: 600 barrels in 2004 (estimated).

Brewpub hours: Seven days a week, 11:30 A.M. to 1 A.M.

Tours: During restaurant hours, subject to brewer availability.

Take-out beer: Growlers.

Food: The John Harvard's menu features upscale pub fare, including Asian Crispadillas, chicken pot pie, catch-of-the-day salad, calamari, and a few local specials.

Extras: Full liquor license. Nice Sunday brunch. Regular happy hour Monday through Friday, 4 P.M. to 8 P.M.

Special considerations: Kids welcome. Handicapped-accessible. Cigars allowed and sold at the bar. Vegetarian meals available.

The Pick: St. Nick's Red Ale was the seasonal on tap when I visited, and it is a rocket. The hop flavor comes through only after your mouth adjusts from the 65+ IBU smack, but there is plenty of real hop flavor and aroma there. Quite the hop monster, this one.

Directions to John Harvard's Brew House, Springfield

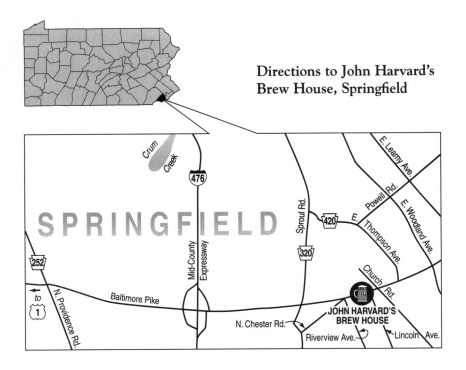

Parking: Plenty of parking in off-street lot.

Lodging in the area: McIntosh Inn of Media, Routes 1 and 352, Media, 610-565-5800.

Area attractions: The large *Springfield Mall* is right across the street. If you prefer small shops and boutiques, there are plenty of them just down the road in Media. *Ridley Creek State Park* (1023 Sycamore Mills Road, 610-892-3900) has fishing and trails for biking, walking, cross-country skiing, and horseback riding.

Other area beer sites: *Iron Hill,* up the road in Media (see below), is about it.

Iron Hill Brewery and Restaurant, Media

30 East State Street, Media, PA 19063
610-627-9000
www.ironhillbrewery.com

With two Iron Hills down already, you've got pretty much of the story. I'll direct you back to the entries for the West Chester (page 89) and North Wales (page 65) Iron Hills to get that, and we'll just talk about the Media location here.

The first time I went to Iron Hill Media was for one of their Brewer's Reserve nights. They do these less regularly than they used to, but they're a lot of fun, and you should come out if you get a chance (check the website for scheduled events). They invite an outside brewer, such as Stoudt's, Victory, Dogfish Head, or in this case, a distiller, Anchor, to come in and share their finest beer, and all the Iron Hill brewers bring a keg or cask of their finest, and those beers go on special that night. You can tour the brewery, hang out with all the brewers, get a free pint glass, and have a rare chance to taste a bunch of GABF medal-level beers all at once; okay, you actually get that chance at Iron Hill pretty often, but this is more so!

Anyway, it was a cold December night, and Cathy and I went over to Iron Hill, Media. Mark Edelson had told me that the brewery was built in an old supermarket, and I wasn't really expecting much. "Cleanup on aisle 6," I guess. But I was stunned. Iron Hill didn't spare expense on interior architecture in any of its restaurants, but this one was beautiful, easily my favorite in the group. High ceilings give a huge feeling of space that the warm tones of the wood and paint keep from being intimidating. The lighting is subdued and indirect.

"Supermarket?" I asked Mark. "There was a suspended ceiling," he said. "They removed it, and there was all this space up there. The architect loved it and talked us into using it." He shook his head with a painful grin. "It's gorgeous, but it was expensive, and it's a bear to heat it in the winter." Suffering for the art builds character, Mark.

Bob Barrar is the brewer here—"Bob the Brewer," as he's known. I drank his imperial stout that night, and it was a deep, dark, rich beauty of a beer. "I love wintertime," Bob confided to me. "I like big Belgians, I like Russian Imperial stouts, the big beers you can make in wintertime." With Bob's bushy black beard, the Russian Imperial stouts are a natural, but I have to question how much a man who consistently wears a pair of cargo shorts regardless of the temperature (he was wearing them when the crew rigged in the tanks at North Wales last January and the temperature was about 22 degrees F) really *likes* winter!

It does show in his beers. Bob's regular beers are well-made, competent brews, but his passion and craft are lavished on the bigger beers. Even his Pig Iron Porter shows evidence of that love. His West Coast Gold is a light golden ale with a barge-load of hops in it—completely unbalanced, and that's the point. Bob really loves the Belgian types: His Dubbel was deep and sweet, yet complex and structured—much nicer than most other American-brewed dubbels I've had—and his Tripel was similarly deep, spiked with bright spice and yeast notes, a beautiful masterwork of a beer.

Beers brewed: Year-round: Iron Hill Light Lager, Raspberry Wheat, Lodestone Lager (GABF Gold, 1997; GABF Bronze, 2000), Anvil Ale, Ironbound Ale, Pig Iron Porter (GABF Bronze, 2002; RAF Silver, 2002, 2003). Seasonals: Altbier, Barleywine, Belgian White, Bohemian Pils, Bourbon-aged Russian Imperial Stout (GABF Bronze, 2004), Dry Stout, ESB, Hefeweizen, Imperial IPA, India Pale Ale, Lambic de Hill (GABF Gold, 2003), Maibock (GABF Bronze, 2000; GABF Gold, 1999), Munich Dunkel (GABF Bronze, 2003), Nut Brown Ale, Oatmeal Stout, Oktoberfest, Old Ale, Russian Imperial Stout (GABF Gold, 2003), Saison (GABF Bronze, 2003), Dubbel, Tripel (GABF Bronze, 2002, 2004), Vienna (GABF Bronze, 1999), Wee Heavy (GABF Bronze, 1998, 2001), Oud Bruin, Doppelbock, Weizenbock. (*Note:* The medals were won at brewpubs within the group, not necessarily at this particular pub.)

The Pick: Bob's Pig Iron Porter is righteous, a wild boar of a Pig Iron Porter, heavy, gutsy, and maybe even a little threatening—beer with a bite to it. Hops, chocolate, fruit, weight, alcohol: Take a sip—it's all in there, waiting. Take one on.

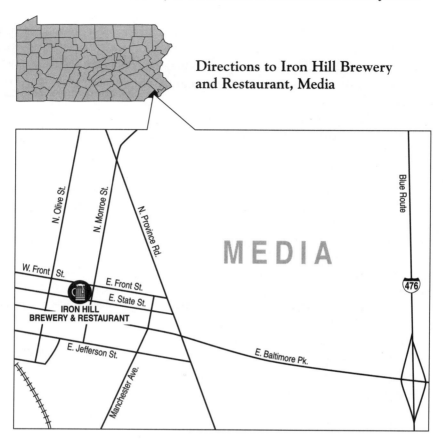

Directions to Iron Hill Brewery and Restaurant, Media

I've been to Media in the summer, and Bob's big hoppy beers are great in the heat. But I think I'm going to make a habit of going to Media in the winter, to see what big, deep beers Bob has to sip on while I look out the front windows at the cold, cold weather that can't touch me in that extravagantly heated beauty of a brewpub.

Opened: June 2000.
Owners: Mark Edelson, Kevin Finn, Kevin Davies.
Brewer: Bob Barrar.
System: 10-hectoliter Specific Mechanical brewhouse, 1,000 barrels annual capacity.
Production: 820 barrels in 2004 (estimated).
Brewpub hours: Monday and Tuesday, 11:30 A.M. to 12:30 A.M.; Wednesday through Saturday, 11:30 A.M. to 1:30 A.M.; Sunday, 11 A.M. to 11:30 P.M.
Tours: Upon request.

Take-out beer: Growlers.

Food: See Iron Hill, West Chester (page 90).

Extras: Pool tables. Like the other Iron Hills, this one has a regular weekly schedule of specials: Fat Tuesday, a Creole-style prix fixe dinner; Thursday, seafood; and Sunday, brunch and a special prime rib dinner.

Special considerations: Kids welcome. Handicapped-accessible. Vegetarian meals available. Cigars allowed at the bar.

Parking: Street parking, plus public lots on both sides of the restaurant.

Lodging in the area/Area attractions/Other area beer sites: *Quotations* (37 East State Street, 610-627-2515) is right across the street and is developing a steadily improving selection of hard-to-find beers. Definitely worth the walk. Also see the John Harvard's, Springfield, entry (page 94) for suggestions.

Victory Brewing Company

420 Acorn Lane, Downingtown, PA 19335
610-873-0881
www.victorybeer.com

Victory is aptly named. It is a victory of beer geek over marketer. The two principals, Ron Barchet and Bill Covaleski, are childhood friends who homebrewed together for years. Then, through an odd set of circumstances, they wound up brewing at the same microbrewery. One thing led to another, and they decided to open their own. After years of plans, salesmanship, and sweat, Victory was born.

Now that they are running their own show, they have decided to give their beer a fair chance. Victory doesn't compromise for the market, because Ron and Bill believe that there is a market for uncompromising beer. "Everyone else is brewing what they think the market wants," said Ron. "We're brewing what we want, and we're beer geeks."

They're uncommon beer geeks, at that. Victory brews lager as well as ales, bucking the national trend in microbrewing (although Pennsyl-

vania has the greatest concentration of lager microbrewers in the country). Victory's unabashed Prima
Pils is a bold statement of mission, a beer that blows
away any lame ideas about being "just another pilsner" in a powerful gust of Saaz hop aroma. Late
winter is fortified by the arrival of St.Victorious
Doppelbock, a big d-bock with a surprising hint of
beech-smoked malt. And the steady anchor in the
brewpub lineup is the Victory Lager, recently reformulated as a helles from its previous incarnation as
a Dortmunder Export style.

Beers brewed: Year-round:
Victory Lager, Prima Pils,
HopDevil India Pale Ale,
Golden Monkey. Seasonals:
Hop Wallop Ale , Mad King's
Weiss, Kölsch, Vienna Lager,
Old Horizontal Barleywine,
St. Victorious Doppelbock,
St. Boisterous Hellerbock,
Whirlwind Wit, Sunrise Weiss-
bier, Sunset Dunkleweizen,
Moonglow Weizenbock, Uncle
Teddy's Bitter, Workhorse
Porter, V-10, V-12, Grand Cru,
Festbier, ESB, Storm King Impe-
rial Stout, Victory Dark Lager.

Don't think it's all cold tanks and long waits,
though. After all, Victory's flagship beer has turned
out to be the bedazzlingly powerful HopDevil IPA, a
beer that builds a tower of hop power on a rock-solid
base of German malt, with the beguilingly smooth
(and whackingly strong) Belgian-style Golden Monkey coming in a
strong third. Geeks wait impatiently for the annual release of Hop Wallop
Ale, a beer Victory describes stylistically as "a big hoppy ale." You'll find
German-based ale magic in the duo of Sunrise Weissbier, a soft classic
weissbier, and its Mr. Hyde-like companion Moonglow Weizenbock, a
very nice, very big wheat bock. Topping it off is Victory's one-two punch:
Old Horizontal Barleywine and Storm King Imperial Stout.

Victory's beers were winning critical acclaim across the country
even when they were available only within about 150 miles of the
brewery. Locals mailed samples to their friends in other states. I know
one guy who drove from Indiana to Harrisburg just to get some Victory
beer. Now wider distribution—to Chicago, Boston, and California—
has made it easy for people to find Victory.

Victory's growth has pushed into the adjoining bay of the building,
giving them room for a big bottling line that has all the necessary doodads to keep Victory's beer fresh as long as possible. They have replaced
their solid 25-barrel brewhouse with a new 50-barrel one (the old one
served as an upgrade for Weyerbacher). But don't even think that the
beer has changed, or dropped one notch in geekly intensity. Quality has
not been compromised for quantity. Ron Barchet told me quite happily
that the automation of the new system will actually allow him to regain
more personal control of the brewing process.

The pub in Downingtown does represent some compromises. The
brewery was built in part of an old Pepperidge Farm complex, so it's very
much an industrial space. When I was first there, the concrete floor and

cinderblock walls were exposed. High, echoing ceilings had been hung with empty malt bags in an attempt to deaden the sound. Since then, Victory has put in carpet and acoustic tile.

The industrial feel is easily overlooked, however, because the service is friendly and the food is as fresh and carefully made as the beer. The big, wood-fired brick oven in the pub goes through about a cord of wood each week. From its flaming maw come crisp-crusted pizzas with imaginative ingredients—try the multi-mushroom pie in this fungus-happy area. This is definitely a place for families. My kids love Victory's size, the brewed root beer, and the kids' menu.

Plant yourself at the bar, made from the wooden crates in which the original brewhouse was shipped. Get a glass of cask-conditioned HopDevil from the handpump, and get an eyeful of those big tanks behind the bar—a lot more of them than there were in 1996. They're full of Victory . . . though not for long. Time for the next batch to arrive; drink up!

The Pick: One ale, one lager—that's fair. HopDevil IPA is the East's answer to the western hop-monster beers, but with the East's trademark balance. HopDevil has a bedrock foundation of malt that makes its wildly aromatic hoppiness even more appealing. Outstanding, galactic-class beer. Victory Lager has undergone a change from my beloved export style to a helles, which I like every bit as much. Victory has mastered the malt character of the Munich helles, a beer that evaporates from your glass. This is my dad's Pick, too, one of the few craft beers he truly enjoys. It's part of the greatness of this beer that he and I can both love it.

Opened: February 1996.

Owners: Ron Barchet, Bill Covaleski, and private investors.

Brewers: Brian Hollinger, Rob Cassel, Luke Lindsey, John Baer, Scott Gilbert, Dave Schurr, Steve Zweir, Greg Papp.

System: 50-barrel Rolec brewhouse, 35,000 barrels annual capacity.

Production: 15,520 barrels in 2003.

Brewpub hours: Monday through Saturday, 11:30 A.M. to midnight; Sunday, 1 P.M. to 10 P.M.

Tours: Friday and Saturday at 4 P.M.

Take-out beer: Growlers, six-packs, cases, kegs.

Food: Victory's wood-fired oven bakes great pizzas. You can get fresh salads and sandwiches and some of the best fries around. At dessert time, be sure to check the menu for the occasional batch of Storm King ice cream, rare and delicious. If you just want a snack, try the homemade, home-rolled soft pretzels. Victory also brews a great root beer.

Extras: Victory has darts and regulation-size pool tables. You can also check the well-stocked gift shop for a huge range of V-gear.

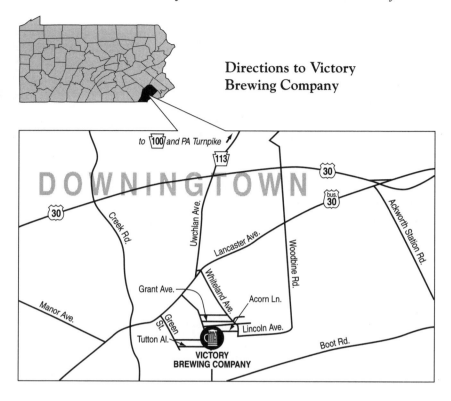

Directions to Victory Brewing Company

Special considerations: Kids welcome. Handicapped-accessible. Cigars allowed and sold. Vegetarian meals available.

Parking: Free off-street parking; please stick to the lined spaces!

Lodging in the area: Desmond Great Valley Hotel, 1 Liberty Boulevard, Malvern, 610-269-9800; Duling Kurtz House and Country Inn, 146 South Whitford Road, Exton, 610-524-1830; Holiday Inn Express, 120 North Pottstown Pike, Exton, 610-524-9000; Marsh Creek Campground, Route 282, Lyndell, 610-942-2282.

Area attractions: If it's apple season, go to **Highland Orchards** (610-269-3494) to pick your own. If you have younger kids, you'll want to visit **Springton Manor Farm** (5 miles west on Route 322, on Springton Road, 610-942-2450), a demonstration farm with pigs and poultry in a petting area. Admission is free. **Stargazer's Stone,** at Route 162 and Stargazer Road, was an observation point for the surveying of the Mason-Dixon line. The Brandywine Valley Association watershed advocacy group purchased a 300-acre property, the **Myrick Farm Center** (610-793-1090), and has set aside the former farm for hiking and children's education. If you want to see how things used to be done on the farm, back in the days of steam, you'll want to hit the Old Thresherman's Reunion at the **Rough and Tumble Engineers Historical Association** (on the eastern edge of Kinzers, on the north side of Route 30; full schedule at www.roughandtumble.org). Everyone just calls it the Rough and Tumble, and they have a number of events during the year. The Old Thresherman's Reunion, in mid-August, is one of the biggest collections of steam tractors, steam shovels, early gas and diesel tractors, stationary steam engines, and "hit and miss" engines that you'll find anywhere—everything from a huge stationary Corliss engine to a tiny Sterling cycle engine you could hold in the palm of your hand. I told Bill Covaleski about this place, he took his kids, and now he's hooked, too.

Other area beer sites: *The Epicurean* (Route 113 and Township Line Road, Phoenixville, 610-933-1336), a very nice restaurant with six good taps and a wide bottle selection, also has a six-pack store that sells bottles to go. See and be seen with a glass of great beer at the **Drafting Room** (635 North Route 113, Exton, 610-363-0521), a neon-lit, designer-friendly bar. Bill and Ron also recommend the **Half Moon Restaurant and Saloon** (108 West State Street, Kennett Square, 610-444-7232).

McKenzie Brew House

451 Wilmington Pike, Glen Mills, PA 19342
610-361-9800
www.mckenziebrewhouse.com

On the morning of September 11, 2001, Scott Morrison was breaking camp in the Poconos. He was taking a break from heavy work getting the brewery ready for a late-fall opening at McKenzie Brew House: a short camping trip, then out to the far end of Long Island to do a little brewing with his friend Phil Markowski at Southampton Publick House. He got close enough to Manhattan to see the smoke from the World Trade Center before he turned on the radio and learned what had happened.

"Everyone else was trying to get off the island," Scott recalled; "I was trying to get on, and they wouldn't let me!" He was getting nowhere, so he swung northeast to Groton, Connecticut, and took the ferry across to the northeastern tip of Long Island. A surprised Markowski answered his door at 9 that night to find Morrison on the step. "It took me twelve hours," Morrison said, laughing as he remembered that day, "but I made it."

Morrison (or "Dude," as most of the brewing community calls him) makes his own path in most things. Originally from Chester County, Morrison moved up to Connecticut to brew at Elm City Brewing with the legendary Ron Page. He met Markowski there, while Phil was at New England Brewing in Norwalk, Connecticut, and became a bit fanatical about his brewing. Consistency is the number-one goal at production breweries like Elm City, and that was a mindset that Morrison had to break to some degree at McKenzie.

"When I was a microbrewer," Morrison said, "it was four beers, and you did everything for consistency. At a brewpub, consistency is still important, but the most important thing is making new beers." It didn't come easily. I remember Morrison explaining early on how he intended to change one variable per batch on a beer he wasn't quite pleased with, while I thought of how most brewpub brewers would simply throw in another 10 pounds of hops and half a bag of specialty malt and see how that batch came out.

But the Dude's been loosening up and flexing his brewery muscle since that first year, and things have gotten downright funky. Literally funky, as in the *brettanomyces*-laced bone-dry Trappist Pale Ale that snagged him a bronze medal at the Great American Beer Festival. He's also regularly brewing an Abbey 11, which he describes as like an abbey 12 with more residual sugar, and a big Double White, a supercharged *witbier*. He's also been doing a "Burton series": an ESB, an IPA, and possibly a barleywine, all patterned on the kind of over-the-top brewing tone set by the legendary Ballantine Burton Ale, which was super-hopped and aged for years.

Scott's realized that being close to the action is a good thing. "There are great advantages to a brewpub," Morrison told me with a big grin. "I don't have to worry about how the beer's handled at retail outlets. I lost a lot of sleep over that at Elm City. But here, all I have to do is pull the tap!"

Beers brewed: Year-round: Light Lager, Unicorn Amber, O Rogue Pale Ale, Shane's Gold, Black Lab Stout. Year-round specialty bottles: Farmhouse Saison (GABF Bronze, 2003), Bavay Biere de Garde (GABF Bronze, 2004), Raven Baltic Porter. Seasonals: O'Reilly's Irish Red, Pumpkin Ale, Octob Fest, East Kent IPA, Maibock, Brandywine Gold (helles), Sun mer Wheat (American-style), Hefe Weizen, Double White, Raspberry Wheat, Blackberry Wheat, Belgian Pale Ale, Alt Beer, "Steam" Style Beer, Burton Ale. Rotating specialty bottles from "The Beer Cellar" Super Wit, Belgian Xmas, Grand Cru, Abbey 8, Abbey 11 Triple, Trappist Pale Ale (GABF Bronze, 2003), 5 Czars Imperi Stout, Belgian Gold.

When they pull the tap for you in McKenzie's spacious barroom, or downstairs in the friendly confines of the Underground, you'll get either one of Scott's solid basic beers or one of a set of more adventurous seasonals. They're clean, solidly in style—and consistent! But to get the bold stuff, you'll have to go to the bottled specialties, where you'll find everything from a big lager-brewed Baltic porter to a stunningly solid barleywine, with a big range of Belgian styles in between. Think of them as growlers you can drink at the bar.

Things have gone so well that a second brew-pub is in the planning stages. There were a few snags with the original building, and things were on hold when I wrote this, but it's almost inevitable, given the demand at the current location. Morrison's ready for now with some new used tanks. "There's no new equipment in the business anymore," he said with a laugh. "Those tanks are from New England Brewing, and this one," he said as he slapped a white-painted classic 7-barrel Grundy tank, "was made in 1948! Think of all it's been through!"

Kind of like Morrison himself, who's been in eastern microbrewing since the early days. Morrison is modest, but it's clear that he is becoming one of Pennsylvania's top brewers, a respected name like that of his friend Brian O'Reilly at Sly Fox, or his buddy Phil Markowski. I'm very pleased to see brewers getting recognition for doing more than just throwing bales of hops in the kettle.

The Pick: There are plenty of opportunities to pick beers that are easy to drink and quite accessible; there aren't many opportunities to pick a beer like The Dude's Trappist Pale Ale. I'm actually surprised that the GABF judges had the guts to give it a medal; this is a challenging beer, one with piercingly dry character, a bit of a nose-wrinkler, but very rewarding once you get to know it.

Opened: December 2001.
Owners: Bill Mangan.
Brewers: Scott Morrison.
System: 10-barrel Specific Mechanical brewhouse, 1,400 barrels annual capacity.
Production: 1,350 barrels in 2004 (estimated).
Brewpub hours: Seven days a week, 11:30 A.M. to 2 A.M.
Tours: Please call ahead and talk to Scott; he prefers at least forty-eight hours' notice.
Take-out beer: Growlers; some 750-milliliter specialty bottles available by singles or case (ask about case discount).
Food: The menu is wide-ranging, from wild mushroom and asparagus pasta (done with truffle oil and dry vermouth), to lobster pot pie, to a big old New York strip. Ease up to the big meal with one of

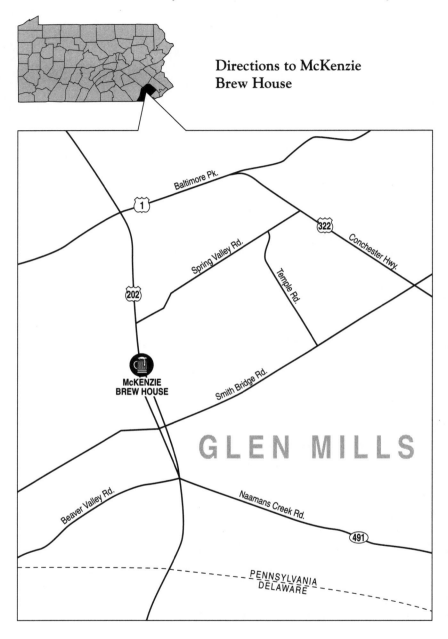

Directions to McKenzie Brew House

seven rotating soups (go Sunday for the Very Wild Mushroom) or something as exotic as the Tapas Trio or as simple and delicious as steamed littlenecks.

Extras: The Underground downstairs has a game room with pool tables, darts, and shuffleboard—a very popular room after dinner.

Special considerations: Kids welcome. Handicapped-accessible. Cigars allowed. Vegetarian meals available.

Parking: Large free on-site lot.

Lodging in the area: Brandywine River Hotel, Routes 1 and 100, Chadds Ford, 800-274-9644; Park Inn and Suites, Brandywine Valley, 1110 Baltimore Pike, 610-358-1700; Best Western, Routes 1 and 322, Concordville, 610-358-9400.

Area attractions: See the listing for Iron Hill, West Chester (pages 91–92).

Other area beer sites: Scott recommends the *Half Moon Restaurant and Saloon* (108 West State Street, Kennett Square, 610-444-7232). *Firewaters* (inside the Park Inn and Suites, see address above, 610-459-9959) has fifty taps and more than a hundred bottles, another like the highly successful and geek-beloved Firewaters in Atlantic City.

Pennsylvania Hotel Bars

The pint is not always the point. That's something you should keep in mind as you are beer traveling. While great beer is a goal in itself, I have found that there is equal pleasure to be found in the hunt for great bars. Some of them may serve nothing more lofty than Yuengling Lager and offer simple fare of hot dogs and cheese plates. Yet for me there is a sheer joy to walking into a place where I feel instantly at home, or where I find neons for beer brands long passed away, or an ornately carved wooden backbar with a hunting scene painted fifty years ago.

I love these great Pennsylvania bars as much as the great Pennsylvania beers. There are some beauties in the cities. Chiodo's, in Pittsburgh, is about as friendly as it gets. The Northeast Taproom, in Reading, pulls off being a great bar with great beer, something that is all too rare. McGlinchey's, in Philadelphia, will serve you good cheap beer and good cheap food, and you might meet anyone there. But my real love is reserved for the great bars out in the hills and forests of Penn's Woods.

I tended bar outside of Strasburg, Pennsylvania, back in the 1980s. I banked some money for graduate school and learned a lot about people and drinking. I always suspected that a lot of the reason the owner built the bar was so that his friends could come by and have a beer with him. As I served these guys, most of them World War II and Korea vets, I kept hearing about drinking "down at the hotel."

The hotel (which they pronounced "HO-tel," as opposed to a Hilton or Ritz-Carlton "ho-TEL") they were talking about was a hotel bar, in this case the Strasburg Hotel or sometimes the Rawlinsville Hotel. These were not hotels in the normal sense; I don't know of anyone ever staying overnight in one . . . at least, not intentionally. They were simply bars, watering holes, although they used to be much more.

The Pennsylvania hotel bar is a holdover from Colonial and stagecoach days. Colonial travel was appallingly difficult and expensive because of the hills, ridges, and waterways that began just outside of Philadelphia. Philadelphians considered a voyage to England easier than a journey to Reading, and they were right. Taverns, inns, and hotels opened through the southeastern part of the commonwealth to sustain the traveler with a bed, hearty road-worthy fare, and a pot of restorative cider, ale, or whiskey.

As roads were built and railroads replaced stagecoach lines, the hotel evolved into a restaurant and saloon. It became more a place for the local worker than for the traveler. European immigrants provided the workforce that carried America into the industrial age, and they also provided the thirsty throats that propelled us into the lager age. The hotel bar, complete with cuspidor and "free lunch," kept the beer cold and flowing.

After Prohibition's gloomy days, when drinking went undercover in the speakeasies, the pool halls, and the so-called "seafood houses," the hotel bar was back, at least in upstate Pennsylvania. But soon after World War II, Americans started to cocoon themselves in living rooms lit by the blue glow of televisions and cooled by central air, quaffing easily available packaged beer. The hotel's appeal slipped. It was no longer the center of socializing, that role usurped by fire halls, American Legion and VFW clubs, and bingo halls.

The upshot of these trends is that genuine hotel bars are a vanishing breed, and unchanged examples are a little harder to find every year. Almost as many have been ruined by ham-handed "restorations" as have been turned into homes, shops, and hardware stores. But some beauties still can be found out in the ridge country of Berks, Schuylkill, and Lehigh Counties. We'll take a quick tour through some of the best.

High on the list is the **Kempton Hotel** (610-756-6588). Located at the intersection of Routes 737 and 143, east of Hawk Mountain, the Kempton has been renewed without losing its "real deal" appeal. It was built in 1874 to house and feed the men building the railroad between Berks and Lehigh Counties and it survives as the local bar, restaurant, and meeting place for a large, thinly populated area. The kitchen serves up regional fare like chicken and waffles, pig stomach stew, and hickory nut pie. Look up to admire one of the unique attractions of the Kempton. Two local artists have painted three murals on the hotel ceiling: *Kempton History* in the bar, the *Pageant of American History* in the dining room, and the *Life of Christ* in the back banquet room. It's worth the trip.

If you head south on Rout 737 about 3 miles or so, you will come to the little village of Stony Run. The **Stony Run Hotel** (610-756-4433) sits on the corner, a big white building with green trim. New owners Jerry and Marie Boltz took over in 1998, intending to restore the hotel. I honestly worried, but what they have done should be a model for such restoration. The bar is almost untouched, including the massive back-bar, hand-carved in nearby Topton more than a hundred years ago. If you order a bottle, it will be opened with a Stegmaier promotional bottle opener from the 1940s; Marie said they found a box of them in a back room. The major change was a spotless new modern kitchen, a welcome addition to any bar. They've even left the outhouse in the backyard, although indoor plumbing has been added.

If you want to try some of the hearty and filling Pennsylvania Dutch hotel food, you can't do better than **Haag's Hotel** in Shartlesville (just off Exit 8 of I-78 west of Allentown, 610-488-6692). The family-style tables at Haag's are authentically laden, brimming over with ham, chicken, sausage, beef, gravy, potato filling, sweet potatoes, green beans, chicken potpie, dried corn, pickled beets, pepper cabbage, pickles, applesauce, large-pearl tapioca, stewed apricots, sugar cookies, shoofly pie, cherry and apple pies, and ice cream, with plenty of bread and butter, cottage cheese, and apple butter on the side. This is solid food that lines the belly like bricks and mortar.

For those who would rather go at it just a bit less full-bore, **Hubert's Inn,** on the left side of Route 183 coming into Cressona from Pottsville (570-385-3613), has a fine menu of down-to-earth eating. The dining room is nice enough for taking out the in-laws. (Don't worry, the bar is close enough to slip out for a quick one during dinner!) This is a nice, cozy little bar, with a compact yet impressive backbar and the cleanest men's room you'll find around.

One of my favorite spots in upstate Pennsylvania is the town of Jim Thorpe. There's lots to do here, but the must-see for the beer traveler is the Hotel Switzerland, right at the square under the hill. Though the name has been changed to **JT's Steak and Ale** (570-325-4563), it's still the Switzerland to me. Belly up to the dark wooden bar and imagine yourself a coal magnate, surveying the world over a cold mug of lager. Come hungry; the place serves a fine steak dinner and usually has some good beer to go with it.

You can get the best of both worlds at the **Douglassville Hotel** (Route 422 East, Douglassville, 610-385-2585). The big porch outside and the big menu inside will tell you it's a real hotel, and the beer list, sporting imports and micros from all over, will make you a happy geek. The bar gets a little loud and smoky at night, so I usually stay in the dining room. Hog into the salad bar, where you'll find things like chow-chow (pickled vegetables) and Froot Loops, then get a big plate of the house special, Veal Gruyère.

These hotels are not all in the Pennsylvania Dutch Country, either. I found a real gem while poking around Altoona after visiting Marzoni's: the **U.S. Hotel** (401 South Juniata Street, Hollidaysburg, 814-

695-9924), dating from 1835. It has a solid twin-pillar backbar lit by original glass marble "bunch o' grapes" lights, tile walls, a footrail, and even a tiled trough with intact plumbing at the foot of the bar, so that "gentlemen" wouldn't have to search for a spittoon. Belly up to this one and you'll really know what it was like back when.

There are more fine old hotel bars out there. If you can find an out-of-print book called *Bars of Reading and Berks*, by "Suds" Kroge and "Dregs" Donnigan, buy it. It's a somewhat dated but invaluable guide to these old bars and a hilarious read to boot.

Try any small town along the Appalachian front and chances are you'll find a hotel. You'll know the thrill of discovery, whether it features an original pressed-tin ceiling, an ornately carved or painted backbar, or just a fresh, clean squirt of Yuengling. It's out there, waiting. Go and find it.

A PATCHWORK OF FARMS
Pennsylvania Dutch Country

Most people think of Lancaster County alone as Pennsylvania Dutch Country, thanks to the county's busy tourist bureau. There are indeed a lot of Amish farms and "Dutchie" accents in Lancaster, but you'll find them up through Lebanon and Berks Counties as well, and on into the Lehigh Valley. This is my home territory. I was born and raised in Lancaster County, like all my family since 1741, so I'm a bit nuts about the place.

The small cities of the area—Lancaster, Reading, Allentown, Bethlehem, and Easton—were at first market towns. They became industrial towns, and now they are finding their own ways in the shifting economy of the twenty-first century. All of them have come to realize that their heritage is bankable, so you will find them eager to please tourists. Lancaster has been this way for years, but Reading and the towns of the Lehigh Valley also have learned the art of promotion and the value of tourism.

This is Pennsylvania's breadbasket. Watered by rivers like the Schuylkill, Conestoga, and Lehigh, small farms cover the landscape, producing milk, fruit, vegetables, soybeans, and even cigar tobacco. There are some fine restaurants here, serving everything from nouvelle cuisine to massive, multicourse "Pennsylvania hotel" dinners. The regional fare is hearty and simple, with farmboys' delights such as chicken potpie, dripping with gravy and freighted with great raftlike noodles, and molasses-and-cake-filled shoofly pies.

You'll also find good beer here, thanks to some great little breweries. Carol and Ed Stoudt started things in northern Lancaster County back in 1987, with Pennsylvania's first microbrewery in modern times.

They have since been joined by a bevy of brewers, all making fine products. True to their heritage, some of them brew German-style lager beers, and the local population laps it up.

Visiting these breweries will give you an opportunity to take a leisurely drive through gently rolling hills and past beautifully kept farms. One of my favorite drives is to head east from New Holland on Route 23, along the ridge through the Twin Valley area to Morgantown. You can also take a shopping trip from the factory outlets along Route 30 in Lancaster up Route 222 to the factory outlets in Reading. And if you get thirsty on the way, Stoudt's is just off Route 222.

There is also the attraction of the Amish themselves. They live among us "English," as the Amish call all people outside the faith, but they strive to keep themselves separate. Please respect their privacy. Although the Amish of Lancaster County are more worldly than some of their brethren in upstate New York or Indiana, they still try to live in accordance with their beliefs. There are plenty of Amish attractions; some are better than others. The Amish Farm and House is one of the more accurate ones, on Route 30 east of Lancaster (717-394-6185).

There are two other areas in Pennsylvania Dutch Country that you should visit. The high bluffs on the lower Susquehanna near Holtwood Dam are breathtakingly beautiful in spring and fall. Trails there range from easy strolls by Pequea Creek along old trolley beds to soaring climbs that challenge the experienced day hiker. Far to the east is the Delaware River, curving quietly with gentle splendor through some of the prettiest countryside in Pennsylvania. Taking a drive along the Delaware is a wonderful way to spend the afternoon.

Wherever you go in Pennsylvania Dutch Country, take your time; the pace is wonderfully slow here. You'll find plenty to see, lots of shops to visit, and countless backroads to explore. You may come for the Amish, but be sure to take a look around. You'll come back for the beauty.

Lancaster Brewing Company

Plum and Walnut Streets, Lancaster, PA 17603
717-391-6258
www.lancasterbrewing.com

I grew up in Lancaster County. Our line of Brysons have lived there since 1741. My mother's side of the family has farmed in the county for more than two centuries, and her father and my father ran a general store outside Strasburg. My father and I both went to Franklin and Marshall College in Lancaster, where I met my wife. My parents still live there, in the little town of Paradise, and my children have played in the fields where I played.

I want you to understand how much this land means to me. I don't live there now—which is not to say that I don't live there anymore. But I know and love the farm-dotted valleys and ridges of Lancaster, the woods of the southern end, the river hills and the tiny roads of the northern reaches. It's my home, and it always will be.

I tell you all this because I want you to understand how deep-down glad and proud I am that Lancaster Brewing survives. I've always felt a connection to the brewery. Back when it was Lancaster Malt Brewing, we shared initials; buying LMB gear was like getting free monogramming. I was at the brewery's opening; I signed books there. I lost touch at times, but I was always interested, and when they fell into bankruptcy, I was aghast.

John Frantz, the man on the spot who rose from sales director to run the brewery and restaurant, reassured me then that they fully intended to survive, to come out of bankruptcy and rise again. With new investors, new management, a new menu, and even a couple new beers, it looks like he might be right.

"Things have changed, and for the better," Frantz told me. "We went bankrupt, and this is a new company. LMB ceased to exist, and Lancaster Brewing started that same day. We have new equipment, a new bottling line, and new cooperage [kegs]. We've been getting sixtels; it's a great way for a bar to sample a beer."

Beers brewed: Year-round: Gold Star Pilsner, Amish 4-Grain Pale Ale, Milk Stout, Litening Lager, Hop Hog IPA, Red Rose Amber Ale. Seasonals: Strawberry Wheat, Spring Bock, Hefeweizen, Baltic Porter, Gueuze, Oktoberfest, Winter Warmer, Dunkel Weizen, Lancastrator Doppelbock.

The Amish 4-Grain Pale Ale is the big seller, a solid pale with a good scoop of esters. The Strawberry Wheat is the biggest seasonal by far, although the Oktoberfest runs wild for two months. There's no fear of the bigger beers, either. I've had my head ripped off by a couple pints of Lancastrator, and the Gueuze is a piercing strike to the tongue.

"We quit bottling for a while," John said, referring to the period when their old bottling line left a lot of bad fills, sliced caps, and bad beer in general. "We went all draft, so there was no more bad beer. Our reputation seems to have weathered that: The draft is doing well; 2004 will be our best year ever, and the restaurant's doing well again."

The Pick: The Milk Stout is a sweet stout that is still somewhat roasty, a drink refreshing yet rich. My wife would walk over my back to get this beer. It's embarrassing to admit, but the combination of Milk Stout and Strawberry Wheat is truly delicious. And it is *not* a "girl beer"! Get some Gold Star, too, it's smooth and creamy, then comes through with a hoppy middle and a long bitter finish.

Stop by the restaurant and look around. The brewery is located in a renovated tobacco warehouse. The historic brick building has dark wood floors, massive wooden beams, high intricate brick ceilings, and copper accents. The warehouse works well as a showcase for the beer. The bar and the casual dining area wrap around an open drop to the attractive 15-barrel JV NorthWest brewhouse below, an interesting change from the usual behind-the-bar setup.

Brewing in Lancaster is a natural. The county once had fourteen breweries and was known nationwide as a brewing center. H. L. Mencken favored beer from the city's Rieker Star Brewery. Lancaster beers sold in Boston in the 1940s for $10 a keg, a princely sum for beer. But the last brewery went silent in 1956. Locally made beer finally made a comeback when Lancaster opened in 1995.

And now it's done it again. Lancaster's well on the path to recovery. I don't know if it's going to last as long as my family has in Lancaster, but I intend to retire here, and I'm hoping Lancaster Brewing will be around when I do. Keep at it, boys!

Opened: April 1995.
Owner: Private corporation; owners include the city of Lancaster.
Brewers: Christian Heim, Joe McMonagle.
System: 15-barrel JV NorthWest brewhouse, 8,000 barrels annual capacity.
Production: 4,000 barrels in 2004 (estimated).
Brewpub hours: Monday through Thursday, 11:30 A.M. to 11 P.M.; Friday and Saturday, 11:30 A.M. to midnight; Sunday, 11 A.M. to 10:30 P.M.
Tours: Daily 10 A.M. to 5 P.M., please call ahead.
Take-out beer: Growlers, six-packs, cases, kegs.

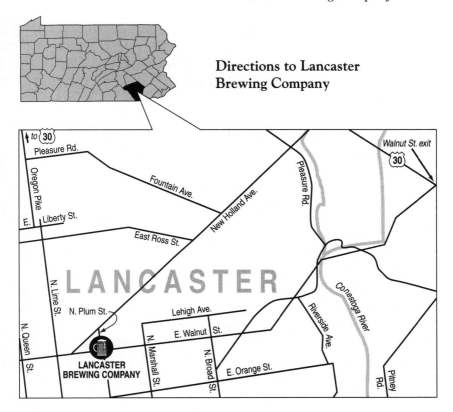

Directions to Lancaster Brewing Company

Food: The Walnut Street Grille is a busy restaurant and a popular spot for private parties. It features a full menu with ale-simmered mussels, grilled meatloaf, white chili, and the delicious Lamb Burger made with feta and tzatziki sauce. Vegetarians will enjoy the Mediterranean Vegetable Grille. Most entrées have suggested beer pairings—hint to other brewpubs!

Extras: There is a dartboard, and backgammon and chess-checker boards are built into the bar tables. Live music (acoustic and electric) on Fridays.

Events: Lancaster is starting to sponsor beer festivals again; check the website for further info. The first in years was a Blues and Brews Fest in October 2004, which is planned as an annual event.

Special considerations: Kids welcome (special menu). Restaurant is handicapped-accessible, but access to the brewery is limited. Cigars allowed in the bar area; selection of fine cigars for sale. Vegetarian and specially prepared meals available.

Parking: Small lot on Plum Street. Street parking can get tight at times. Weekends and evenings, you can park across the street.

Lodging in the area: Host Resort, 2300 Lincoln Highway East, 717-299-5500; Travelodge, 2101 Columbia Avenue, 717-397-4201 or 800-578-7878; Gardens of Eden B&B, 1894 Eden Road, 717-393-5179; The King's Cottage B&B, 1049 East King Street, 717-397-1017 or 800-747-8717.

Area attractions: Call the Pennsylvania Dutch Visitors Bureau (717-299-8901) to get a large package of literature about their many attractions. Lancaster's selection of factory outlets rivals Reading's these days. You'll find most of them on Route 30 east of Lancaster. *Reading China and Glass* in Rockvale Center (717-393-9747) has cheap pint glasses and sometimes sells "yards of ale" glasses. *Dutch Wonderland* (2249 Lincoln Highway East, 866-386-2839) is an amusement park just for the little ones, with scaled-back flumes, roller coasters, and bumper cars ideal for kids under ten; recently rated the fifth-best kids' amusement park in the world. *Wheatland* (1120 Marietta Avenue, 717-392-8721), the home of James Buchanan, Pennsylvania's admittedly not-very-notable contribution to the presidency, is a beautifully restored Federal-era mansion with original furniture. For tubers, a float down the Pequea Creek is a great way to cool off in the sticky heat of a Lancaster summer. You can rent tubes at *Sickman's Mill* (717-872-5951) in Conestoga; you can camp there, too. Take old sneakers and don't wear a white suit; the river's muddy sometimes. Just north of Ephrata, the *Green Dragon Farmers Market and Auction* is open every Friday, with a livestock auction, food stands, and more interesting people than you can shake a shoofly pie at. Stop by for a tour of the *Julius Sturgis Pretzel House* in Lititz (219 East Main Street, 717-626-4354). Then walk over to the *Wilbur Chocolate Company* (48 North Broad Street, 717-626-3249).

Other area beer sites: *Quips Pub* (457 New Holland Avenue, 717-397-3903) is not far and has been serving up great British and British-style beers since I was at Franklin and Marshall . . . er, a long time. The *Lancaster Dispensing Company* (33-35 North Market Street, 717-299-4602) has been one of Lancaster's best watering holes for years and has finally caught up to the better-beer idea. I had my first nonmainstream beer at the *Blue Star* (602 West King Street, 717-509-5095) way back in 1981, when it was still the Lauzus Hotel; before that, it was the Rieker Star Brewery. The beer selection's not bad at all, and the bar itself is a classic beauty. Be aware that now, as then, the crowd can be a bit rowdy at times! If you want someplace very nice to eat with a couple good beers and a wine list with more than fourteen hundred selections, **Strawberry Hill** (128 West Strawberry Street, 717-393-5544) fits the bill. You'll find a small but select draft and bottle selection; they love wine, but they've had good beer for more than fifteen years.

Bube's Brewery

**102 North Market Street,
Mount Joy, PA 17552
717-653-2056
www.bubesbrewery.com**

Six blind wise men went to Bube's to find out what it was like. When they returned, the people asked them, "What is Bube's like?"

The first man said, "Bube's is a brewpub, with well-made and tasty beers, a great semidry cider, and friendly bartenders."

The second man said, "No, Bube's is a unique set of lodgings, with rooms arranged as adventures, lavishly decorated with a sense of drama and humor, and one large suite of rooms like a cosmopolitan apartment, complete with kitchen."

The third man said, "Fool! Bube's is a hip martini bar, with an astonishing array of fine gins and vodkas, vermouths, bitters, and accoutrement, run by an obsessed and entertaining czar of martinis."

The fourth man said, "Where did you go, dotard? Bube's is a beer garden, an exceptionally lovely green oasis in the middle of town where people enjoy beer in relaxed informality and good cheer."

The fifth man said, "Verily, you're all nuts. Bube's is a deep set of catacombs, antique lagering cellars where people dine and celebrate, often entertained by mummery and music."

The sixth man said, "Mummery, flummery! Bube's is a nightclub, a warm, friendly bar with good beer and spirits, that turns into an intimate venue for live music as the night lengthens."

Beers brewed: All beers rotate; always five of the following, plus Bube's Hard Cider on tap at any time: Red Ale, Kölsch, Hefeweizen, IPA, Bavarian Lager, Nut Brown Ale, Imperial Stout, Honey Cream Ale, Scotch Ale, Porter, Belgian Strong Ale, Steam Beer. "We will always be adding to this list," Sam Allen says.

And the people said, "How can this be? Bube's is a brewpub, a nightclub, a hotel, a martini bar? Are these not wise men? How could they all find Bube's so different?"

And Lew said, relax, they are all correct, for Bube's is a big place, a fun place, a place that sizzles with imagination and drama and the never-ending energy that keeps it evolving for the pleasure of its guests. And besides, the blind guys missed the home-brew shop, the antique brewery tour, the art gallery, the banquet room upstairs, and Alois's Restaurant on the first floor. You need some new wise men, folks.

The Pick: Well, to be honest I really liked all six taps I trie at Bube's. Let's pick the Hard Cider, because it's so much better than most hard ciders on the market. It's semidry, not apple-soda sweet, has a decent depth to it, and is wa way too drinkable.

I probably missed a couple things myself, because Bube's (it really is pronounced "boobies"; it's German), at the Central Hotel in Mount Joy, is a rambling complex that is always expanding at the behest of proprietor Sam Allen. Allen is a former actor who has found his niche and his calling creating a series of wonders and comforts here at this old brewery and hotel complex.

It really is a historic brewery, run by Alois Bube in the 1800s. The full history is in a small museum upstairs from the lobby—there, I told you I missed something. Bube made lager beer, beer for which the brewery was well known. "We called it Bube's Brewery when we opened," Allen said. "But people kept calling and coming to visit and asking, 'Where's the brewery?' We did a study with the business department at Lebanon Valley College, and after we did all the work, they told us we had an image problem: People expected a brewery, and there was none." He grinned and chuckled. "No kidding!"

Allen wanted to brew, wanted to add a brewery, but how to do it in the room he had? I first reported on their intent to add a brewery in the mid-1990s, and a few more times in the late 1990s. "We spent the first four years doing all the legal paperwork," said Allen. It was a problem with the Pennsylvania Liquor Code (stop me if you've heard *that* one before). The property had a liquor license, and originally, Pennsylvania code didn't allow brewers to hold liquor licenses, and vice versa. When the law changed and brewpubs were allowed to hold licenses, licensees also were allowed to brew. Allen was off and running, and on November 28, 2001, the brewery served its first legal, house-brewed beer since 1917.

The beers are brewed in a tiny room by two not-so-tiny guys, brothers-in-law Doug Binkley and Tim McMullen. Tim was a homebrewer who'd dragged Doug into the pernicious hobby (just kidding, guys!), and when they heard that Bube's was putting in a brewery, they talked

Allen into giving them a shot. "We're not pros," said Doug. "We both still have our full-time jobs." Maybe so, but the beer has always been good, at least, from the time I stopped in a month after they opened to the last time I dropped by and ran the taps, five beers plus the cider.

Bube's is an experience, run like few other places in the East. What it really reminded me of was the McMenamin's brewpubs and bars in Oregon and Washington, inspired reusers of solid old buildings and patrons of incidental art. We could use a few more Bube's around these parts. Stop in and see what I mean, and be wiser than the blind men: explore. I've been going to Bube's for years (I started dating my wife there), and I never knew they had a beer garden till last month. Huh. Blind man!

Opened: Brewery reopened November 2001.

Owners: Sam Allen, Tobin Garber.

Brewers: Doug Binkley, Tim McMullen.

System: 3.5-barrel Specific Mechanical brewhouse, 350 barrels annual capacity.

Production: 200 barrels in 2004 (estimated).

Brewpub hours: Seven days a week, 11:30 A.M. to 2 A.M.

Tours: 5 P.M. to 10 P.M. tours of the historic brewery area are available seven days a week. The "modern" brewers are available for tours on Wednesday evenings ("and happy to meet you!").

Take-out beer: Growlers.

Food: Depending on where you dine, there are a number of menus, with items ranging from Mango Fritters to Sausage en Croute to start, followed by entrées that feature both serious vegetarian dishes and honking big cuts of meat and fish. There really is something for everyone here . . . as long as you're hungry.

Extras: Live music Thursday through Sunday evening, jazz in the front bar. Bube's is almost a theme park: There's the brewing museum, a very serious and well-armed martini maven in the front bar (just ask for Andrew), art gallery, gift shop and homebrew supply shop, beer garden (with outdoor pool table), The Catacombs for private parties and banquets, and rather uniquely decorated lodging upstairs.

Special considerations: Accommodations for kids, smoking, vegetarian meals, and the handicapped vary by restaurant; please call with specific concerns.

Parking: Good free street parking and small lot.

Lodging in the area: The Olde Fogie Farm B&B (106 Stackstown Road, Marietta, 877-653-3644) is a working farm, and a rare B&B

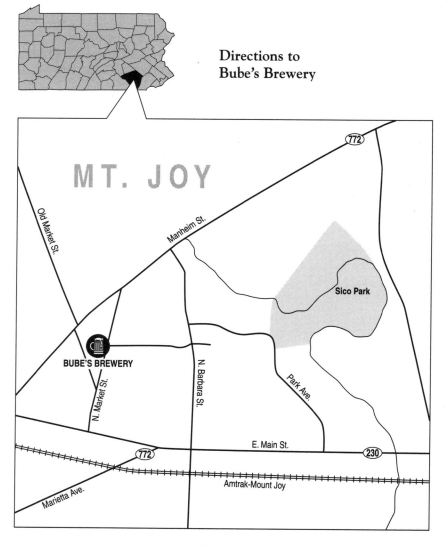

Directions to Bube's Brewery

that's perfect for small children. Olde Square Inn, 127 East Main Street, Mount Joy, 800-742-3533; Holiday Inn Express, 147 Merts Drive, Elizabethtown, 717-367-4000.

Area attractions: Hershey is not far away, and I think we all know what that means; if you don't, roll down the window and sniff. This is the home of **Hershey's Chocolate World** (HersheyPark Drive, 717-534-4900), a ride through the making of chocolate and a huge chocolate gift shop. **HersheyPark** amusement park (100 West HersheyPark Drive, 800-HERSHEY) has *eight* roller coasters and a water park, or you can just walk around and feed the carp in the stream. The **ZooAmerica Wildlife Park** (HersheyPark Drive, 717-534-3860), included in admission to HersheyPark, focuses on the animals of North America. Or you can just stop alongside the street and breathe deeply, till you gain a pound or two.

The **Cornwall Iron Furnace** (off Route 322, follow signs on Route 419 to Rexmont Street, 717-272-9711) is a restored iron mine and furnace; these are actual, original restored buildings, not re-creations. This was an important source of iron during the Colonial period and operated as a furnace through 1883.

Other area beer sites: Sam Allen notes that while Bube's bars are the most beer-oriented in town (and he's dead right), "Mount Joy has many other bars within walking distance, each with a distinct (non-chain) personality, and they are great for a pub crawl." Also consider **Shank's Tavern** (36 South Waterford Avenue, Marietta, 717-426-1205), a longtime spot for better beer that's holding up well. See the listings for Harrisburg (pages 153–54) and Lancaster (pages 116–17) as well.

Swashbuckler Brewing Company, Ltd.

83 Mansion House Road (on the Renaissance Faire grounds),
Manheim, PA 17545
717-664-3930
www.swashbuckler-beer.com

The last time I wrote about Scott Bowser was in the first edition of *Pennsylvania Breweries*, brewing so-so beers (and a pretty darned good cider) at the Summy House in Manheim. The Summy House is still around, but Scott's little brewery is gone, and so is Scott. In a plot reminiscent of *A Connecticut Yankee in King Arthur's Court*, Scott left Summy House, took a right turn on Route 72, and disappeared into the Renaissance.

What really happened is that Bowser got a call from Chuck Romito at the Mount Hope Vineyards, home of the Pennsylvania Renaissance Faire. "How

Beers brewed: Seasonal: Swashbuckler's Gold, Red Sea Amber Ale, Plank Walker's Pale Ale, Old Peg Leg Stout. (*Note:* All beers are brewed from May through October.)

can we get your beer up here?" Romito asked. "We've got no beer here, but we get 150,000 people a year."

Scott Bowser maybe didn't make the best beer, but nobody ever accused him of being slow on the uptake when there was a buck to be made. "A hundred and fifty thousand people in the summer and no beer?" he said to me with a big grin and a snort of laughter. "How can you go wrong!"

The Pick: Call me predictable, but I liked the Old Peg Leg Stout, Scott's bigger beer. It was chocolaty, roast and just pretty darned good drinking. But I feel I should mention that all the beers really were good; like Scott said, not medal winners, but definitely good pints of beer.

He almost did, but only by aiming too low. He took his Prussian Street Brewing system up to the Faire, a 3-barrel brewkettle and a couple of 7-barrel tanks. "We got behind after a week!" Scott told me. Time to get serious. He scanned the boneyard section of brewers' forums and found a system. "We went out to Las Vegas and bought Holy Cow's 12-barrel system and six tanks. That gave us 80 barrels tank capacity. By week seven of the Faire, we're still scrambling. We sell more beer in fifteen weeks than some restaurants do in two years."

Like some Pennsylvania brewpub owners, Romito wanted to take advantage of the quirks of Pennsylvania law to sell his wine. Brewpubs are allowed to sell their own house beer and Pennsylvania wines without a liquor license. He sells a lot of wine now, but Scott's beer outsells it by four to one.

"We've got three bars, serving six to eight thousand people a day during the Faire," Scott said. "But they're coming for the Faire, not for our beer. So we have to please them. We're middle of the road, we're not going for medals. We can't; we can sell out completely on a big, hot weekend."

He laughed and shrugged. "Hey, I'm still just a homebrewer on a commercial system," he admitted. "We screw up sometimes, but the equipment is great, it covers for us. We've come leaps and bounds from the Summy House days." He passed me a cup of Gold, the biggest seller, and gave me a knowing grin. "Go ahead, try it. It's a lot better than it used to be."

Okay, I thought, I'll be the judge of that. Scott laughed at the look on my face: Hey, it really is better! "I told you," he said. "There's even some hops in there, huh? We're real brewers here!" They sure enough are, and they were brewing their brains out when I was there, the day before Day One of the 2004 Faire. Things were about to explode the next day.

The whole Faire grounds was bustling with workers, and Scott was moving the entire time we were talking. He's not just the brewer, he's the

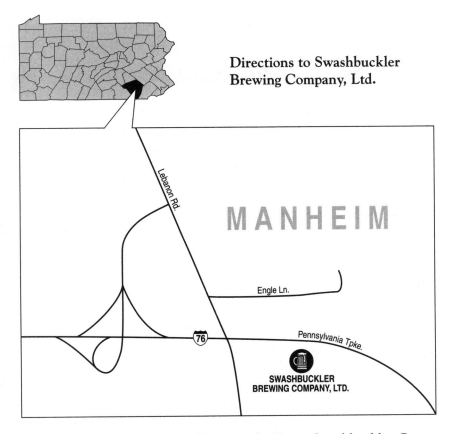

Directions to Swashbuckler Brewing Company, Ltd.

Lebanon Rd.

MANHEIM

Engle Ln.

76

Pennsylvania Tpke.

SWASHBUCKLER
BREWING COMPANY, LTD.

general contractor for the buildings at the Faire. Swashbuckler Grove, the brewery/bar/eats pavilion complex, and the big red pirate ship are all his, as are two other bars in the Faire. He's even got his empire well protected by a curtain wall with crenellated battlements: the Walled City.

Between the beer sales, the food sales (Scott runs a barbecue beef pit, a pizza oven, and a seafood stand), merchandise, and the construction and rentals, Scott's got all he can handle. For now, anyway. "We're considering bottling some 750-milliliter bottles next year," he said, "so people can take the beer to go. I don't really see us in outside accounts." Don't even suggest brewing year-round; he's too busy building and repairing in the off-season.

Like Twain's Hank Morgan, Scott Bowser did well among the denizens of another time. And he's achieved the dream of many a small boy: his own pirate kingdom, Swashbuckler Grove. If you can get past the defenses of the Walled City (I hear the guards can be bribed on a fairly regulated basis . . .), you can join him for a flagon of his much-improved ale. Yo ho!

Opened: March 2000.

Owner: Scott Bowser.

Brewer: Scott Bowser.

System: 12-barrel Century Manufacturing brewhouse, 1,200 barrels annual capacity.

Production: 350 barrels in 2003.

Hours: 11 A.M. to 6 P.M. while the Faire is on, mid-August through October (see www.parenfaire.com for event dates). Also open during theater hours, October through December (see website for dates).

Tours: Subject to brewer availability . . . and that's pretty slim while the Faire's on. Call ahead.

Take-out beer: Not available.

Food: Brick-oven pizza, rotisserie beef and chicken, and broiled seafood are all available throughout Swashbuckler Square.

Extras: Enjoy the Renaissance Faire—25 acres of medieval theater!

Special considerations: Kids welcome. Handicapped-accessible. Cigars allowed. Vegetarian meals available.

Parking: Large free lots.

Lodging in the area: Hampton Inn, 2764 South Lebanon Road (Route 72), 717-665-6600; Rodeway Inn, 2931 South Lebanon Road (Route 72), 717-665-2755; Rose Manor B&B, 124 South Linden Street, 717-664-4932.

Area attractions: To get to the brewery, you're going to have to go to the **Pennsylvania Renaissance Faire** (717-665-7021, www.paren faire.com), which features jousting, balladeers, wizards, shops, artisans, and of course, pirates! The Faire's more than just the Faire. Events continue past mid-October, with Edgar Allan Poe Evermore through mid-November, followed by a Victorian Christmas through New Year's. And Scott sells beer throughout the whole time.

Besides the Faire, the **Mount Hope Estate Winery** is right there on the grounds. Also see the suggestions at Bube's (page 120), Tröegs (page 156), and Lancaster Brewing (page 116) for the attractions that surround Swashbuckler.

Other area beer sites: The **Summy House** (31 South Main Street, 717-664-3333) still has a decent selection of beer, and the food's quite good. See Bube's (page 120), Appalachian (pages 153–54), and Lancaster Brewing (page 116) for other suggestions.

Stoudt's Brewing Company

Route 272, Adamstown, PA 19501
717-484-4386
www.stoudtsbeer.com

Carol Stoudt is a pioneer. When she founded Pennsylvania's first micro-brewery in 1987, she was one of the country's few female brewers. She followed her own course, brewing the German-style lagers she and her husband, Ed, adored. She set high standards and met them. Stoudt's is one of the winningest breweries in the history of the Great American Beer Festival, with a total of twenty medals.

I was at a tasting of Belgian beers with Carol and Ed just before they left for a long tour of Belgium about ten years ago. They didn't know a lot of technical information about Belgian beers, but they liked what they tasted. Carol came back from Belgium ("With a full beer notebook!" she told me) and started the wheels turning.

Stoudt's doesn't brew a huge amount of beer; it definitely is still a micro. The effect that Carol and her brewery have always had on the industry, however, is macro. She makes good beer. The Stoudts don't hold with average; they want the best. The Great Eastern Invitational Microbrewery Festival lives up to this standard. Carol and Ed host the event, which has grown to three festivals each summer. They are not the biggest; each session is limited to twelve hundred people. But they are some of the best on the East Coast. The brewers are well taken care of, and they are easily accessible to visitors. Carol and Ed try to make it fun for everyone.

The brewery hall at Stoudt's is a spacious roofed area with a small, open courtyard. When you enter it, two things are clear. First, signs of the Stoudts' German heritage are proudly displayed. Coats of arms from German cities and provinces adorn the

Beers brewed: Year-Round: American Pale Ale, Scarlet Lady ESB, Pilsner (six GABF medals), Gold (five GABF medals), Fest (two GABF medals), Fat Dog Stout, Double Bock, Double IPA. Seasonal: Oktoberfest (GABF medal), Blonde Double Mai-Bock (three GABF medals and an honorable mention), Abbey Triple, Weizen (two GABF medals), Winter Ale, plus three more GABF medals on beers no longer brewed. All beer is now brewed on premises.

walls. Trestle tables enhance the "permanent tent" beer-hall aura of the place.

Second, the Stoudts have willingly embraced the idea that the beer hall can be a place for the whole family. Children are welcome at the Bavarian Beer Festivals, which fill the hall on weekends in July, August, and October. These are not sloppy, beat-the-clock swill fests, but a time for people to enjoy good company in the warm glow of a few mugs of festbier and the comfort of a plate of wurst and potato salad. As the accordion plays and feet stamp on the dance floor, you can forget the world outside in the happy whirl of skirts, a beer, and a cigar.

It's not your average beer fest, but Carol Stoudt's not your average brewer. She makes whatever suits her fancy. "We keep experimenting. I guess we're one step above some crazy homebrewer," she said with a laugh. "At our size, our beers need to be assertive. They need to stand out. If you aren't making aggressive beers, then you're trying to compete with the bigger, broader-market breweries."

The Pick: Just look at all those GABF medals! This is a tough call, but for me it has to be the Weizen. Ever since 1995, Stoudt's has nailed this beer solidly. It is richly refreshing, with classic clove and banana aromas and swirling flavors of peach and red plum. An unmatched after-the-fest beer. I've also been drinking a lot of Stoudt's Pilsner lately, now that I can get it in 12-ounce bottles. This is roaringly great beer, with a teetering balance of hops and malt that seems born to drink with red meat. Reacquaint yourself with this one.

There was a big change at Stoudt's in 2004, a change that had been hinted at over the past year. All beer production was brought in-house. Previously, the 12-ounce bottled beers had been brewed under contract at Frederick Brewing or The Lion. Now, with the addition of a large refrigerated warehouse, an additional bright tank, and a bottling line, Stoudt's was ready for action.

Unfortunately, there will be no more 765-millileter bottles; they were just too expensive. But the good news is that finally Stoudt's delicious Pilsner and Weizen are available in 12-ounce size, and that just makes me happy as a lark. It must have made some of you happy as well. When I was up to visit in August 2004, Marc Worona told me that the Pilsner has moved up the sales positions, and that they were running the brewery near capacity for the first time in years. Far from the drop in sales they were concerned about with the switch in production, sales have surged to the point where a brewhouse expansion is planned for 2005.

The re-tooled Fat Dog Stout and Triple, and the new Double IPA have helped that growth. These three beers are hotter than a pistol in the Pennsylvania market right now. The Triple carves a malty middle course between the traditional sweet tripels on one hand and herbally dry tripels

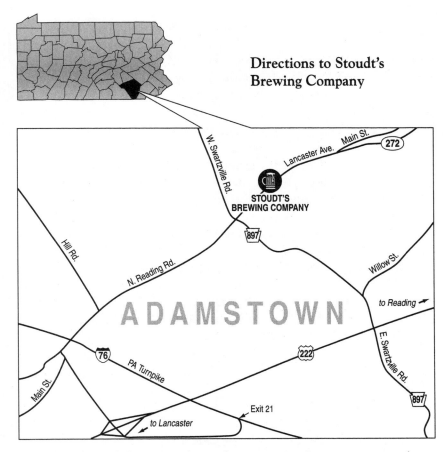

Directions to Stoudt's Brewing Company

on the other, and the Dog is fatter than ever as a 9 percent imperial oat-meal stout. But the Double IPA is a real head-banger, unlike anything Stoudt's has ever brewed before, 10 percent huge and audaciously hoppy.

"We want to maximize what we have," Worona said. "We did some expansions in the past that we maybe shouldn't have, like the lagering cellar, but now we can use it all. We have a full-service lab on-site, bet-ter than some regional brewers I've visited. And finally the consistency of flavor will be there between draft and bottle. It's been a long time coming, but it's finally here."

All Stoudt's, all house-brewed, all excellent. Stoudt's microbrewery was Pennsylvania's first, and Carol and Ed are making sure it remains one of Pennsylvania's best.

Opened: May 1987.
Owner: Carol Stoudt.
Brewers: Marc Worona; John Matson; Brett Kinzer

System: 30-barrel Century/Criveller brewhouse, 9,000 barrels annual capacity.

Production: 9,000 barrels in 2004 (estimated).

Brewpub hours: Monday through Thursday, 4:30 P.M. to 11 P.M.; Friday and Saturday, noon to 11 P.M.; Sunday, noon to 9 P.M.

Tours: Saturday at 3 P.M.; Sunday at 1 P.M.

Take-out beer: Cases or six-packs of all varieties.

Food: Light fare at the pub—soup, sandwiches, and munchies. The bock-wurst is exceptional! Fine dining can be had at the adjacent Black Angus restaurant, which is owned by Carol's husband, Ed Stoudt.

Extras: Rock'n'Brew nights in the brewery hall every Friday starting at 6:30 P.M. (ages twenty-one and up).

Bavarian Beer Festival in July and August (Saturdays starting at 5 P.M., Sundays starting at 2 P.M.), and in October (Sundays starting at 2 P.M.). Both feature a variety of bands; call for bands and schedules. Great Eastern Invitational Microbrewery Festivals in summer and fall (call for schedule and tickets). On the five Sundays before Christmas, the beer hall becomes a traditional German Christkindlsmarkt, selling antique toys and Christmas items and serving German holiday specialty foods. The Black Angus restaurant has a full liquor license.

Special considerations: Kids welcome in the brewery hall. Handicapped-accessible. Cigars allowed. The Black Angus restaurant is also handicapped-accessible and has a special children's menu. Cigars allowed in the bar.

Parking: Plenty of parking in the big side lot.

Lodging in the area: Holiday Inn Lancaster County, Route 272, Denver, 717-336-7541; Black Forest Inn, Route 272, 717-484-0122; Adamstown Inn, 62 West Main Street, 717-484-0800. Camping is available at Shady Grove Campground, Route 897, just north on Route 272, 717-484-4225.

Area attractions: The antique markets in Adamstown, including one in the same compound as the brewery, are regionally renowned. *Stoudtburg,* a planned European-style community started by the Stoudts, is an experimental shopping and living area behind the Black Angus complex. The Stoudts have constructed and sold buildings to artisans, who set up shops on the first floor and live on the second floor, much as in European towns. Down the hill in Adamstown is the *Bollman Hat Company*'s outlet shop (717-484-4361), with cowboy hats, Stetsons, fedoras, berets, and orange hats with pull-down flaps—if it's a hat, they sell it here. The Reading and Lancaster factory outlet stores are within easy driving distance. A guided tour of the restored buildings at the **Ephrata Cloister** (632 Main Street, Ephrata, 717-733-6600) gives tourists insight into a communal religious society founded in the 1730s. The **Green Dragon Farmers' Market and Auction** is held every Friday just north of Ephrata, where the area's Amish and Mennonite farmers mingle with antique hunters and grocery shoppers, the song of the livestock auctioneer lifting over the din of the crowd.

Other area beer sites: The **Alpenhof,** a traditional German *gasthaus*-type restaurant with a good stock of German beers, is 2 miles south of Shillington on Route 10 (610-373-1624.). Also see the listings for Legacy (page 132) and Lancaster (page 116).

Legacy Brewing Company

545 Canal Street, Reading, PA 19602
610-376-9996

Reading has always been a German town. German immigrants worked in its factories along the Schuylkill River. When I was growing up near there, some of the Reading churches still held services in German. And German traditions, of course, mean beer. Reading was home to a number of breweries, all of which eventually died out. When that happened, German-Americans took to drinking national brands and Yuengling like the rest of us.

When microbrewing came to Pennsylvania, Reading jumped on board with three: Camelot, Pretzel City, and Neversink . . . all of which eventually died out.

Well, not exactly. Pretzel City and Neversink survived, at least in a once-removed set of circumstances. The two partners who formed Pretzel City, Scott Baver and David Gemmell, recently formed a new company, Legacy Brewing. After starting out brewing under contract at Ortlieb's in Sunnybrook (which has since closed), they wound up in the brewery under the Canal Street Pub, where Neversink used to be. You can see why they called themselves Legacy.

Beers brewed: Year-round: Euphoria, Hedonism, HHH IPA, Reading Pils, Legacy Pale Ale. Seasonals: Festbier.

"We came in with our eyes wide open," said Dave, referring to their experience with the ups and downs of the beer business with Pretzel City. "But we came in without a lot of debt, either." They're leasing the brewery from Bill McShane, the original owner of Neversink, who never sold the brewery after Neversink sank. He actually leased it to another brewery in the interim, Fancy Pants, which never caught on.

The Pick: I've got to have the Reading Pils. It's clean, well-balanced, firmly hoppy, and devilishly drinkable, a real throwback to the glory days of brewing in Reading. Get out the liter mugs, boys and girls!

Scott and Dave aren't quitting their day jobs this time: Scott's a driver for New Penn Motor Express, Dave's a finance officer at an insurance company. "Yes, we want to keep doing this, because we love it," said Scott. "But we need to get serious about it. We need a full-time salesperson, we need someone on the street in the local market. Your backyard should be your strongest area. We need to work on Reading." Bill Moore, former brewer at Ortlieb's, Sly Fox, Independence, and Stoudt's, is doing some part-time sales work for them and having a great time with it.

But if you, like me, were hankering for the return of any of the Pretzel City beers—and I was absolutely jonesing for some Duke of Ale IPA—well, they tried that, but it just didn't work out. "We tried Steamhorse, and that didn't sell," said Scott. "We brought back the Duke, and, well, IPAs have moved on in the five years since we last made it. It's just not considered that exciting anymore. We discontinued it. I'd just as soon be done with Pretzel City."

That was tough for me to take, until I tried a glass of Legacy's new Reading Pils. This is liter beer, solid body with a firm bitterness that isn't overwhelming. Given the recent long-overdue success of Stoudt's Pils, this beer could work for them, and I hope it does, if only so it hangs around and I can drink all I want of it. Legacy Pale Ale is getting its share of taphandles just by being a simply good drinking beer.

Yet the beer that's getting the most attention for Legacy is their big 9 percent Euphoria, a Belgian-type that's fun, with a big citrus character, a great full mouthfeel, and gripping psychedelic graphics. It's the centerpiece of their website, it's the beer that's got the buzz in Berks County, it's the beer people know Legacy for.

So what's the focus at Legacy? Belgians? "Concentrating on Belgians narrows our appeal," said Dave. "We make *quality* beers. We've settled on these three beers, and now we can focus and our distributors can focus."

"That's right," said Scott. "We stay the course. We make good beers. I don't want huge success; I just want to make beer and have a comfort-

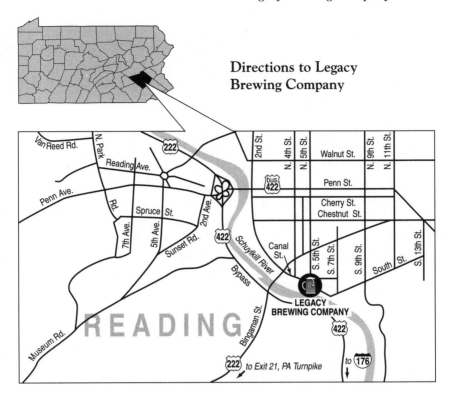

Directions to Legacy Brewing Company

able life. I've been reading about Frederick Lauer, the great nineteenth-century Reading brewer. He did nothing but give back to the community. I want us to have strong ties to the local community; we need to give back to it." He paused, then continued enthusiastically: "And we need to give them a really great beer garden!"

Scott, old buddy, I like the way you think. Every town, every brewery needs a beer garden. That would be a monumental legacy to leave behind: great beer, an enriched town, and a hell of a nice beer garden.

Opened: May 2003.
Owners: Scott Baver, Dave Gemmell, Mark Hoover.
Brewers: Mark Hoover, Scott Baver.
System: 15-barrel Pub Brewing System brewhouse (modified for step infusion or decoction brewing), 2,000 barrels annual capacity.
Production: 1,500 barrels in 2004 (estimated).
Tours: Saturday, 1 P.M. to 3 P.M.; it's best to call ahead.
Take-out beer: N/A
Special considerations: Kids allowed. Handicapped-accessible.
Parking: Large well-lit lot.

Lodging in the area: Sheraton Berkshire Inn, 422 West Papermill Road, Wyomissing, 610-376-3811; Econo Lodge, 635 Spring Street, Wyomissing, 610-378-5105; Country Inn and Suites, 405 North Park Road, Wyomissing, 610-373-4444; Inn at Center Park, 730 Center Avenue, 610-374-8557.

Area attractions: Reading is known for its outlets: **VF Outlet Village, Reading Outlet Center, Reading Station,** and others. Just follow the signs. The **Reading Public Museum** (500 Museum Road, 610-371-5850) has a planetarium and sculpture garden. For a great view of the city, make your way up to the **Pagoda,** a Japanese-style tower, albeit one trimmed in pink neon, that sits on Mount Penn. It's breathtaking at night. The route to the Pagoda defies written description, so call 610-655-6374 for directions. The **Daniel Boone Homestead** is about 9 miles east of town on Route 422 and includes the restored birthplace of Boone, a blacksmith shop, sawmill, and barn. The **Mid-Atlantic Air Museum** at the Reading Airport (610-372-7333) displays restored military and commercial aircraft and puts on an annual air show. Also contact the Visitors Bureau at 610-375-4085.

Other area beer sites: The **NorthEast Taproom** (Twelfth and Robeson Streets, 610-372-5284) has been Reading's best beer bar for years, a uniquely characterful place with excellent draft and bottles. Founder Pete Cammarano has left, but the Taproom has lost none of its magic. **Third and Spruce** (Third and Spruce Streets, West Reading, 610-376-5254) is that rare find—a sports bar with great beer taps. They have thirty-six taps, twenty-three TVs, and five satellite dishes. **Bixler's Lodge** (1456 Friedensburg Road, 610-779-9936) has been a Reading staple for years, and it's got good beer, too. The **Speckled Hen Cottage and Alehouse** (30 South Fourth Street, 610-685-8511) is right in front of what used to be Pretzel City Brewing, in a restored eighteenth-century log house, and boasts good British imports and a former NorthEast Taproom bartender behind the stick. The **Ugly Oyster** (21 South Fifth Street, 215-373-6791) has plenty of beer in an actual transplanted Yorkshire pub . . . look, ordinarily I hate this kind of thing. But unlike most of these "pub in a box" deals, the beer's too good to ignore. I can't believe that I never included **Bruno's Pizza and Beers of the World** (4500 Perkiomen Avenue, Reading Mall, 610-779-4443) in these books before. It's one of the very first good beer places I went to in Reading, sent there by a bartender at the Taproom. Big, hot slices of Sicilian pizza and a pretty decent selection of bottles, all in a no-nonsense pizza parlor that gets real busy on a Friday night. The friendly **Douglassville Hotel** (Route

422 East, Douglassville, 610-385-2585) serves huge dinners and has a hefty beer list. The small towns north of Reading also have a number of excellent old hotel bars: Fleetwood, Krumsville, Bowers, Virginville, and Kempton are the homes of some of my favorites. Also see the Stoudt's listing on page 129.

Kutztown Tavern/ Golden Avalanche Brewing Company

272 West Main Street, Kutztown, PA 19530
610-683-9600
www.kutztowntavern.com

Kutztown, no matter what anyone from Lancaster will tell you, is in the very heart of Pennsylvania Dutch country. I say this as a Lancaster native who grew up in a home with a backyard bordered by an Amish farm. But there are more real Pennsylvania Dutch people in Kutztown and nearby towns than there are Amish in Lancaster. Everyone talks with a "Dutchie" accent up here, whether they're discussing the relative merits of different butchers' ring bologna or the computer needs of their law firm. They're big eaters, frugal with their money, and loyal to a fault.

Kutztown Tavern is aimed right between their eyes. The food is solid, with an in-house bakery for pies and cakes, and it comes in bountiful portions. Allen Young, the brewer who set up the Beraplan brewhouse at Kutztown, was shocked by that. "The dinners are huge," he told me, "and they expect to get more than they can eat." If they're the Dutchmen I know, they probably tucked in and finished it anyway. Then they washed it down with very affordable beer. The Blonde Lager sells for $2 a pint in the downstairs Shorty's Bar area, which indeed is the lowest nonpromotional price I've ever heard for brewpub beer.

Beers brewed: Year-round: Blonde Lager, Youngallen's Lager, Olde Brick Alt, Onyx Cream Stout, Donner Weiss. Seasonals: Winter Bock, Oktoberfest, Spring Bock, Maibock, Fruit Weiss.

Shorty's was a bar in Kutztown before the Grid-ers came along. They saw a big cash flow and a liquor license, and invited Shorty's owner Harry Bieber in as a partner and set up Shorty's in the basement. Shorty's is a perfect college bar. The wide-open main room is superb for mad dancing when the bands and DJs kick in. The back room, with its brick walls and low ceiling, manages to make pool tables and video games almost cozy, a good place to retreat from dance fever.

The Pick: The Olde Brick Alt is tasty, aromatic, and solid as its namesake. I'd like to see a few more beers like this under the "alt" handle in American brewpubs.

Up above is where things are about dinner, and conversation, and beer. Here the long bar, spacious dining room, and glass-enclosed brew-house set the tone, and the tone is cool. The atmosphere is sophisti-cated, with an artfully designed new-construction backbar and attractive placement of bottles, yet they have managed to retain the familiar air of the Pennsylvania hotel bar. Those hearty meals and fresh-baked pies, cakes, and muffins help a lot.

Familiar air or not, you won't find beer like this at too many hotel bars. The Donner Weiss is a spot-on rendition of a Bavarian weissbier, light, spritzy, and full of the distinctive banana-clove aromas. Onyx Cream Stout is a smooth mouthful of black, without all the roasty bite of a dry stout. "They love their bocks," noted Chris. "Winter Bock, Spring Bock, Maibock—if they're not on, the regulars are asking for them."

"The beer profiles are a bit understated," Chris allowed. "But there's always something interesting; there's always something there for everyone. I have a lot of latitude to make it the way I want to. The Griders are very hands-off when it comes to the brewery." As long as the beer sells and people are happy, Chris just keeps making beer with no worries. I'll bet there are some jealous brewpub brewers reading this paragraph right now.

By the way, the Golden Avalanche of the brewing company name is the former Kutztown University team name. No one's quite sure what a "golden avalanche" is, which is probably why these days the teams are known as the Golden Bears.

The brewpub has met the Dutchman and adapted. I doubt you'll see too many Amish in the Kutztown Tavern, but open an ear as you sit at the bar, and you'll hear the voice of the true Pennsylvania Dutch. Get one of the big meals inside you and some of that reasonably priced beer, and you'll know you're in a true Pennsylvania Dutch brewpub.

Opened: August 1999.
Owners: Don and Matt Grider.
Brewers: Chris Rafferty, Bob Sica.

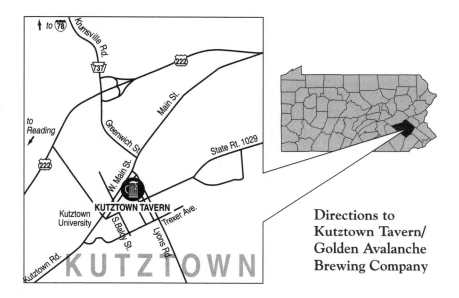

**Directions to
Kutztown Tavern/
Golden Avalanche
Brewing Company**

System: 10-hectoliter Beraplan system, 1,000 barrels annual capacity.
Production: 700 barrels in 2003.
Brewpub hours: Daily, 11 A.M. to 11 P.M.
Tours: On weekdays, please call ahead.
Take-out beer: Growlers, quarter and half kegs.
Food: Full menu is offered: seafood, chicken, steaks, pizza, sandwiches,
daily lunch and dinner specials. Pies, cakes, and muffins baked on-
premises.
Extras: The action is downstairs at Shorty's. Live music on weekends,
no cover, large dance floor. Pool tables, video arcade, nineteen TVs,
and thirty-six taps of house and guest beers.
Special considerations: Kids welcome. Handicapped-accessible. Cigars
allowed at bar. Vegetarian meals available.
Parking: Plenty of free parking in community lot behind the brewpub.
Lodging in the area: Campus Inn, Route 222, 610-683-8721; Die Bauerei
B&B, Route 222, 610-894-4854; New Smithville Country Inn, 10425
Old Route 222, 610-285-2987; Around the World B&B, 30 South
Whiteoak Street, 610-683-8885.
Area attractions: *Kutztown Airport* (15130 Kutztown Road, 800-
SOAR-999) offers glider, airplane, and open-cockpit biplane rides at
extremely reasonable prices. *Crystal Cave* (610-683-6765) is north
of town; just follow the plentiful signs. The cave has a large forma-
tion of delicate crystalline growths, as well as the usual "this forma-

tion looks like an ear of corn" stuff, although the Jack Frost formation at the end of the tour is striking. The **Kutztown Pennsylvania German Festival** (888-674-6136 or www.kutztownfestival.com) in July celebrates fine craftwork, including quilts, folk art, toys, and furniture, plus antiques, music, storytelling, and hearty Pennsylvania Dutch food. This is different from the original Kutztown Folk Festival, which is now called the **Pennsylvania Dutch Folk Festival** and is held in Schuylkill County (www.dutchfest.net). Both are fun, but don't get the locals started on the topic.

Antiques are big in the area. **Renninger's Antique and Farmers Market** (740 Noble Street, 610-683-6848, www.renningers.com) has many different dealers in one spot on weekends. **Antique Complexes I and II** are two large antique markets a bit south along Route 222, near Fleetwood (610-944-0707 or 610-944-9661, www.antiquecomplex.com). Up Route 737 north of town, you'll find the **Wanamaker, Kempton and Southern Railroad** (610-756-6469), one of the oldest steam excursion lines operating in the United States. Ride the steam train 3 miles from Kempton to Wanamaker.

Other area beer sites: *Kutztown Bottling Works* (78 South Whiteoak Street, 610-683-7377) makes their own birch beer, cream soda, and sarsaparilla. It's also a beer distributor and sells a good selection of micros and imports. The **Pricetown Hotel** (3674 Pricetown Road, Pricetown, 610-944-9368) is not a preserved gem of an old hotel, and it doesn't have a great beer selection, but it's been a regular stop for us for years. It's clean, it's friendly, it's an institution. The **Bowers Hotel** (610-682-2900) is a preserved gem, south of Kutztown in Bowers, a town too small to be on most road maps. The original hotel was built around 1822; the large addition that remains was built in the late 1800s to serve the Reading Railroad stop. The bar has been carefully restored without losing its personality. Call for directions.

Bethlehem Brew Works

569 Main Street, Bethlehem, PA 18018
610-882-1300
www.thebrewworks.com

The Bethlehem Brew Works is a classic example of a phenomenon you could call "brewpub anchoring," when a brewpub establishes the core for a neighborhood revitalization. The initial idea is often met with a degree of skepticism, because a substantial part of the population believes that letting a brewery into the neighborhood will lead to public drunkenness, wanton and willful destruction of property, a decline in social values and school test scores, human sacrifice . . . But a brewery is foremost a production business with good wages and local responsibilities, something most communities encourage. A brew*pub* offers all that and more: It has a vested interest in developing and maintaining a good neighborhood that will attract customers.

Brewpubs make very good neighbors, and that's what has happened in Bethlehem. "There wasn't anywhere to go for a nice evening out in downtown Bethlehem," brewer Jeff Fegley told me. "We took the chance. We came to downtown Bethlehem, and we made it. We gave people someplace to go. There's a cluster of good restaurants around here now. Sometimes I worry that we showed the corporate restaurants the way, but we're different from them. We'll always be different."

They are that. The menu's different, with adventurous appetizers like the Meze Hummus assortment (that includes the popular garlic ale hummus and a black olive tapenade), roasted red pepper miniwraps, Brewschetta, and an ever-changing selection of fabulous house-made soups "that aren't really low-fat at all," said Peg Fegley with a laugh.

The decor is different, tied to the image of Bethlehem as the home of Bethlehem Steel. The trim is skid-proof diamond plate, the booths are topped with steel pipe dividers, and the walls are

Beers brewed: Year-round: Valley Golden Ale, Fegley's ESB, Steelworker's Oatmeal Stout. Seasonals: Hefeweizen, Belgian Kriekbier, Belgian Dubble, Belgian Wit, Bagpiper's Brew Scotch Ale (bestseller), IPA, American Pale Ale, Summer Wheat, Honey Brown Ale, Flemish Ale, Shilling Light Ale, Oktoberfest, Pumpkin Ale, Cream Kölsch, Framböse (three on at any time).

studded with old hand-carved casting patterns. It is an industrial look, but the warmth of dark wood and the street-side windows make it a sheltered gathering place.

Then there's the beer. Bethlehem has turned out to be a malt-loving kind of town, and the Fegley's ESB and Bagpiper's Brew Scotch Ale are very popular taps. Don't worry, geeks: Jeff knows what to do with hops, too, and you'll always find something aromatic and bitter on, like the razor-sharp IPAs that come on quite often. Jeff is also unafraid of less conventional styles; I had a rewardingly funky and sour Belgian Kriekbier when I visited, and he's done a number of other Belgian styles since.

The Pick: I'll take a walk on the wild side and pick the Belgian Kriekbier. I thought it would be a somewhat tart cherry beer, but this one has some real funk and sour cherr flavor. It's not over the top at all, although I've had less assertive Belgian imports. Jeff used Wyeast's lambic culture yeasts, and they worked fine. Not for the beginner, but the geek will find this rewarding.

The brewpub is located in the heart of downtown and so is a popular site during Musikfest, the hot nine days in August when six hundred-plus musical acts of all types come to Bethlehem. It's New Orleans on the Lehigh as beers hit the streets in plastic cups and cops look the other way. You'll find more music in the Brew Works at that time—folk, country, rock, blues, what have you. It's a wild time, and a lot of fun.

The rest of the year, this is a family-friendly place for lunch and dinner. "At six o'clock, every high chair in the place is full," Peg said. The crowd just doesn't seem to want to get crazy. "We tried music," Rich recalled, "but the people would rather sit and talk over a few beers."

That changed when the Fegleys went downstairs in 2001 and opened the Steelgaarden Lounge, a Belgian beer bar that has become one of the most popular spots in Bethlehem, a spot that outdraws the brewpub at times. After a recent expansion, more than a hundred Belgian bottled beers, comfy couches and armchairs, three pool tables, and a sophisticated sound and lighting system make this one cool place for the sophisticated beer lover.

The success of the brewpub and the Steelgaarden have given the Fegley family the confidence to open a second Brew Works. That's planned for downtown Allentown, at 812 Hamilton Street, in the fall of 2005. Jeff's probably going to be brewing there, possibly assisted by Sven Vollmert, a German brewer who's been coming over in the summers to brew authentic Kölsch with Jeff, while Lewis Thomas continues brewing in Bethlehem. Busy times ahead for the family.

Things have changed significantly in Bethlehem. Sometimes all it takes is a couple beers among friends to make everything look a bit more cheerful, a bit more settled. Stop by the bar at the Steelgaarden, and you'll find out just what I'm talking about.

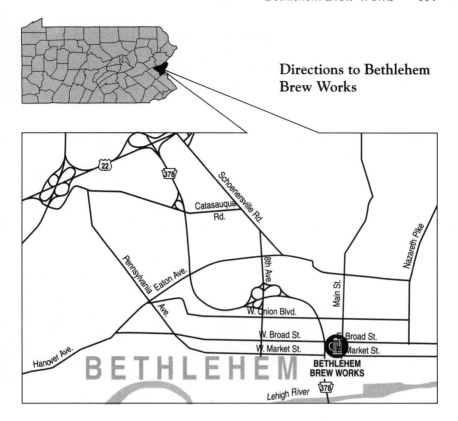

Directions to Bethlehem Brew Works

Opened: April 15, 1998.

Owners: Peg, Dick, Rich, Nicole, Dave, Jeff, and Mike Fegley.

Brewers: Jeff Fegley, Lewis Thomas.

System: 15-barrel Pub Brewing System brewhouse, 1,500 barrels annual capacity.

Production: 1,100 barrels in 2004 (estimated).

Brewpub hours: Sunday through Wednesday, 11 A.M. to midnight; Thursday through Saturday, 11 A.M. to 2 A.M.

Tours: Every day, by request.

Take-out beer: Growlers and 12-ounce bottles.

Food: The popular garlic ale hummus has become part of a tapaslike assortment of hummus, tapenade, and beer-soaked tomatoes, served with warm pita wedges. The beer and cheese soup still rocks, and you can pig out on Diamond Plate Pork or Wiener schnitzel. It's a full menu, folks, and one with real vegetarian choices.

Extras: Cask ales on Thursday nights, with one-cask special batches like whiskey stout or chocolate ESB. Mug Club is very popular but limited in membership; call for details. Full liquor license, with a good selection of single malts. Live music on select nights (call for schedule). Private dining room available for private parties and business functions. The Steelgaarden Lounge downstairs has more than a hundred Belgian beers available (plus BBW Belgian-types), three pool tables, no TVs, a top-of-the-line sound system, lounge furniture, and a funky lighting system that slowly changes colors; available for private parties.

Special considerations: Kids welcome. Handicapped-accessible. Cigars allowed at bar. Vegetarian meals available.

Parking: Free and pay lots nearby; validation stamps available.

Lodging in the area: Radisson Hotel Bethlehem, newly renovated, 437 Main Street, 610-867-2200; Comfort Suites, 120 West Third Street, 610-882-9700; Courtyard by Marriott, 2160 Motel Drive, 610-317-6200.

Area attractions: There are three big annual events in Bethlehem. The nine days of *Musikfest* draw approximately 1 million people to Bethlehem every August to hear performances by more than six hundred musical acts. It's a big, big deal, and the Brew Works is right in the middle of it. Christmas is also huge in Bethlehem, as you might guess from the permanent electric star on the hill over town. Two hundred thousand visitors enjoy candlelight walks and a traditional *Christkindlsmarkt* featuring Christmas handicrafts. The *Celtic Classic Games* in September, featuring traditional Highland games and Irish, Scottish, and Welsh music, is not as well known as the other two events but is getting big; ESPN covers it these days. *The Smithy* (425 Main Street, 610-332-6247) is a restored, working 1750s-era blacksmith shop right next to the *Hotel Bethlehem*. It's a new attraction, call for hours of operation.

For hootin', hollerin' fun, get out to *Dorney Park and Wildwater Kingdom* (on Hamilton Boulevard west of Allentown, 800-386-8463). You'll find four roller coasters, including the Steel Force and the new Hydra, the Peanuts playland for the kids, and an extensive water park. One more thing: The *Martin Guitar Company* (610-759-2837) is just up the road at 510 Sycamore Street in Nazareth. If features a collection of vintage Martin guitars, acknowledged as some of the best in the world, and a free tour at 1:15 on weekdays. Get more information from either the Bethlehem Visitors Center (610-868-1513) or the Lehigh Valley Convention and Visitors Bureau (800-747-0561; www.lehighvalleypa.org).

Other area beer sites: *The Sun Inn* (564 Main Street, 610-974-9451) isn't a bar, but you might want to stop anyway, just for the atmosphere. Other people have, like George and Martha Washington, Ben

Franklin, John Adams, and the Marquis de Lafayette. You can eat that history with a spoon. Allentown is not far away, and you'll find more bars there. The **Sterling Hotel** (343 Hamilton Avenue, 610-433-3480) a beautifully restored Pennsylvania grand hotel, is a must. The Long Bar is a single 64-foot-long piece of Honduran mahogany, with an architectural plaster ceiling overhead and a classic carved backbar. The Sterling has two other full bars—the Neuweiler Pub and the outside bar built of Mercer tile from Doylestown—usually with good beers on tap. The big draw is the bands: national and regional acts play here. Open Wednesday through Sunday, 4 P.M. **J. P. O'Malley's** (1528 Union Street, Allentown, 610-821-5556) is a comfortable, happy multitap that pays attention to local beers. For a real treat, slide by **Cannon's** (448 North Ninth Street, 610-820-9313), a neighborhood corner bar with a great selection of tap and bottled beers, including some unusual Belgian ales. The food is adventurous, tasty, and reasonably priced. You can also head the other way to Easton (see the beer sites listed on page 145).

Weyerbacher Brewing Company

905 Line Street, Easton, PA 18042
610-559-5561
www.weyerbacher.com

Weyerbacher
Brewing Company, Inc.

Dan Weirback used to sell swimming pools. But when he got bit by the brewing bug, he just had to go with it. The brewery name he chose reflects his German ancestry. "The family name was Weyerbacher before the immigration officers got hold of it," Dan explains.

Weyerbacher started in an old livery stable on Sixth Street. After running it for a few years as a production brewery, Dan opened a tiny pub right next to the brewery. It was a huge success, at least in the eyes of the people who loved hanging out there. It was a chance for Dan and his brewers to get a nice little cashflow, great word-of-mouth advertising, and instant feedback on new beers. One after the other, beers were formulated, brewed, and market tested, taking advantage of the quick decision cycle of a microbrewery.

As the cycles turned, it became clear that Weyerbacher's customers liked big beers. The Raspberry Imperial Stout had always been popular, a big raspberry chocolate truffle of a beer. Over the winter of 1998–99, Dan took the plunge and cut loose with three new big beers. The imperial stout was released on its own, without the raspberries. A dryish, herbal Belgian-style Triple, similar to the famed Triple of Westmalle, was next.

But the beer that Dan told me later was the one that saved the brewery was a huge, malty, 12 percent ABV barleywine, whimsically named Blithering Idiot. Things were tight, things were close, and they'd always wanted to brew a barleywine . . . this might be their last chance. What the heck. They told their wholesalers about the beer, and the reaction caught them all by surprise: It sold out in two weeks. Retail sales once the beer hit the floors were just as immediate. People loved the Idiot. I've seen lines twenty deep at beer festivals, waiting for Dan to hook up a keg of it.

Faced with success and the need to come up with the next big thing, Dan reasoned that big hops should sell as well as big malt and hit the summer market with the blatantly geek-tilted Hops Infusion. The bold orange label, adorned with an atom-styled hop cone, screamed a challenge to hopheads: seven varieties of hops! Four times the hops of our IPA! It was a big hit, and Weyerbacher was ahead of projections in the middle of their best year ever.

One thing up, one thing down: Weyerbacher lost their lease the next year. After flirting with the idea of moving into a downtown movie theater and going with a much bigger pub, Dan made the call to go back to a production situation and moved to the current location on Line Street. I was there for the last night at the pub, and it was insane: an upside-down Christmas tree hanging from the ceiling, wall-to-wall mug clubbers, frenzied waitresses, and busy bartenders. People still miss the pub. (If you'd like to recapture the experience, Which Brew is run by the same people; stop in and tell Kelly Jo I said hi!)

New building, new ideas, and eventually new yeast. Weyerbacher had trouble with their beer's longevity over the years, and after continual attempts to fix the problem, they finally gave up and switched to a

Beers brewed: Year-round: Blithering Idiot Barleywine, Scotch Ale, Old Heathen Imperial Stout, Merry Monks Ale, Hops Infusion. Seasonals: Winter Ale, AutumnFest, Hefeweizen, Raspberry Imperial Stout, Blanche, Insanity Barrel aged Barleywine, Heresy Barrel-aged Imperial Stout.

The Pick: It's not just the label, though it's one of the best around. I've always loved Dan's imperial stout, and Old Heathen carries on almost unchanged: big, bitter, almost austere. I don't like a sweet imperial stout; as I heard one geek say, "No thanks, I like my beer fermented." But when they take it that one vanilla- and oak-laced, boozy step further and make Heresy it brings to mind a quote from *Patton:* "God help me, I do love it so."

new yeast. The effects were significant and instantaneous, and sales stabilized. Dan invested in some new packaging and gave some of the beers new names. The Triple became Merry Monks Ale; the Imperial Stout got a beautifully haunting label and the name Old Heathen. Things got better, and the big beers sold.

Weyerbacher is more settled now and ready to grow. Dan hired a new brewer, Chris Wilson, from Bayhawk Brewing in California, a brewery that had just grown at a furious pace. There was a launch party for a new beer, a bourbon barrel-aged version of the Old Heathen named Heresy, and the beer's selling so fast they can't brew enough of it. There's a barrel-aged version of Blithering Idiot—called Insanity—lurking in the wings that's simply delicious. Volume shouldn't be a problem after 2005 opens up, either. Weyerbacher bought Victory's previous brewhouse, a 25-barrel workhorse that will provide all the wort they need.

What's next? Dan's planning an overhaul of Hops Infusion. A beer with a name like that ought to really grab the ganglia, and that's what he's aiming for. Dan Weirback and his brewery have been surviving for almost ten years, staving off the fate that awaited many craft brewers. He's finally got the critical and popular acclaim he's been looking for, a solid brewhouse, and a solid staff to run it. The time for survival is over. It's time to thrive.

Opened: August 1995.

Owners: Dan Weirback and private investors.

Brewers: Chris Wilson, John Parsons, Craig Schneiderwind, Dan Weirback

System: 25-barrel Century Manufacturing brewhouse, 7,000 barrels annual capacity.

Production: 2,650 barrels in 2003.

Tours: Saturday, noon to 3 P.M.

Take-out beer: Cases, growlers, and kegs during tours.

Special considerations: Kids welcome. Handicapped-accessible.

Parking: Off-street lot.

Lodging in the area: Lafayette Inn, 525 West Monroe Street, 610-253-4500; Best Western Easton Inn, 185 South Third Street, 610-253-9131; Days Inn, Route 22 and Twenty-fifth Street, 610-253-0546, 800-329-7466.

Area attractions: Easton is home to Binney and Smith, maker of Crayola crayons. *The Crayola Factory* at Two Rivers Landing (30 Center Square, 610-515-8000) is the company's public face. Kids can draw on the walls, make crayons, and do other colorful stuff. In the

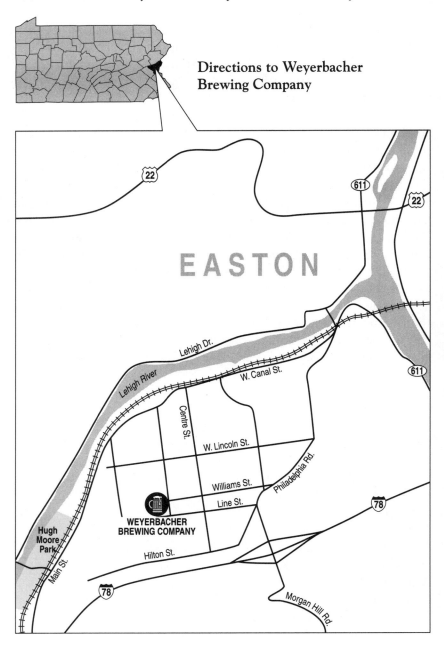

Directions to Weyerbacher Brewing Company

same building is the **National Canal Museum** (610-515-8000), celebrating the history of America's canals. You can get a canal boat ride during the summer. Easton's **Shad Fishing Tournament and Festival** is held in April and early May (call 610-258-1439 for precise dates) and ends with a big celebration of planked shad, lots of other good eats, and plenty of carnival fun. You'll find good canoeing opportunities on both the Delaware and Lehigh Rivers. Get the latest information on Easton happenings at www.easton-pa.org or by calling 610-515-1200.

Other area beer sites: *Pearly Baker's* (Center Square, 610-253-9949) is a somewhat fancy but never snooty multitap, with first-class dining. *Which Brew* (665 Northampton Street, 610-330-2666) is run by the folks who used to work Weyerbacher's pub. Its great tap selection (which is coordinated with Porter's, across the street, to avoid too much duplication) and excellent atmosphere make this a bar I wish I lived next to. *Porter's Pub* (Seventh and Northampton Streets, 610-250-6561) is a neighborhood bar that boasts twelve taps and a good selection of Belgian bottles. Across the Delaware in Milford, New Jersey, is the *Ship Inn* (61 Bridge Street, 908-995-7007), a brewpub with good British-style ales.

Brewing Beer

You don't need to know much about beer to enjoy it. After all, I don't understand how the electronic fuel injection on my car really works, but I know that when I stomp on the accelerator, the car's gonna go!

Knowing about the brewing process can help you understand how and why beer tastes the way it does. It's like seeing the ingredients used in cooking a dish and realizing where the flavors came from. Once you understand the recipe for beer, other things become more clear.

Beer is made from four basic ingredients: water, hops, yeast, and grain, generally barley malt. Other ingredients may be added, such as sugars, spices, fruits, and vegetables, but they are extras. In fact, the oft-quoted Bavarian Reinheitsgebot (purity law), first promulgated in 1516, limited brewers to using only water, hops, and barley malt; yeast had not yet been discovered.

In the beginning, the malt is cracked in a mill to make a grist. The grist is mixed with water and heated (or "mashed") to convert the starches in the grain to sugars (see *decoction* and *infusion* in the Glossary). Then the hot, sugary water—now called wort—is strained out of the mash. It is boiled in the brewkettle, where hops are added to balance the sweetness with their characteristic bitterness and sprightly aroma. The wort is strained, cooled, and pumped to a fermenter, where yeast is added.

A lager beer ferments slow and cool, whereas an ale ferments warmer and faster. After fermentation, the beer will either be force-carbonated or naturally carbonated and aged. When it is properly mature for its style, the beer is bottled, canned, kegged, or, in a brewpub, sent to a large serving tank. And then we drink it. Happy ending!

Naturally, it isn't quite that simple. The process varies somewhat from brewery to brewery. That's what makes beers unique. There are also major differences in the ways microbrewers and mainstream brewers brew beer. One well-known distinction has to do with the use of non-barley grains, specifically corn and rice, in the brewing process. Some microbrewers have made a big deal of their Reinheitsgebot, proudly displaying slogans like "Barley, hops, water, and yeast—and that's all!" Mainstream brewers like Anheuser-Busch and Pennsylvania's regional brewers all add significant portions of corn, rice, or both. Beer geeks howl about how these adjuncts make the beer inferior. Of course, the same geeks often rave about Belgian ales, which have a regular farrago of ingredients forbidden by the Reinheitsgebot.

Mainstream brewers boast about the quality of the corn grits and brewer's rice they use, while microbrewers chide them for using "cheap" adjunct grains and "inferior" six-row barley. Truth is, they're both right . . . and they're both wrong.

Barley, like beer, comes in two main types: two-row and six-row. The names refer to the rows of kernels on the heads of the grain. Six-row grain gives a greater yield per acre but has more husks on smaller kernels, which can give beer an unpleasant astringency. Two-row gives a plumper kernel with less husk but costs significantly more. Each has its place and adherents.

When brewing began in America, farmers and brewers discovered that six-row barley did much better than two-row in our climate and soil types. Two-row barley grown the same way as it had been in Europe produced a distinctly different malt. This became especially troublesome when the craze for pale lagers swept America in the mid-nineteenth century. The hearty ales they replaced had broad flavors from hops and yeast that easily compensated for these differences. But pale lagers are showcases for malt character, and small differences in the malt mean big differences in beer taste.

Brewers adapted and used what they had. They soon found that a small addition of corn or brewer's rice to the mash lightened the beer, smoothed out the husky astringency of the six-row malt, and gave the beer a crispness similar to that of the European pale lagers. Even though using these grains required the purchase, operation, and maintenance of additional equipment (cookers, storage silos, and conveyors), almost every American brewer did it. Some say they overdid it, as the percentages of adjuncts in the beer rose over the years. Is a beer that is 30 percent corn still a pilsner?

Microbrewers say adjunct grains are cheap substitutes for barley malt. In terms of yield, corn and brewer's rice are less expensive than two-row barley, but they are still high-quality grains. Similarly, six-row barley is not inherently inferior to two-row; it is just not as well suited to the brewing of some styles of beer. Mainstream brewers have adapted their brewing processes to six-row barley. The difference is in the beer those processes produce.

Another difference between microbrewers and mainstream brewers is the practice of high-gravity brewing. The alcohol content of a beer is mainly dependent on the ratio of fermentable sugars to water in the wort, which determines the specific gravity of the wort. A higher gravity means more alcohol.

Large commercial brewers, in their constant search for ways to peel pennies off the costs of brewing, discovered that they could save money by brewing beer at a higher alcohol content and carefully diluting it later. To do this, a brewer adds a calculated extra amount of malt, rice, corn—whatever "fuel" is used—to boost the beer to 6.5 percent alcohol by volume (ABV) or higher. When the fermented beer has been filtered, water is added to bring the ABV down to the target level of 4 to 5 percent.

How does this method save money? It saves energy and labor costs during the brewing process by effectively squeezing 1,300 barrels of beer into a 1,000-barrel brewkettle. Although 1,000 barrels are boiled, 1,300 barrels are eventually bottled. It also saves money by allowing more efficient use of fermentation tank space: 10,000-barrel fermenters produce 13,000 barrels of beer. It sounds great, so why not do that with every beer? Because the high-gravity process can produce some odd flavor and aroma notes during fermentation. That's what brewers aim for in big beers like doppelbocks and barleywines. But these characteristics are out of place in a pilsner. I also feel that beer brewed by this high-gravity method suffers from a dulling phenomenon similar to "clipping" in audio reproduction: The highs and lows are clipped off, leaving only the middle.

With a studied nonchalance, big brewers keep this part of their brewing process away from the public eye. To tell the truth, of all beer styles, American mainstream lager is probably the style least affected by this process. It is mostly a practice that just seems vaguely wrong, and you won't see any microbrewers doing it.

So now you know how beer is made, and a few of the differences in how the big boys and the little guys do it. It's probably time for you to do a little field research. Have fun!

The Capital Corridor

Route 15 runs north from the Mason-Dixon line, past Gettysburg, through farms and orchards, meets the Susquehanna across the river from Harrisburg, and then follows the river north, running alongside the western branch right into Williamsport. To the east lies Pennsylvania Dutch country and the coal region of the Wyoming Valley; to the west, the land is furrowed in seemingly endless green ridges and valleys. But Route 15 and the Susquehanna wend their way north, piercing the ridges, seeing farms, busy rail lines, and the increasingly heavy traffic of the state's capital.

The major industries here are government and tourism; agriculture plays a picturesque third place. Tourists are drawn to the area because of its history and its geography. Significant historic sites from the Revolutionary War, the Civil War, and wars with the American Indians are found here. The Susquehanna River and the Appalachian Mountains, traced by the Appalachian Trail, appeal to lovers of the outdoors.

Harrisburg celebrates the Susquehanna with Riverfront Park, 5 miles of gardens and memorials along the river. The seat of government offers tourists the architectural glories of the state capitol and a look at the history of the state at the State Museum of Pennsylvania. Once a year, the state's farmers come to Harrisburg for the six-day Pennsylvania Farm Show, complete with animals, vegetables, crafts, and outstanding food.

Gettysburg is the foremost historic attraction in the area, drawing thousands of visitors every day in the summer to relive the pivotal battle of the Civil War. You can walk or drive the battlefield and see what small accidents of geography made the battle: the high ground of the series of ridges that would allow the hard-pressed Union forces to fall back to successive positions of strength, the shattered rocks of Devil's Den that made such perfect protection for Confederate sharpshooters, and the cool flow of Spangler's Spring that legendarily brought temporary truce to the battle of brothers. The Appalachian brewpub in town is right beside Lee's Gettysburg headquarters; Gettysbrew is located in a barn that was used as a Confederate field hospital.

Carlisle is a beautiful little town with a history of its own. It was the home of two signers of the Declaration and the location of the Carlisle Indian School, where Jim Thorpe got his education. At Carlisle Barracks, you can visit the army's Military History Institute, a library with a huge collection of Civil War photographs.

The western and northern reaches of the corridor are liberally scattered with state forests, game lands, and well-stocked streams and lakes. Two of my favorite state parks, Colonel Denning and Gifford Pinchot, tempt the summer traveler with lakes perfect for swimming and canoeing.

Farther north in the corridor, the population density thins out rather dramatically, and it's a matter of small towns separated by wide stretches of farms and forests. Then you climb over North White Deer Ridge and see Williamsport and the whole valley spread out before you, a view that stretches for miles.

This area is more often driven through than driven to. With the Pennsylvania Turnpike and Interstates 80, 81, and 83 passing through, the area is continually crisscrossed by travelers. But take an exit, take a drive, then stop for a beer. You may just find something you like.

Appalachian Brewing Company, Harrisburg

50 North Cameron Street, Harrisburg, PA 17101
717-221-1080
www.abcbrew.com

Old and worn but beautiful. That describes the Appalachian Mountains. These folded ridges, eroded remnants of sky-piercing peaks, thrust north into the state from Maryland and then make a bend to the northeast, curving around the state capital at Harrisburg. Compared to mountain chains in the West, and even to New Hampshire's Presidential range,

Pennsylvania's mountains stand head and shoulders below the rest in terms of sheer altitude. But they bow to no mountains when it comes to the beauty of their vistas and foliage.

Appalachian Brewing Company is strangely similar to its namesake. Although it's less than ten years old, it is in some ways old and worn. The brewhouse is recycled from Vancouver Island Brewery in British Columbia. The Canadian brewery sold Appalachian the equipment when it upgraded to a substantially larger system. The Harrisburg building is a print shop dating from 1890 that took two years to renovate. Appalachian's bottler is a used German classic, a Holdefleiss long-tube filler.

Beers brewed: Year-round: Purist Pale Ale, Water Gap Wheat, Jolly Scot Scottish Ale, Mountain Lager, Susquehanna Stout. Seasonals: Abbey Roade, Peregrine Pilsner, Hinterland Hefe-Weizen, Anniversary Maibock, Kipona-fest, Mad Cameron Belgian Wit, Hoppy Trails IPA, Rockville Rye Ale, Pennypacker Porter, Broad Street Barleywine, RiverSide Red, Hibernation Ale, Grinnin' Grizzly, Volks Weizenbock.

Even brewmaster Artie Tafoya is recycled in a way, though I'd be the last to call him old. Tafoya built his reputation in the Colorado brewing scene and has relocated to Harrisburg.

Like the Appalachians, this brewery is also eye-catching. The building was designed for function, to hold massive machinery, and yet there is beauty in its solid construction, huge timbers, glowing hardwood floors, and wide-swinging front doors. The brewhouse is distinctive—the bulbous unitanks look like a formation of great aluminum balloons straining to take flight.

Appalachian has become a sponsor of the Appalachian Trail Conference, a nonprofit organization promoting the use and maintenance of the Appalachian Trail. The trail runs from Maine to Georgia, and that, not coincidentally, is the potential market area for this beer. The Purist Pale Ale is named for "purist" hikers who hike every inch of the trail and don't skip the tough parts. Water Gap Wheat recalls the water gaps along the trail, where rivers cut through the ridges.

Officials in Harrisburg evidently did some research and saw the positive effect that a brewpub can have on its neighborhood. They courted Appalachian's owners and sold them the building for $1. Considering the amount of restoration that was necessary, it was just barely a bargain, but it made the project possible for the brewers. The city viewed the brewpub as the cornerstone of its Paxton Commons project. Reclamation of the area is already starting to ripple outward; it's a lot nicer neighborhood these days.

This is one of the biggest places you'll ever feel comfortable in. With its high ceiling, the great depth of its main room, and the massive tanks behind the glass wall to the right, one thing Appalachian has is plenty of room. The total floor space is 53,000 square feet, making Appalachian possibly the largest brewpub in the United States. Once the third floor is completed, they'll have more than enough room to do whatever they want. This is the only brewpub I know of that is big enough to host a brewers' festival inside the pub; Appalachian holds a great one every fall.

Put on your lugsoles and hike up to the bar at Appalachian. You can even be a purist . . . try all the beers from light to heavy, and don't skip the tough ones.

The Pick: The Hinterland Hefe-Weizen, for sure. Artie Tafoya was the hefe king of the GABF when he was brewing in Colorado, and he hasn't lost a step. This hefe has every bit of cloudiness and cloviness that you're looking for. They must have a gift for wheat at ABC, though, because I was taken aback by how good the Water Gap Wheat was. Time to be honest: It's a wheat ale, generally one of the dullest styles of American craft brewing. But this . . . Water Gap surprises with a fresh graininess and subtle fruity notes. Try one.

Opened: January 1997.

Owners: Shawn Gallagher, Jack Sproch.

Brewers: Artie Tafoya, Jesse Prall.

System: 36-barrel Alliance brewhouse, 15,000 barrels annual capacity.

Production: 4,900 barrels in 2004 (estimated).

Brewpub hours: Sunday through Thursday, 11 A.M. to 11 P.M.; Friday and Saturday, 11 A.M. to 2 A.M.

Tours: Saturday at 1 P.M., or upon request.

Take-out beer: Growlers and six packs.

Food: A full menu of fresh and innovative pub food is available all the time. For starters, ABC features its Tastebud Temptations: oriental lettuce wraps, Cajun Shark Tacos, and Appalachian classics like Brewer's Cheddar Ale Soup, Pennsylvania Dutch pretzels, and crab quesadillas. Fresh salads and hearty sandwiches make up the lunch and light dinner options. The steak and portabella salad, Hog Wild (pulled pork sandwich), and ribeye sandwich will surely fill you up. Really hungry? Try the Pork Schnitzel, beer-battered fish and chips, or the more conventional steaks, ribs, crab cakes, and pasta dishes.

Extras: Full liquor license. The second-floor Sports Pub was replaced by a sophisticated lounge, the Abbey Bar. "We were inspired by Bethlehem's Steelgaarden," Artie said. You'll find 50 Belgian bottles, and Belgian and Belgian-style drafts, including the "Obbie" Belgian-styles being brewed at ABC Gettysburg. Live entertainment and a fondue menu complete the attraction. ABC also offers banquet facilities for parties of 25 to 550 in the Gallery banquet room or on the rooftop deck.

Special considerations: Kids welcome. Handicapped-accessible. Cigars allowed and sold. Vegetarian meals available.

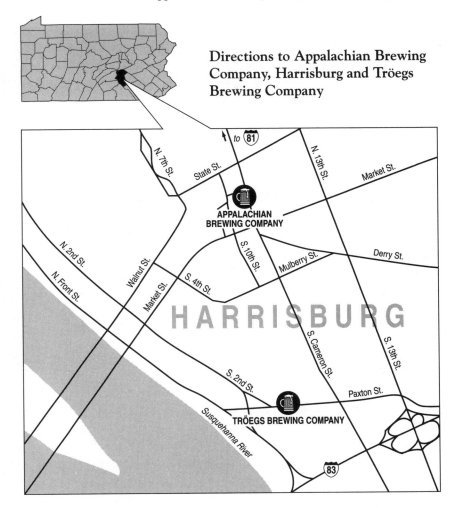

Directions to Appalachian Brewing Company, Harrisburg and Tröegs Brewing Company

Parking: Off-street lot behind building; metered parking on street.

Lodging in the area: Holiday Inn Express Riverfront, 525 South Front Street, 717-233-1611; Ramada Inn on Market Square, 23 South Second Street, 717-234-5021; Comfort Inn East, 4021 Union Deposit Road, 717-561-8100; Harrisburg Hilton and Towers, 1 North Second Street, 717-233-6000.

Area attractions: See Tröegs listing on page 156.

Other good beer sites: The crew at Appalachian recommended the following bars. *McGrath's Pub* (202 Locust Street, 717-232-9914), *Epic Bar and Grill* (25 South Fourth Street, 717-233-0975), *Stocks on 2nd* (211 North Second Street, 717-233-6699), and *Pep Grill* (209 Walnut Street, 717-236-6403). I recommend *KClinger's Pub-*

lik House (895 Old Trail Road, Etters, 717-932-0575), a multifloor (be sure to get down to the basement and hang with the Dead Guy) multitap with beers you just won't see anywhere else in the area. This place is all about beer, and everyone loves it. You're going to feel right at home here.

Tröegs Brewing Company

800 Paxton Street, Harrisburg, PA 17104
717-232-1297
www.troegs.com

What's in a name? Tröegs is certainly an odd one. It's a loose combination of brewery partner Chris Trogner's adolescent nickname "Trogs" and a *kroeg,* a Belgian slang word for pub. Even in central Pennsylvania, where you run across names like Hocker, Ochtemaier, and Fishburn, Tröegs sticks out. How do you pronounce it? You can pretty much say it any way you want, as long as it gets you one of these beers!

Tröegs's logo proudly proclaims "Hand Crafted by Two Brothers." Chris and John Trogner have carefully put together a technically proficient brewery in the middle of the state capital, Harrisburg. There's a well-thought-out brewhouse and fermentation hall, spotless in stainless steel and white plastic and epoxy.

Nothing less is to be expected of John Trogner, who brewed at the well-regarded Oasis Brewing Company in Colorado and later helped design a new brewhouse for them. John is neatly turned out, with short-trimmed hair and an earnest face. With quiet pride, he showed me each innovation in the brewery, from the electronic temperature sensors in the brewkettles, designed to allow precise replication of brewing regimens from batch to batch, to the recycling system for recapturing used cleaning caustic.

Chris Trogner, the hairier, looser brother, handles the sales and marketing end of the business,

Beers brewed: Year-round: Tröegs Pale Ale, Hopback Amber, Rugged Trail Ale, Bavarian Lager, Troegenator Doublebock. Seasonals: Oatmeal Stout, Sunshine Pils, Mad Elf. Single Batch beers: Dreamweaver Wheat, Nugget Nectar, Dead Reckoning Porter

putting thousands of miles on his car as he travels throughout central Pennsylvania. Now, after years of staying clear of the big markets in Philly, Pittsburgh, and Baltimore-Washington, they have decided to move in slowly from the suburbs. John explained their strategy: "We don't want to expand our area just to get more volume. We want to build solid customers. And we won't build a pub. No pub!"

The Pick: Year-round, I'll have to go with the Troegenator, for reasons already noted. My favorite seasonal, despite all the interesting Single Batches, has got to be the Sunshine Pils, a light, bright, clean-as-sunlight pilsner that I've sipped for pleasure and quaffed by the liter for laugh-out-loud good times. These boys have a surprising gift for lager beer.

They've discovered another key lately: size matters. Tröegs has discovered the geekerie, and the geekerie has for sure discovered Tröegs. It took years for John to work up to a big beer, and when he did, he didn't fool around. The Troegenator Doublebock was a huge beer, and a huge success, so much so that it's gone into the year-round rotation, a rare thing for a doublebock. But the Troegenator *is* a rare thing for a doublebock; it's strikingly dry in its maltiness, luring you into drinking more than you would of many heavier, sweeter doublebocks.

Tröegs has another big beer that makes things crazy at the brewery, a little thing made with cherries and honey called Mad Elf. There is only one release each year of this sweet, tasty, 10+ percent Christmas beer, and it is cause for alarm at beer stores and bars as folks stream in to grab it before it's gone.

The brothers keep the excitement tuned up with their single-batch beers, one-offs that they brew just for fun (though the Troegenator was a single-batch beer that kicked and bit its way right out of the category). Dead Reckoning Porter was one, a batch of delicious porter that was released in cask form only. It's a good idea to sign up for their e-letter at the website to keep abreast of the Single Batch releases.

Tröegs has come a long way from its early days of fairly cautious (though always well-crafted) beers: a pale ale, an ESB, a nut brown. These days, a variety pack from Tröegs has a "Wow!" in every bottle.

Opened: June 1997.
Owners: Chris Trogner, John Trogner.
Brewers: head brewer, John Trogner; assistant brewer, Chris Brugger.
System: 25-barrel Braukon brewhouse, 5,000 barrels annual capacity.
Production: 7,000 barrels in 2004.
Tours: Saturday at 2 P.M., or by appointment.
Take-out beer: Growlers, cases, and kegs.
Special considerations: Kids welcome. Handicapped-accessible.
Parking: Large off-street lot.

Lodging in the area: Hilton Harrisburg and Towers, 1 North Second Street, 717-233-6000; Allenberry Resort Inn, 1559 Boiling Springs Road, Boiling Springs, 717-258-3211; Holiday Inn Express Riverfront, 525 South Front Street, 717-233-1611; Hotel Hershey, 1 Hotel Road, Hershey, 717-533-2171.

Area attractions: The *State Museum of Pennsylvania* (Third Street between North and Forster, north of the capitol, 717-787-4978) has a wide range of exhibits on industry, art, science, archeology, and of course, Pennsylvania history. The *State Capitol Building* offers free tours every day of the week to view the grand architectural features of this massive stone structure. *Riverfront Park* hosts a number of festivals; call the mayor's office (717-255-3040) for more information. There's lots going on over on *City Island* (717-255-3020), in the middle of the river: trails, swimming, and the ballpark of the Harrisburg Senators AA baseball team. You may want to time your visit for January to catch the *Pennsylvania Farm Show* (717-255-3040), a huge and friendly display of the state's agricultural bounty, from fancy chickens to butter sculptures to draft horse pulling competitions—and the food is fantastic! Fair warning, though: Pennsylvanians have a superstition about "Farm Show weather." Winter often seems to save its worst for that week. Nearby *Hersheypark* (800-437-7439) is a treat for roller-coaster fans. *Hershey's Chocolate World* (800 Park Boulevard, 717-534-4900) offers a tour ride that exhibits the chocolate-manufacturing process in a nonfactory setting.

Other area beer sites: *Zembie's* (226 North Second Street, 717-232-5020) was one of my farthest-flung regular stops when I lived in Lancaster. It has a great marble bar and is very cool and soothing in the summer. The Trogner brothers suggested *Cragin's Brickhaus* (229 North Second Street, 717-233-4287), *O'Reilly's* (800 East Park Drive, 717-564-2700), and the *Marysville Tavern* (13 South Main Street, Marysville, 717-957-9900), mentioned by John Frantz at Lancaster Brewing, too.

Appalachian Brewing Company, Gettysburg

401 Buford Avenue, Gettysburg, PA 17325
717-334-2200
www.abcbrew.com

Gen. Robert E. Lee led his Army of Northern Virginia up the Appalachian front to Pennsylvania in 1863, in an attempt to bring the war to the North. It was a bold, swift stroke, the kind he was known for. But his genius failed him at Gettysburg, as the Union forces gathered swiftly to block his advance and tenaciously held the high ground against all assaults. The cream of Lee's army was broken in the battle, and he would never attempt to take the war north again.

Lee watched the battle unfold and fall apart from his headquarters, a stone house rented at the time by Mary "Widow" Thompson and her family, and ironically owned by the fiercely antislavery, anti-Confederacy politician Thaddeus Stevens. Whether this occupation contributed to Stevens's radical plans for the subjugation of the South after the war is a teasing question.

Artie Tafoya led Appalachian Brewing Company down Route 15 almost exactly 140 years later in an attempt to bring ABC's style of brewpub to more communities. It also was a bold, swift stroke: The whole thing took place in a matter of weeks. As I write this, the Pennsylvania Liquor Control Board is still holding the high ground, but Artie's army should prevail. If they do, it will be symbolically right in Lee's face: ABC's new Gettysburg brewpub is only a few steps from the museum that Lee's headquarters and Stevens's house has become.

"We had always hoped to franchise the Appalachian brewpub idea," Artie explained. "But you can't really franchise until you've done it yourself; you have to be multiunit first. No one wants to be the beta site for your expansion plans. So we did that. This was an operating restaurant, and we came in and made it an ABC brewpub in a month.

"We're looking for more opportunities like this," he added. "We're looking at some right now.

Beers brewed: See the Harrisburg ABC list on page 151 for available beers. Once brewing starts, expect some of those "big beers" Artie was talking about.

We intend to put a brewery in each one. We had a chance to pick up two small systems recently, and we've put them in storage till we need them." There are also plans for a fairly large ABC brewpub across from the new minor league baseball park in Lancaster.

For now, though, all the Gettysburg pub needs to become a *brew*pub is final licensing clearance from the PLCB. Once that happens, they can fire up their 10-barrel Mueller brewhouse ("Mueller," Artie noted, "that's the good stuff") and start making beer. "We'll still have the majority of the beers brewed in Harrisburg," Artie said. "But we'll be able to do smaller batches here, so we can make the big beers we couldn't really do at Harrisburg: doublebocks, imperial stouts, tripels." Now that sounds interesting.

The origins of that Mueller brewhouse are interesting, too. Mueller is a company known for their work making tanks for the dairy-farming industry; they are accomplished master at stainless steel fabrication. There aren't many Mueller brewhouses out there, and this one has an interesting provenance. It was originally built for the Jack Daniel's brewery. The Jack Daniel Company jumped into microbrewing back in the mid-1990s—when it seemed like everyone was jumping into it—and for three years produced some pretty darned good beers. The Christmas beer was exceptional, a cherry-spiked malt mama that aged well . . . till I drank the last of my stash three years ago. So I'm expecting good things from this brewery!

Don't expect the same size as the brewpub in Harrisburg. This one's much smaller, though there is a large banquet room downstairs. There's a game room, too, right beside the brewhouse. But you'll find the main bar and dining room upstairs, looking out across the battlefield.

Out across the battlefield . . . Artie, like Lee, sees the battle shaping and knows it's all on his shoulders. "I figure I can go do something else," he said, shrugging, "or I can take this as far as it can go. I've got great staff. We work hard at excellence. My partners are great; they trust my decisions and help out where they can. This brewpub, the planned brewpubs, open new ground for the bottle and kegged product; people see it, drink it, and then go buy it. Our off-premise sales are up 30 percent this year so far."

The Pick: Big beers, eh? Harrisburg managed to squeak out a few, and one of them was on when I visited Artie: Broad Street Barleywine, a whopper of a beer, aged for a year and a half in oak cask used for cabernet at the Presque Isle winery in Erie, and another year and a half in the keg. This was remarkable beer, not over-oaked, but winey, smooth, smoky, sweet and fruity, broad and mature. Fantastic stuff.

It doesn't sound like this bold, swift stroke is going to be sent home reeling in disarray. Artie Tafoya and ABC have taken the high ground in Gettysburg, and they're staying till the fight's won.

Opened: August 2003.
Owners: Shawn Gallagher, Jack Sproch.
Brewers: Artie Tafoya, Jesse Prall.
System: 10-barrel Paul Mueller Company brewhouse, 1,200 barrels annual capacity.
Production: None in 2004.
Brewpub hours: ABC at Gettysburg, like Gettysburg, is quite seasonal, and hours change with the tourist flow. From March 1 to June 30, hours are Tuesday through Thursday, noon to 9 P.M.; Friday and Saturday, noon to 11 P.M.; closed on Sunday and Monday. From July 1 to September 30, hours are Sunday through Thursday, noon to 9 P.M.; Friday and Saturday, noon to 11 P.M. From October 1 to November 24, hours are Sunday and Tuesday through Thursday, noon to 9 P.M.; Friday and Saturday, noon to 11 P.M.; closed on Mondays. At least that was the plan; business was so good, the pub was open all year on longer hours, and it's still flexible. Best to just call ahead.
Tours: Every day at 5 P.M., plus 1:00 P.M. on Saturday.
Take-out beer: Growlers and six-packs.
Food: See ABC Harrisburg on page 152 for identical menu.
Extras: Full liquor license. Billiard room (pay by the hour for tables), with darts. ABC also offers banquet facilities for parties of 25 to 125 in the Gallery banquet room. Located just steps from General Lee's headquarters and museum at the edge of the historic battlefields.
Special considerations: Kids welcome. First floor handicapped-accessible. Vegetarian meals available. Cigars allowed.
Parking: Lots beside the building and across the street.
Lodging in the area: Comfort Inn, 871 York Road, 717-337-2400; Best Western Gettysburg Hotel, historic hotel on Lincoln Square, established 1797, 717-337-2000; Herr Tavern and Publick House, 900 Chambersburg Road, 800-362-9849; Quality Inn Larson's, on Seminary Ridge, 401 Buford Avenue, 717-334-3141. Lightner Farmhouse, historic B&B, 2350 Baltimore Pike, 717-337-9508.
Area attractions: The *Gettysburg National Military Park and Cemetery* are naturally the main draws in Gettysburg. The park visitors center is across from the cemetery on Route 134 just south of town. Guided and self-guided walking and auto tours are available there,

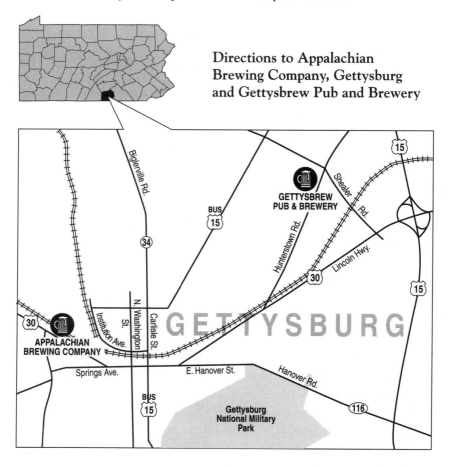

Directions to Appalachian
Brewing Company, Gettysburg
and Gettysbrew Pub and Brewery

including private tours with licensed battlefield guides. The center also has a museum, the Cyclorama; a 365-foot painting of Pickett's Charge; and the Electric Map, a large relief map of the area that uses colored lights to show the ebb and flow of the three-day battle. *Note:* You may want to call ahead or check the park's website (www.nps.gov/gett); the Cyclorama is under restoration, the Electric Map is being considered for restoration, and there are plans to build a new visitors center.

Another site of interest to military history buffs of a different era is Dwight D. Eisenhower's Gettysburg farm, preserved as the **Eisenhower National Historic Site.** There is a shuttle bus to the site from the National Park Visitor Center (717-334-1124). Off the battlefield, there's good antiquing in New Oxford (about 8 miles east on Route 30).

When you're tired of battles and history, relax at **Thistlefields** (29 Chambersburg Street, 717-338-9131), a quite authentic British tearoom. In nearby Hanover, **Utz Potato Chips** (900 High Street, 717-637-6644), offers free tours showing the production of its delicious chips. **Ski Liberty** in Fairfield (southwest on Route 116, 717-642-8297) has a 606-foot vertical drop, snowmaking, ski school, night skiing, restaurant and lounge, and day care. **Caledonia State Park** (west on Route 30, 717-352-2161), offers camping, fishing, swimming, hiking, golf, and 10 miles of cross-country skiing trails.

Other area beer sites: The **Blue Parrot Bistro** (35 Chambersburg Street, 717-337-3739) is a relaxed oasis off the square, away from the hustling tourist trade. You'll find a couple local taps and Guinness, as well as some good whiskeys. I was quite taken by the Springhouse Tavern at the **Dobbin House** (89 Steinwehr Avenue, 717-334-2100), built in 1776. The Springhouse Tavern is downstairs in a rough stone cellar, where the bar itself (complete with after-hours wooden "fences" to lock up the liquor) dates from before 1818. It's illuminated with low lights and lots of candles, and you can hear the actual spring trickling in the corner. Surprisingly, the costumed barmaid was able to draw me a fresh glass of Tröegs Hopback Amber; the fellow beside me heartily recommended the locally made Lucky Leaf sparkling cider (nonalcoholic). The Dobbin House is pretty touristy, but the tavern offers a unique drinking experience. Artie also recommended **Mamma Ventura's Restaurant and Pizzeria** (13 Chambersburg Street, 717-334-5548) as a friendly place for a quick bite and a beer; the bar's downstairs.

Out of town, you'll find an outstanding selection of German and German-style beers at the **Hofbrau Haus** in Abbottstown (just west of the town square on Route 30, on the north side, 717-259-9641). It's clean and neat, and the food is delicious. **KClinger's** (304 Poplar Street, Hanover, 717-633-9197) is an excellent big city–level multitap beer bar with limited-release beers, vintage beers, and a whole boatload of attitude. It's a must-stop.

Gettysbrew Pub and Brewery

248 Hunterstown Road, Gettysburg, PA 17325
717-337-1001
www.gettysbrew.com

It's an oddly perfect situation at this pub and brewery, located near one of the nation's most revered historic battlefields, Gettysburg. It's housed in a historic building used as a field hospital by the Confederate Army during the battle, and it's owned by a retired U.S. Army medical researcher. Dr. Paul Lemley loves Gettysburg, loves the building, loves his work, and loves to talk about it. A wiry bundle of energy, Paul is always looking for ways to improve his pub.

Paul brews his beer on a little extract system shoehorned into a historic brick-end barn, part of the Monfort Farm. During the battle of Gettysburg, the Confederates brought casualties to the farm to be treated. After Lee's retreat, the Union Army's doctors continued to care for the hundreds of men who were too injured to travel. The only conditions treated at the Monfort Farm these days, of course, are hunger and thirst.

The pub has been minimally reconstructed. The dining room is under the soaring rafters of the barn overhead. Ventilation holes in the brick-end walls, common to Pennsylvania barns of that period, have been glassed over for comfort's sake. Underfoot are rough-hewn planks solid enough to hold a troop of Confederate cavalry. Paul has added gallery seating on the front of the barn and enclosed the back patio to create a cozy piano bar that maintains the authentically rough look of the barn. There are not many restaurants outside restored communities that offer this kind of simple, homespun beauty.

The ceramic tower taps will pour whichever brew you care to try. Paul's been homing in on what he wants to brew as year-round beers and points unabashedly to his Gettysbrew PA Blonde as a 3.3 percent ABV light beer. "Some brewpubs

Beers brewed: Year-round: Gettysbrew PA Blonde, Big Red One, Blew Kilt, Dark Horse, Black Knight. There is also an assortment of house-made sodas.

The Pick: Gettysbrew uses an all-extract system and no specialty grains at all. This is a limiting factor; you can make good beers with extracts, but you are going to have a hard time making excellent ones.

won't serve light beer," he said scornfully. "It costs me less to make it, and people want it and will pay the same price for it. That's an expensive principle."

Meanwhile, the brewpub continues to attract tourists and reenactors. When the place is full of reenactors, as it was one Remembrance Day when I drank with the 2nd Wisconsin, you can feel the age of the place and what it's seen. Monfort Farm is an authentic piece of Gettysburg battlefield history. It's lucky that the man who built a brewpub here respects the history and the hallowed nature of this ground.

Opened: Brewery, August 1996; restaurant, July 1997.
Owner: Dr. Paul V. Lemley, Lt. Col., USA (Ret.).
Brewer: Paul Lemley.
System: 7-barrel Specific Mechanical brewhouse modified for extract brewing, 1,000 barrels annual capacity.
Production: 120 barrels in 2004 (estimated).
Restaurant hours: Monday through Friday, 4 P.M. to 8:30 P.M.; Saturday and Sunday, noon to 8:30 P.M.
Tours: By appointment only.
Take-out beer: Growlers.
Food: Gettysbrew has a full-range menu: appetizers, salads, sandwiches, steaks and seafood, and desserts.
Extras: Live music (call for schedule); big-screen TV sports. Gettysbrew can accommodate large groups, including bus tours, wedding receptions, and reunions, for a buffet with prior coordination.
Special considerations: Kids welcome. Handicapped-accessible. Cigars allowed on deck. Vegetarian meals available.
Parking: Large, lighted free lot.
Lodging in the area: See Appalachian Brewing Company, Gettysburg listing (page 159).
Area attractions: See Appalachian listing (pages 159–161).
Other area beer sites: See Appalachian listing (page 161).

Market Cross Pub and Brewery

113 North Hanover Street, Carlisle, PA 17013
717-258-1234
www.marketcrosspub.com

This is the brewery that refused to die. Before Jeff Goss talked Kevin Spicer into brewing in it (and it doesn't sound like it took much talking), this was the brewhouse for Whitetail Brewing, a brewery that had at least two lives. Whitetail brewer Wade Keech told me that before that, the brewery had been the original brewhouse built by English microbrewing pioneer Peter Austin, back in the late 1970s, and used in his first microbrewery, The Long Barn.

That's some pedigree, but Market Cross is up to it. Jeff Goss was a food services major from Penn State who wound up working for a computer company. Then he got married and had a daughter, and decided he wanted to settle down and watch his daughter grow up. Market Cross was the result. He named the pub for the main square in the United Kingdom's Carlisle, also an old market town.

It was a conscious decision he made after having been there. "I wanted to re-create that community feel in the pubs in the UK," he told me, "and I like to think we succeeded. Our customers, our regulars, are lawyers, plumbers, colonels from the Barracks, truck drivers."

It's certainly a lot better now than it was when Goss bought the building. His wife, JoAnne, is from Carlisle and remembers what it was. "The Boiler Room," Jeff told me, laughing. "They had Bud, Busch, and fights every week." There hasn't been a fight in here in years, but it's still all about beer: Market Cross has one of Pennsylvania's increasingly rare beer-only licenses, and Jeff proudly points out that it is malt beverage license E2, the second one issued by the state after Repeal.

So why the emphasis on beer variety that would finally lead to a brewery out back? "I thought, if we only have beer, let's do the best we can," said Jeff. They opened with a selection of 60 beers that has grown to more than 250, plus the house beers.

The house beers have been around longer than the brewery. "I hooked up with Wade when

Beers brewed: Year-round: Market Cross Red English Ale, Olde Yeller IPA, Pub Porter. Seasonal: "Tell Me Rye" Golden Ale, Midsummer Knights Wheat, Excalibers Imperial Stout.

he was still brewing down in York," said Jeff. "Kevin came up with the recipes for the Red Ale and the Porter, and Wade brewed them for us." When Keech lost his lease in York, Goss offered the back building as a new home for Whitetail. And when Keech finally gave up after much heartache, Goss took over the brewery and let Spicer, a local high school geo-environmental science teacher, take over the brewing.

The Pick: "Tell Me Rye" indeed; tell me rye so many other beers like this at other brewpubs taste like tainted fizzy water, when this tastes like beer. Distinctive beer, and pint-poundable. If you've never had a rye beer before, this is a good place to start.

"We go to the festivals," Goss said. "We're the little guy, not like the big craft brewers with the fancy logos and glassware. But we don't have to be financially cautious about our beer. It's just part of what we do. So Kevin can stretch a little."

That's where beers like "Tell Me Rye" come from, a hazy "American rye" beer that lets the flavor of the grain come through. Kevin's Olde Yeller IPA ("You'll cry when the beer's over" is the standard joke on that one) is a light yellow beer that shocks you senseless with 7+ percent ABV and hops sticking out all over.

What's it like, brewing on Peter Austin's original system? "It really is home brewing. It's a *very* manual system," Kevin said. "I carbonate the beer by rocking the kegs; about 250 rocks does it."

But that's not Ringwood yeast in there anymore. "We get yeast from Appalachian Brewing," Kevin said. "Appalachian and Tröegs have been a big help. Artie Tafoya told me when I started, 'I *want* you to brew good beer, right out of the gate!' He knows that good beer at every brewpub helps every brewpub."

It's true, but at least for now, this brewpub is the only place you'll get this good beer—except for the occasional festival—because Market Cross's license doesn't allow outside sales. That's going to have to change, because Goss is taking Market Cross and the gift of good beer to Shippensburg. "We'll be opening another Market Cross at 105 West King Street in Shippensburg," he said. "We'll start with a big beer selection while we work on the federal paperwork to allow us to ship our own beer down there."

Opening another place, shipping beer around . . . I don't know, Jeff; that sounds just like a big craft brewer. It surely tastes like one.

Opened: Pub opened April 1, 1994; brewery resumed operations as Market Cross in September 2002.
Owner: Jeff and JoAnne Goss.
Brewer: Kevin Spicer.

Directions to Market Cross
Pub and Brewery

System: 10-barrel Peter Austin brewhouse, 1,000 barrels annual capacity.

Production: 125 barrels in 2003.

Brewpub hours: Sundays, noon to 10 P.M.; Monday through Thursday, 11 A.M. to midnight; Friday and Saturday, 11 A.M. to 1 A.M.

Tours: Monday and Thursday evenings, otherwise as brewer is available.

Take-out beer: No house beers sold for off-premises consumption; six-packs of other beers available.

Food: Market Cross has the usual bar food, well executed and fresh, as well as a strong selection of the best of English pub food: fish and chips, cottage pie, shepherd's pie, bangers and mash, and beef and Guinness. Solid, belly-mortar food.

Extras: Real darts, big-screen TV, live music on Saturdays, and "Singin' Wingin' Wednesdays." Really.

Special considerations: Kids welcome. Handicapped-accessible. Cigars allowed. Vegetarian meals available.

Parking: On-street and off-street parking is easy to find.

Lodging in the area: Carlisle House B&B, 148 South Hanover Street, 717-249-0350; Econo Lodge Carlisle, 1460 Harrisburg Pike, 717-249-7775; Jacob's Resting Place B&B, 1007 Harrisburg Pike, 717-243-1766; Yellow Breeches House B&B, 213 Front Street, Boiling Springs, 717-258-8344.

Area attractions: Carlisle is well known for an annual series of automobile flea markets, where car enthusiasts buy and swap car parts from vintage autos and hot rods. There is a different market each month from April to October. Call **Carlisle Productions** (717-343-7855) for current information on schedules and locations. The **Trout Art Gallery** (High Street on the Dickinson College campus, 717-245-1711) has a variety of art, including classical Greek, African, Oriental, and modern American. **Carlisle Barracks,** one of the oldest permanent army posts in the United States, is home to the Army War College, the Army Heritage Educational Center, and the Army's Military History Institute. The institute (717-245-3611) houses a deep collection of military history texts, including U.S. and foreign regimental histories, and one of the most extensive collections of Civil War photos in the world. Carlisle also is simply a nice town to stroll through, nicely kept with an attractive town square. The fly fishing on the Yellow Breeches Creek is world-class. Contact the **Allenberry Resort Inn** (1559 Boiling Springs Road, Boiling Springs, 717-258-3211) about trout-fishing seminars and weekend packages—or dinner theater specials at the Allenberry Playhouse. The **Yellow Breeches House** (213 Front Street, Boiling Springs, 717-258-8344) has similar fishing packages. If you'd rather wade in on your own, get in touch with the **Cold Spring Anglers,** a fly-fishing shop at 419 East High Street in Carlisle (717-245-2646, www.coldspringanglers.com) that will guide you to the local fishing areas. You can get regularly updated detailed fishing reports by clicking on "Stream Reports" on the website.

Other area beer sites: The other good bar in Carlisle is the **Gingerbread Man** (5 South Courthouse Avenue, 717-249-6970), where it's loose, informal, and fun. **KClinger's** (304 Poplar Street, Hanover, 717-633-9197) is a must-stop. This is probably the best spot for beer in Pennsylvania, outside of Pittsburgh and Philadelphia, because of their selection, the staff's beer knowledge, and how they handle their beer.

Selin's Grove Brewing Company

**119–121 North Market Street,
Selinsgrove, PA 17870
570-374-7308**

"What do you think of this one?" "How are you figuring to vote this year?" "Look at that!" "They were great, I want to hear more." "This one's pretty good." "Is that one ready yet?" You try sitting at the bar at Selin's Grove without hearing other people's conversations!

One of the reasons I like this little basement brewpub is the low-volume background music and lack of television. Steve Leason and Heather McNabb say they want people to "practice the art of communication," something that all too many pubs make impossible.

Steve and Heather are like that. They work with what they have to get the results they want. They don't—*can't*—throw money at every problem, so a lot of thought goes into everything. Until recently, they worked on a self-built 3-barrel brewhouse, because that's what they had. With more than twenty years' brewing experience between them, though, the size of the system didn't matter.

The beer is knock-your-socks-off stuff. Heather and Steve both brew, and it's impossible to tell who brews which beer. I tried nine beers the first time I visited Selin's Grove (the plain black taps marked with masking tape and marker), and seven of them were exceptional. My notes have phrases like "reaches out and grabs you" (Old Trail ESB), "real beer" (Cream Ale), and "Wattabeer! Smooth and silky, yet fathoms deep" (Shade Mountain Oatmeal Stout).

My most recent trip repeated the experience. The Pale Ale: "Very full flavor, rich malt, deep character." The Milk Stout: "Creamy, smooth, just a touch of mild chocolate flavor." I took a growler of the Kriek to a beer event at the Grey Lodge Pub in Philly, and people got down on their knees and bowed down to the beer.

Beers brewed: Year-round: Shade Mountain Oatmeal Stout, White Horse Porter, Captain Selin's Cream Ale, a pale ale, a Scottish-style ale, and a fruit beer. Seasonals: A wheat beer of some type, St. Fillin's Barleywine-style Ale, Market Street Fest, Kriek, Milk Stout, and the list is still growing; call for current taps. Selin's Grove has two beer engines and cask-conditions some of its beers for hand dispense.

The food's pretty great here, too. The kitchen is tiny but as tightly organized as a ship's galley, and only the necessary appliances fit in. "Just because it's a micro*brewery* doesn't mean you have to have a micro*wave*," Steve noted acerbically, and I applaud the sentiment. Some of that good stuff is bought with sweat equity. The brewpub belongs to an organic farm co-op and gets fresh vegetables in exchange for three hours of work on the farm each month.

Financial reasons originally forced the two to locate in Selinsgrove, but they have made the best of it. The brewpub occupies the basement of the Snyder mansion, which until recently was run as a museum attraction by Heather's parents. "We're here because we could afford it," Heather cheerfully admitted.

The Pick: The Shade Mountain Oatmeal Stout is a lighter-bodied yet intensely flavored stout, possessed of smooth body with a real roasted-barley bite—a great all-around stout. The St. Fillin's is very broad and full of malt, with a pleasing touch of butterscotch, fruitiness, and alcohol heat, and it only gets better as it ages. And that Kriek was just phenomenal, like eating a sour cherry pie. Once I tasted it, I knew I was leaving the pub with a growler of that beer, one way or another.

Any qualms they may have had about their location were settled early by a little thing Heather saw in a local church cookbook. "We realized the brewpub would be within 100 feet of a church," Heather recalled. This proximity would allow the church to block the brewpub. "We went over to see if we could talk to them about it," she continued, "and I saw the church cookbook, one of those community projects. I opened it, and on the first page was a homebrew recipe. We thought that looked like we had a pretty good chance!"

The couple delved into Selinsgrove history, looking for evidence of a brewing heritage. They came across a few mentions but were more interested in something else they found. It seems a man named Mathias App had a distillery in Selinsgrove in the early 1800s. He had a water pump at the distillery that was powered by stray dogs in a wheel, and he paid small boys to catch dogs for him. Heather and Steve liked this image of a dog-powered distillery so much that they made it the symbol of the brewery.

Things have gotten a bit larger at Selin's Grove. Heather's parents closed the gift shop upstairs in the mansion, and the brewpub will be expanding into the first floor, with seating for about forty and a full-size kitchen. Steve's nervous, but I think it's going to be a fantastic success.

They recently retired the 3-barrel "Franken-brewery" after purchasing a used 7-barrel system from Avery Brewing in Colorado. "We couldn't keep up; we just never got ahead," said Steve. Heather added "The physical toll it was taking . . . it just wasn't as much fun anymore.

All that moisture in an 1816-era house wasn't good, either." The last batch on the old system was Scotch Ale, just like the first batch, way back in 1996.

The new system is out back in a former garage, a setting that is practically industrial compared to the old tucked-in-the-basement brewery. "We can use more whole hops in this system," said Steve, "and the flow goes by gravity, no pumps. It's gentler on the beer." Don't laugh, it really does make a difference.

But don't think Steve's going to get carried away with all those whole-leaf hops and build ever-bigger IPAs like some brewers. "Just throw more hops in," he carped about the way beer geeks have taken to massively bitter beers lately. "They think you're a god, and it's the dumbest beer you can make!"

Just another reason why Selin's Grove is very much out of the ordinary for a brewpub. Its intimate size, fireplace, vegetarian entrées, smoke-free environment, wide range of excellent beers—and the brewers' refreshingly contrarian attitudes—help set it apart. That's precisely why I like it.

Opened: December 1996.

Owners: Heather McNabb, Steven Leason.

Brewers: Heather McNabb, Steven Leason.

System: 7-barrel CDC brewhouse, 380 barrels annual capacity.

Production: 180 barrels in 2004 (estimated).

Brewpub hours: Wednesday and Thursday, 4 P.M. to 11 P.M.; Friday and Saturday, noon to midnight. Sunday hours may happen; call ahead.

Tours: Anytime the staff is not too busy, they are happy to give tours; best to call ahead.

Take-out beer: Growlers.

Food: Sandwiches, soups, and salads make up the bulk of the menu, along with one weekly hot entrée special. The emphasis is on healthy vegetarian items. (In a brewpub? Amazing!) Good, house-made root beer, organic coffees, and teas round out the menu for kids and nondrinkers.

Extras: Selection of Pennsylvania wines available. Live music every other week: bluegrass, swing, folk, blues, and much more. Call for schedule. Assorted books, magazines, tavern puzzles, backgammon, and chess. "We're too small for darts," says Steve Leason. Now that's a microbrewery!

Special considerations: Kids welcome. Handicapped-accessible. Interior completely smoke-free, but cigars and cigarettes allowed in out-

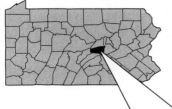

**Directions to Selin's Grove
Brewing Company**

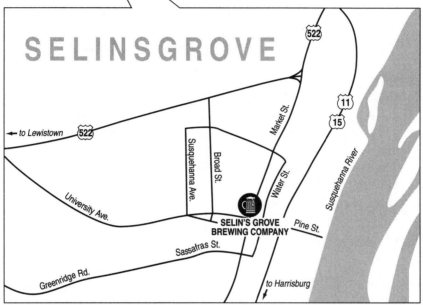

side beer garden. Many vegetarian meals available, including selections to suit full vegans.

Parking: The entrance to the brewpub is actually in the rear, not on Market Street. Parking is available on Market, then you simply walk through the side garden to the rear entrance. There is also a parking lot off Strawberry Alley.

Lodging in the area: Potteiger House B&B, 8 West Chestnut Street (half a block from brewpub), 570-374-0415; Comfort Inn, 710 South Route 11/15, 570-374-8880; Phillips Motel, Route 11/15 and Eleventh Avenue, 570-743-3100.

Area attractions: Small museums and restored homes abound in the central Susquehanna Valley. The *Mifflinburg Buggy Museum* (523 Green Street, Mifflinburg, 570-966-1355) displays carriage-making techniques. The *Joseph Priestly House* (472 Priestley Avenue, Northumberland, 570-473-9474), the home of a wide-ranging thinker who discovered oxygen, founded the Unitarian Church in America, and influenced the writing of the Constitution, has been restored for visits. For more outdoorsy fun, the Susquehanna has plenty of boat ramps; Middle Creek Lake, south of Selinsgrove, is a stocked fishing lake; and state game lands are scattered along the river. If you want to be a hero to the kids, take them to **Knoebel's Amusement Resort** (east of the river in Elysburg, 800-487-4386). It's not expensive (you pay by the ride), you can bring in food and picnic, you can swim, you can even camp there. My kids love it, and so do a lot of others; it was recently rated the fourth-best amusement park in the world, and its Phoenix coaster was rated fourth-best wooden coaster in the world.

Other area beer sites: *BJ's* (one block from the brewpub at 17 North Market) is a steak and rib restaurant with several micros on tap. *Botdorf's Café* (7 South Market, 570-374-9074) is a comfy local hangout. *Russell's* (117 West Main Street, Bloomsburg, 570-387-1332) is a bit of a haul, but it is an outstandingly civilized restaurant and bar with excellent beer and whiskey. Heather recommended *Mastracchio's Restaurant and Lounge* (344 Juniata Parkway East, Newport, 717-567-7511) and other reports back her up; a nice beer oasis on the Juniata River.

Bullfrog Brewery

229 West Fourth Street,
Williamsport, PA 17701
570-326-4700
www.bullfrogbrewery.com

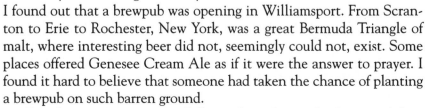

I knew the American brewing revolution was finally in full swing in Pennsylvania when I found out that a brewpub was opening in Williamsport. From Scranton to Erie to Rochester, New York, was a great Bermuda Triangle of malt, where interesting beer did not, seemingly could not, exist. Some places offered Genesee Cream Ale as if it were the answer to prayer. I found it hard to believe that someone had taken the chance of planting a brewpub on such barren ground.

But the rumors were true: Billtown has a brewpub. One man's barren ground is evidently another man's open market. I stopped in for the first time shortly before Bullfrog opened, when the gleaming Bohemian brewhouse had been installed in the front windows. I took a look around as brew-master-to-be Charlie Schnable (now brewer-partner at Otto's in State College) sanded the hardwood floors. The old building was well constructed, with glass all around the dining area and solid beams down below. The sunlight through the glass made the place cheery, even though it had no furniture or lights and the walls were unpainted.

Now that the Bullfrog has been up and running for almost ten years, it's an even happier place. It's become a big part of Williamsport's cultural scene, and business is good. I was in on a Friday night recently, running samples with Terry Hawbaker, when a woman at one of the "high-hat" tables nearby saw the multitude of little beers on our table. "What's that?" I heard her say. "I want some of those little beers!" Not only did she get a sampler, but she also passed it around to her tablemates as the waitress, busy though it was, cheerfully stood by and explained every beer to them.

It's quite a beerlist, too. Bullfrog has had some retention problems with brewers, including one who stayed less than a week. Terry came in from Black Rock, a failed brewpub in Wilkes-Barre, where he shook things up something fierce, brewing anything that took his fancy and brewing it well. He got up to speed on Bullfrog's system with the help of a walk-through with Charlie Schnable. Terry told me he liked Williamsport, liked the Bullfrog, and plans to stay awhile. They're lucky: He's one of the better brewers in Pennsylvania, and with the competition, that's saying something.

But a sip or two here and there will confirm it. Try the Smoked! Amber, an amber beer with a mellow bacony smoke to it, flawless and refreshing. Want big? Try the Edgar IPA, an 8 percent dry-hopped punnish homage to Edgar Allan Poe's last story, *Hop Frog*, and just brimfull with hop aroma. His Saison de Frog is big and spicy, fruity and yeasty, real farmhouse stuff.

New brewer, maybe, but the Bullfrog still has the touches, the menu, the attitude that makes it one of my favorites. The doubled beer boards are still there: Blackboards hang from the ceiling with the current house beers and upcoming events written on them, and someone cleverly writes backward on the backside of the slates so that they are

Beers brewed: Year-round: Billtown Blonde, Ribbit Red Ale, Susquehanna Stout, Edgar IPA, Friar Frog Dubbel, Fruit Wheat. Seasonals: Hefeweizen, Smoked! Amber, 90/ Scottish Ale, Blitzen's Nutcracker, All-American Hop Rod, Double Bock, Witbier, Saison de Frog. Expect more as Terry settles in.

The Pick: I don't get to pick a smoked beer too often, so I gotta grab it: Smoked! is a flawless *rauchbier,* made with Weyermann beechwood-smoked malt from Franconia, Germany, the world's epicenter of smoked beers. It's mellow, it's bacony, it's powerfully refreshing.

legible in the large back mirror! The doodads and giftshop items are above the usual grade, and the taphandles are hand-carved by a local woodworker. My favorite is the one for the root beer: simply a spreading root, sanded and polished.

From the gleaming brewkettle to the hand-carved taps, Bullfrog is a brewpub that would look good anywhere. With other breweries popping up in the old "Beermuda Triangle" (you'll find some good ones down the river and over the line in New York), it's definitely worth the trek.

Opened: August 1996.

Owners: Bob Koch, Harriet Koch, Steven Koch, Barbara Whipple.

Brewer: Head brewer, Terry Hawbaker; Dan Holmes.

System: 10-barrel Bohemian brewhouse, 1,500 barrels annual capacity.

Production: 720 barrels in 2004 (estimated).

Brewpub hours: Monday through Thursday, 11 A.M. to midnight; Friday through Saturday, 11 A.M. to 2 A.M.; Sunday, 9 A.M. (brunch) to midnight.

Tours: Call ahead; tours are available whenever the brewer is in.

Take-out beer: Growlers, quarter and half kegs (call ahead for keg availability).

Food: Bullfrog is serving up some great food these days, including a smoked salmon penne pasta dish that won a countywide "fete de cuisine" competition. You'll find hand-cut steaks, innovative sandwiches, a range of extraordinary salads, and fresh seafood. Bullfrog also serves some very healthy items, including a range of vegetarian dishes and fresh-squeezed juices (I had an apple-carrot-ginger juice that was great).

Extras: Full liquor license with a fine selection of wines and the area's most extensive selection of scotch, tequila, and bourbon (including a rare Pennsylvania bourbon). Private rooms available for parties and banquets. Live music several times a week (call for schedule).

Special considerations: Kids welcome. Handicapped-accessible. Cigars allowed. Vegetarian meals served.

Parking: On-street parking. Municipal parking lot one block south.

Lodging in the area: Genetti Hotel and Suites, 200 West Fourth Street, 570-326-6600; Econo Lodge, 2401 East Third Street, 570-326-1501; Reighard House B&B, 1323 East Third Street, 570-326-3593.

Area attractions: The brewpub is right across the street from the **Community Arts Center** (220 West Fourth Street, 570-326-2424), featuring movies, musicals, and cultural shows; call for schedules. Williamsport is the birthplace of Little League baseball and home of

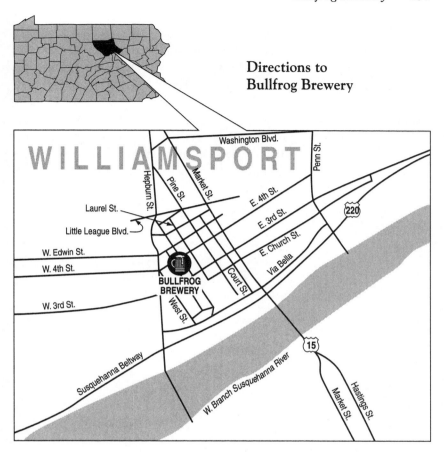

Directions to
Bullfrog Brewery

the annual Little League World Series in August. The **Peter J. McGovern Little League Museum** (next to the World Series field on Route 15, 570-326-3607) has batting cages, Little League history, and major leaguers' Little League uniforms and equipment. Take a Susquehanna River ride on the **Hiawatha,** a paddle-wheel riverboat (800-358-9900). The **Lycoming County Historical Museum** (858 West Fourth Street, 570-326-3326) tells the story of Williamsport's heyday as a lumber boom town and also has an outstanding exhibit of toy trains. As a former librarian, I have to tell you about the **Brodart Company Outlet** (500 Arch Street, 800-233-8467, x76457), a supplier of leased library books that sells the returned titles for insanely low prices. In nearby Woolrich, you'll find the **Woolrich Mills** factory outlet (570-769-7401) and some outstanding bargains. If you go south from Williamsport on Route 15, stop at the scenic overlook, where you can see the whole valley stretching out for miles. Farther down the road near Allenwood is **Clyde Peeling's Reptiland** (800-REPTILAND), a reptile zoo with snakes, lizards, tortoises, frogs, and alligators. It's a Pennsylvania classic. For more ideas, call the Lycoming County Visitor Information Center (800-358-9900).

Other area beer sites: *Russell's* (117 West Main Street, Bloomsburg, 570-387-1332) is an outstandingly civilized restaurant and bar with excellent beer and whiskey. Selin's Grove (page 172) and Russell's are both more than half an hour away, but they're worth the trip.

Beer Traveling

First things first: "Beer traveling" is not about driving drunk from brewpub to brewpub. Beer outings are similar to the wine trips celebrated in glossy travel and food magazines; they're pleasant combinations of carefree travel and the semimystical enjoyment of a potion in its birthplace. To be sure, the vineyards of France may be more hypnotically beautiful than, say, backtown Wilkes-Barre, but you won't get any juicy Krakauer sausage in the Rhône valley, either. Life's a series of trade-offs.

Beer traveling is sometimes the only way to taste limited-release brews or brewpub beers. Beer is usually fresher at bars and distributors near the source. And the beer you'll get at the brewery itself is sublimely fresh, beer like you'll never have it anywhere else—the supreme quaff. You'll also get a chance to see the brewing operations and maybe talk to the brewer.

One of the things a beer enthusiast has to deal with is the perception that beer drinkers are second-class citizens compared with wine and single-malt scotch connoisseurs. Announcing plans for a vacation in the Napa Valley or a couple of weeks on Scotland's Whisky Trail might arouse envious glances. A vacation built around brewery tours, on the other hand, might generate only mild confusion or pity. Microbreweries sell T-shirts and baseball caps, and beer geeks wear them. I've never seen a Beringer "Wine Rules!" T-shirt or a Chandon gimme cap. Beer-related souvenirs are plastic "beverage wrenches" and decorated pint glasses. Wine paraphernalia tends to be of a higher order: corkscrews, foil cutters, tasting glasses.

How do you as a beer enthusiast deal with this problem of perception? Simple: Revel in it. The first time my family went on a long camping trip with an experienced camper friend, we were concerned about wearing wrinkled clothes and sneakers all the time. Our guide had one reply to all our worries: "Hey! You're campers! Enjoy it!" It worked for us, it will work for you: "Hey! I'm traveling to breweries!" How bad can that be?

When you're planning a beer outing, you need to think about your approach. If you want to visit just one brewery, or perhaps tour the closely packed bars around Nodding Head in Center City Philadelphia, you can first settle in at a nearby hotel. Get your cab fare or your walking shoes ready, and you're set to work your way through the offerings. If you plan to visit several breweries in different towns, it is essential that you travel with a nondrinking driver. And when you're looking for that brewery in a mess of industrial buildings, here's a tip for you: Look for the grain silo; it's a dead giveaway.

You should know that the beer at brewpubs and microbreweries is sometimes stronger than mainstream beer. Often brewers will tell you the alcohol content of their beers. Pay attention to it. Keep in mind that most mainstream beers are between 4.5 and 5 percent ABV, and judge your limits accordingly. Of course, you might want to do your figuring before you start sampling.

About that sampling: You'll want to stay as clear-headed as possible, both during the day so you can enjoy the beer and the morning after so you can enjoy life. The best thing to do is drink water. Every pro I know swears by it. If you drink a pint of water for every 2 pints of beer you drink (one to one's even better), you'll enjoy the beer more during the day. Drinking that much water slows down your beer consumption, which is a good thing. Drinking that much water also helps keep away the *katzenjammers,* as the Germans call the evil spirits that cause hangovers. Just remember that if you do, you'll probably also want to follow the sage advice apocryphally attributed to President Ulysses S. Grant: "Never pass up an opportunity to urinate." There is, however, no substitute for the simple strategy of drinking moderate amounts of beer in the first place.

Beer traveling is about enjoying beer and discovering the places where it is at its best. You could make a simple whirlwind tour of breweries, but I'd suggest you do other things too. I've always enjoyed trips to breweries more when we mixed in other attractions. Beer is only part of life, after all.

Upstate Beer Adventure

Upstate Pennsylvania has a natural beauty to make most states envious. It's graced by the high lakes and birches of the Poconos, the "Grand Canyon of Pennsylvania," the gamelands of Potter County, the ridges and ravines of the Allegheny Forest, and the crashing surf of Lake Erie.

Anglers and hunters will find the state a rich preserve of fish and game in a tranquil setting of pine, oak, and mountain laurel, the state flower. For information on seasons, licenses, state game lands, and stocked lakes, call the Game Commission (717-787-4250) or the Fish and Boat Commission (717-657-4518).

Hikers and campers enjoy Pennsylvania's extensive system of trails and state campgrounds. The Appalachian Trail runs west along the front ridge of the Appalachians, then heads south between Gettysburg and Harrisburg. There are short hikes to scenic sites at Dingmans Falls in the Delaware Water Gap National Recreation Area and at Hawk Mountain Sanctuary. In the skies over Hawk Mountain, autumn migration routes converge, making the sanctuary an ideal spot for observing migratory hawks, eagles, and other birds of prey.

Pennsylvania has an extensive state park system, largely thanks to Gov. Gifford Pinchot, a Reform governor who was a well-known conservationist and one of the commonwealth's great politicians. (Pinchot was also an ardent prohibitionist who presided over the creation of the byzantine regulations of Pennsylvania's Liquor Code, but nobody's perfect.) You can get information about Pennsylvania's state parks from the Bureau of State Parks (800-637-2757). Be forewarned that drinking is forbidden in state parks, and the rangers take it pretty seriously.

Upstate Pennsylvania also offers canoeing on rivers—the Allegheny, the Clarion, the Delaware, and the Susquehanna. For the more experienced white-water aficionado, Pine Creek runs the Grand Canyon of Pennsylvania and is rated as a Class III trip. If you're traveling in winter, take your skis. Pennsylvania has more than thirty downhill ski areas, some with vertical drops of over 1,000 feet.

If you're a more sedentary type, upstate Pennsylvania offers many miles of scenic driving. Beyond the ridges of the Appalachian front lies the ravine and plateau country of the northwest. The fiery fall foliage of the northern tier rivals that of New England but draws far fewer people, leaving roads clear of leaf peepers. Along the way, well-kept small towns like Montrose, Emporium, Warren, and St. Marys, the home of Straub Brewing, shine with quiet beauty.

I've included Erie in this section. Even though it's not a rural paradise, Erie's lakefront site offers a natural beauty unique in the state. And though it's far from the urban bustle of Philadelphia and Pittsburgh, you'll still find respectable shopping and nightlife.

Potter County has been calling itself "God's Country" for years. I think it's safe to say that all of upstate Pennsylvania is pretty close to Heaven.

Barley Creek Brewing Company

Sullivan Trail and Camelback Road, Tannersville, PA 18372
570-629-9399
www.barleycreek.com

Trip Ruvane claims that Barley Creek Brewing Company is housed in a renovated nineteenth-century farmhouse. If you press him on that, he will laughingly admit that the farmhouse was "renovated with extreme prejudice." What he means is that he and his crew intended to restore the building, but once they got into the job, they realized it had to be seriously renovated . . . as in torn down. That's the source of the ball

peen hammer taphandle for Barley Creek's excellent Renovator Stout.

But the structure you see is authentically old,
at least in part. The stone foundation and cellar
remain, making an attractive office wall for Trip
and his wife, Eileen. Upstairs, where you and I
drink Trip's beer and eat his delicious food, much
of the exposed wood—solidly thick beams and
paneling—was salvaged from old buildings. The
bar was recently moved out from the glass wall and
is now a large standing island: more attractive, and
offering more space, too.

Structure-wise, Barley Creek is one of the most
attractive new-construction brewpubs around. It's
designed like a tall-peaked wooden ski chalet, airy
and open with miles of overhead space. Glass walls
at either end let the sun shine on the dining room

Beers brewed: Year-round:
Brown Antler Ale, Renovator
Stout, SuperHOP, Creek Light,
Aussie Gold, IPA, and ESB.
Seasonals: J. B.'s Irish Red,
Albee Bock, Strawberry
Wheat, Hefe Weizen, Cran-
berry Bog Wheat, Barley Wine,
Jenkins Woods Lager, Dunkel-
blitzen Lager, Deacon Dort-
munder, Black Widow Lager,
Wahoo Wheat, Chestnut
Mountain Lager, Export Ale,
Atlas Ale, Apple Creek Ale,
Khunnermann's Cream Ale,
Blackberry Porter, and more
to come.

and provide passing motorists with a striking view of the brewery's tanks.
More than a few of them have stopped. Recent visitors have been treated
to beer that just keeps getting better. I recently had the best batch of
SuperHOP I've ever had, as well as an Atlas Ale that was a huge mouth-
ful of malt and alefruit. You can get the SuperHOP, Brown Antler, Aussie
Gold, and Black Widow Lager in 12- and 22-ounce bottles now.

Visitors to the area abound. The Poconos may not have the biggest
vertical drops or the deepest powder—or any powder, for that matter—
but they are the heart of a gorgeous region located close enough to several urban areas to be an easy weekend trip for many people. You can
ski in the Poconos without fighting your way through an airport with
your skis or white-knuckling it up the interstate to New England with
one ear cocked for the radar detector's whine. You can relax, get in your
skiing, and still have time for a trip to the brewpub.

What a place for a pub to be situated, halfway between a major ski
area (Camelback) and a major outlet mall (the Crossings). The mind
happily waffles: Should we go up the mountain and ski, down the mountain and shop, or just stay here on the side of the mountain and have a
few more of these delicious beers?

You can bring your less beer-enlightened friends along, too: Barley
Creek now has Budweiser and Coors Light. This drives some beer geeks
wild, but Trip's crazy like a fox on this one. "I make no apologies for
having Bud or Coors Light on tap," he told me. "When someone orders
one of them, my bartenders have standing orders to also serve them a 2-

ounce sampler of our lightest beer. If they're not in here because we don't serve the beer they like, they'll never get to try my beer."

The food might also hook them. My favorite over the years is still the Crane's Crazy Chip Dip. Trip claims to have won the recipe in a drunken, late-night game of Blockhead. Served in a hot crock surrounded by a variety of corn chips, Crane's dip is a cheesy, spicy, appealingly gooey mess that is just the thing on a cold day. Or a hot day. Or a rainy day. Any day, so long as you're at the bar with a glass of Renovator.

The Pick: It's Renovator Sto for the dark full body, the pleasant dryness of the finis even the hammerhead tap handle. I pretty much love everything about this beer, and the years have not dimmed its beauty. It is the best stout I've ever had from a Ringwood yeast brewery. Every now and then I find ar excuse to head up to Tannersville to get a fix.

After working hard in banking and public relations, Trip and Eileen Ruvane appear to have found their niche. They run an outstandingly clean, fun, and satisfying brewpub with great food and beer. That it is perched in the Poconos, where they love to be, is a happy bonus.

Opened: December 1995.

Owners: Trip Ruvane, Eileen Ruvane.

Brewers: Tim Phillips.

System: 10-barrel Peter Austin brewhouse, 3,001 barrels annual capacity.

Production: 1,201 barrels in 2004 (estimated).

Brewpub hours: Seven days a week, 11:01 A.M. to "late night."

Tours: Monday through Friday, 12:30 P.M. and 4 P.M.; Sundays, 12:30 P.M.; and by appointment.

Take-out beer: 12- and 22-ounce bottles, growlers, and kegs (call ahead for availability).

Food: It's all pretty good: imaginative appetizers, homemade soups, hearty sandwiches, pub fare, fresh desserts, seafood, pasta, big steaks, daily specials, and a kids' menu.

Extras: Gift shop. Live music on weekends. Outdoor deck. Two full bars (one on deck). Foosball, high-tech video arcade. Bar games and metal ring puzzles. World's first whiffle-ball stadium ("We'll be ready when they start ESPN 5," Trip said). Great Pocono Wing-Off (third Sunday in August) and Chowder-Off (spring). "Far Side" comics in the bathrooms. Eileen Ruvane said, "If you can't find something to do at Barley Creek, seek therapy."

Special considerations: Kids welcome. Handicapped-accessible. Cigars allowed. Vegetarian meals available.

Parking: Plentiful on-site parking.

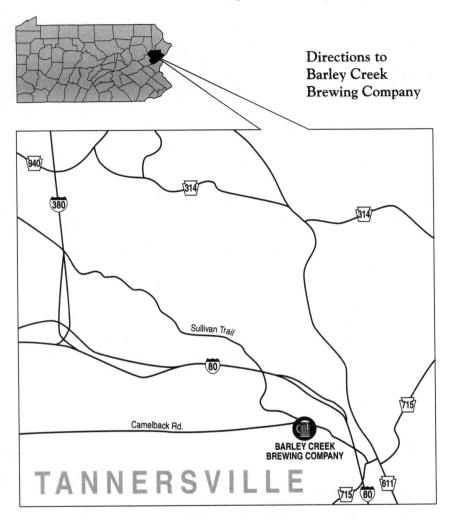

Directions to Barley Creek Brewing Company

Lodging in the area: Pine Knob Inn B&B, Route 447, Canadensis, 570-595-2532; Holiday Inn, Route 611, Bartonsville, 570-424-6100; The Chateau Resort, Camelback Road, Tannersville, 570-629-5900; Comfort Inn, Route 611, Bartonsville, 570-476-1500.

Area Attractions: The major ski areas—***Camelback, Jack Frost, Split Rock, Shawnee,*** and ***Big Boulder***—are all within a thirty-minute drive. Camelback also has a warm-weather water park, ***Camel Beach,*** that adds a few thrills every year. Golf courses dot the area. ***Pocono Raceway,*** home to a number of NASCAR and motorcycle races, is about twenty minutes away. There are state campgrounds and game lands all around, well-stocked lakes and streams, hiking and biking trails, swimming, golfing, canoeing and rafting expeditions. Explore the scenery of the Delaware Water Gap and the mountains, the rushing beauty of Bushkill Falls and Dingmans Falls, and the Appalachian Trail. If it rains, **Summit Lanes** (Route 940 west of Mount Pocono, 570-839-9635) has thirty-six lanes of great bowling. **The Crossings** (570-629-4650) is a major shopping outlet with more than a hundred brand-name stores, and it's right at the bottom of the hill. There are also a yearly jazz festival and blues festival; call the Pocono Mountains Vacation Bureau (800-POCONOS) for more information.

Other area beer sites: **The Swiftwater Inn** ("The Swifty") (6 miles north of Tannersville on Route 611, 570-839-7206) is the classic bar in the area. Yuengling's the beer of choice, and the view is subterranean. Dig it! **Pocono Brewing Company** (just south of the Swiftwater Inn, 570-839-3230) is not a brewpub; it's a multitap bar that books major blues acts and sports a massive videowall TV. **The Deer Head Inn** (5 Main Street, Delaware Water Gap, 570-424-2000) is recommended for its classically huge marble urinal. You gotta see it! Trip tells me that the **Pub in the Pines** (Route 940, Pocono Pines, 570-646-2377) is a good bar and also serves a great breakfast for early risers. If you want to go to "town," the **Sarah Street Grill** in Stroudsburg (5th and Sarah Streets, 570-424-9120) is a nice place for dinner and a beer.

Otto's Pub and Brewery

2105 North Atherton Street, State College, PA 16801
814-867-6886
www.ottospubandbrewery.com

State College was the site of one of the state's first brewpubs, Happy Valley, way back in the late 1980s. With one of the largest college campuses (and faculties) in the state nearby, it would have seemed that Happy Valley would be a natural, but it failed fairly soon. As is often the case, that failure put a bad light on the idea of another brewpub in the area. The continuing farce of the "planned" Red Bell brewpub in the town didn't help people take brewpubs seriously.

So I was kind of surprised to hear that Bullfrog brewer Charlie Schnable had left Williamsport to open a brewpub in State College. Hope it works for him, I thought. I was torn between the pessimism engendered by the bad mojo surrounding brewpubs there and the natural optimism that, darn it, State College was a *perfect* town for a brewpub, hoodoo or not.

Charlie and Otto's broke the hoodoo wide open with a success that just couldn't be stopped. The first time I stopped in was on a bitterly cold and windy night in early 2003, and the joint was jumping. My wife and I thoroughly enjoyed the food, the service was great, but the beer was disappointing. I was perplexed. Did I hit on an off night? I talked to Charlie a few months later, and he said he'd been having yeast problems but had switched to a new yeast and was having better luck.

I stopped in again recently on a "professional" visit and toured the brewery with Charlie. He's working on one of the last of the Bohemian Monobloc systems, with the company's signature gleaming copper cladding, a previously unused model that was used for displays at trade shows. The Monobloc was Bohemian's finest system, when the company finally got it all right, just before it folded. Charlie had brewed on a Bohemian system at Bullfrog and was obviously pleased to have one again.

Beers brewed: Year-round: Helles Lager, Apricot Wheat, Mt. Nittany Pale Ale, Red Mo Ale, Double D IPA, Arthur's Nut Brown Ale, Black Mo Stout. Seasonals: Black Raspberry Wheat, Imperial Stout, ESB, Barley Wine, Oktoberfest, Abbey Dubbel, Apple Barrel Brew, Arthur's Rye Ale, Arthur's Best Bitter, Arthur's Robust Porter, Duffinator Double Bock, Hefeweizen, HellKat, Honey Weiss Triple, Maibock, Mom's Elderberry Stout, Roggen Bier, Spring Creek Lager, Schwarzbier, Sumatra Stout, Winter Warmer, Belgian-style Wit, Pilsener Lager, Flanders Style Red Ale . . . plus more to come.

"I just got a reverse-osmosis water filter," Charlie told me. "The water's very hard here. That brings out hop bitterness really well, but not much hop flavor. I've done one batch with the new filter, and I can taste the difference in the wort. It's great, a lot cleaner, but I'm not sure if I'm going to get the beer tasting the same."

Tour over, we sat down and ran the taps. Wow! "Having better luck" with his new yeast was an understatement. Charlie had better go to Vegas if he's having luck like this. What I tasted was twelve great beers, and one of them, the Flanders Red, was phenomenal. What made it all the more impressive was that the Flanders Red was Charlie's first try at a "bug beer," a beer intentionally inoculated with bacteria to produce effects similar to those in the sour beers of Belgium . . . and he'd nailed it! I'm afraid I might have lost my professional composure and whistled and stamped on the floor.

Charlie, modest as always, changed the subject to his cask ale. It's been going so well that he's getting a second beer engine. "I'll run two at the same time," he explained: "one low-ABV, one high-ABV." At this point, he won't be able to tell you just what that ABV is; Otto's has been warned by the local PLCB enforcement agent not to post the strength of its beers. Even though this is no longer prohibited by the state liquor code, it's better to simply comply than to fight it.

"We're under tight scrutiny here because of the college," said Charlie. With Penn State being the biggest college in the state, the main state-funded college, it's under the eye of the press and the legislature all the time. "All the liquor laws are overenforced," Charlie said, because no one wants to risk an embarrassing headline or an unhappy constituent. Too bad about all the moderate drinkers in the adult population in town.

Next time you get up to State College—to go back to school, take your kid back to school, or go to a Lions game—stop in at Otto's and have some of this great beer. Be loyal and get a Mount Nittany Pale Ale. Be outdoorsy and get a Black Mo Stout. Or you can be eco-conscious and get a Red Mo Ale: "all the fun without the Acid Mine Damage." There's a little something for everyone.

And for the curious, Otto is Charlie's cat. Which is kinda cute, in a good way. Charlie's a good guy, one of the nicest in the biz. And his beer—well, you'll be stamping and whistling too.

The Pick: Man, that's tough Oh, why not: Double D IPA. Just because I think there are too many beers like this around doesn't mean I can't like a good one, and this is. There's a ton of big, fat hop flavor in here, honeyed with malt-a-plenty; it's maltiliciou with plenty of hop dressing; it's bulging with hops, psycho hops, and maniacal malt . . . and I'm rolling in it like catnip I can't stop!

Opened: September 2002.
Owners: Charles Schnable, Derek Duffee.
Brewer: Charles Schnable.
System: 10-barrel Bohemian/Specific Mechanical brewhouse, 1,200 barrels annual capacity.
Production: 900 barrels in 2004 (estimated).
Brewpub hours: Sunday through Wednesday, 11 A.M. to midnight; Thursday through Saturday, 11 A.M. to 2 A.M.
Tours: Upon request, subject to brewer availability.
Take-out beer: Growlers, sixtels, half-kegs; call ahead for keg availability.
Food: Hey, it's a college town; things are a little different. For one, there are some serious vegetarian meals here, not just tossed salad and cheese pizza. Dad's Walnut Barley Burger, vegetarian focaccia,

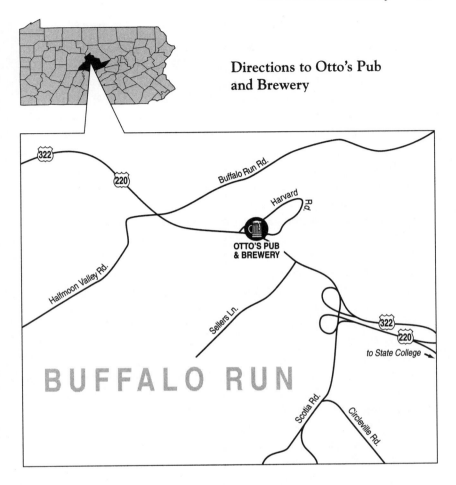

Directions to Otto's Pub and Brewery

tempura tofu skewers, and Farfalle Rosa make for real choices. There's still stuff for Mom and Dad, like the tequila lime chicken and New York strip steak, a Bavarian smoked pork chop, and scallops primavera.

Extras: Live music several times a week (call for schedule or check website). E-mail newsletter (get it; it's funny). Outdoor patio, weather permitting. Penn State football games (and other events, if necessary) on six TVs. Otto's has an interesting twist on the mug club idea: the Pub Club, with a lifetime membership for $125. Beers and growler refills are discounted, club members are allowed to make reservations for dinner for *any* size party, and there are special Pub Club beer dinners.

Special considerations: Kids welcome. Handicapped-accessible. Cigars allowed. Serious vegetarian meals available.

Parking: On-site lot.

Lodging in the area: Carnegie House, 100 Cricklewood Drive, 814-234-2424; The Penn Stater, 215 Innovation Boulevard, 814-863-5000; Motel 6, 1274 North Atherton Street, 814-234-1600.

Area Attractions: The biggest attractions in State College are connected to Penn State, and there are a lot, ranging from museums of football, entomology, and minerals and gemstones to the sports events at the college (and when there's a football game in Happy Valley, you'd better have a ticket and motel reservation lined up well in advance!) to the two college golf courses open to the public (814-865-GOLF for fees and tee times). Get the inside information by calling the Centre County Convention and Visitors Bureau (800-358-5466).

Just because I'm a barbecue hound, I would like to make you aware of **Clem's BBQ** (west of Otto's on Route 322/220, about 2 miles before Port Matilda, maybe twenty minutes from the brewpub on the south side of the road, 814-360-1140), a real slow-smoke barbecue pit with fantastic pork, ribs, and chicken. Be prepared to overeat, because this stuff is downright addictive. **Tussey Mountain Ski Area** in Boalsburg (814-466-6810) has a vertical drop of 550 feet, snowmaking, night skiing, ski school, a restaurant and lounge, and day care. Also in Boalsburg is the **Pennsylvania Military Museum** (814-466-6263). The highlight of the exhibit is a full-scale World War I trench warfare scene with soundtrack. This is a very thoughtful and well-done museum honoring Pennsylvania's soldiers from pre-Revolutionary times to the Persian Gulf War. There's an oddly old piece of history on the other side of Route 322 from the Military Museum: the **Boal Mansion** (814-466-6210), home to the Boal family for nine generations, a family that was related to Christopher Columbus. The altar, religious statues, and explorer's cross from the Columbus family chapel in Spain are in the mansion, as is Columbus's desk.

Follow Route 22 southwest from Lewistown to **Raystown Lake** (888-RAYSTOWN, www.raystown.org), the largest lake inside Pennsylvania and a great hunting, boating, swimming, and fishing area. **Lincoln Caverns** (814-643-0268) are in nearby Huntingdon, with tours through the two caves, gem panning, and picnic areas. **Penn's Cave** (5 miles east of Centre Hall on Route 192, 814-364-1664, www.pennscave.com) is a rare water-filled cave, toured by boat. There is also a wildlife sanctuary with bears, mountain lions, elk, and wolves. Penn's Cave is a little like South of the Border in that the signs are hard to miss once you get northwest of Harrisburg. *Grice Clearfield Community Museum* (119 North Fourth Street, Clearfield, 814-768-7332) has a neat collection of classic cars.

Otto's "Black Mo" Stout is named for Black Moshannon Lake at *Black Moshannon State Park* (4216 Beaver Road, Philipsburg, 814-342-5960). The streams that feed the lake drain through the sphagnum moss of Black Moshannon Bog, picking up so much tannin that the water of the lake is perfectly clear, yet as brown as strong tea, endlessly entertaining to me as a child when I swam here (and still pretty funny two years ago, the last time I did it). The park offers a range of recreation: swimming, camping, rustic and modern cabins, fishing, hunting, snowmobiling, hiking, ice skating, and cross-country skiing.

Other area beer sites: *Zeno's* (100 West College Avenue, 814-237-2857) is the original State College beer bar, with a great selection of draft beer (including a dedicated Yards tap!), "located directly above the center of the earth." The other spot for beer in State College is the *Deli* (113 Heister Street, 814-237-5710), a favorite of Charlie's and just about everyone else with a beer lust. There's a branch of the *Mad Mex* beer-o-philic restaurants (240 South Pugh Street, in the Days Inn Hotel, 814-272-5656). Open up the big wooden door and go below to enter the loud, friendly, subterranean *Phyrst* (111 East Beaver Avenue, 814-238-1406), a rollicking joint with a surprisingly adequate tap selection. If you're looking for something to take back to your room, hit *Sharkies Bar and Bottle Shop* (110 Sowers Street, 814-238-3566) for its array of Pennsylvania micros, the better-known American craft brews, and an okay import section.

I've gone 30 miles out of my way to go to *Schnitzel's Tavern* in the Bush House Hotel in Bellefonte (315 West High Street, 814-355-4230). They serve some of the best German food I've had in the United States, and great German draft beer, in an authentic German setting by the water. *Denny's Beer Barrel Pub* (1423 Dorey Street, Clearfield, 814-765-7190) has a little nonmainstream beer, but that's not why you're going there. It's for the fifteen-pound cheeseburger. I'm not kidding, it's half the size of a case of beer. No one's ever finished it, and I'm kind of glad about that!

Marzoni's Brick Oven and Brewing Company

170 Patchway Rd., Duncansville, PA 16648
814-695-1300
www.marzonis.com

I don't like going to brewpubs until they've been open for at least three months. It gives them a chance to "shake down," learn the quirks of their brewing system, get the whole service picture into focus, and get the menu firmed up. You often get a radically different impression on a second visit if you visit too early.

But when I had a chance to visit Marzoni's less than two weeks after they opened, I grabbed it. I'd heard about Marzoni's—that it was a new idea, a new *concept* from the Hoss's restaurant chain—and I was intrigued by the whole idea of a brewpub in Altoona (or really close to Altoona; Marzoni's is in Duncansville, just south of Altoona, where the Hoss's headquarters is located). This would be the third time someone tried to open a brewpub in Altoona, and I wanted to see if these guys actually had opened their doors, unlike the other two.

They were open, all right. They were so darned open that we wound up three rows back in the parking lot in the middle of a cold, windy day. Hey, good sign!

It was prophetic. Uncle Don and I walked past an antique delivery truck into a gleaming restaurant, past a hostess station perched under an immense suspended locomotive driving wheel, and through to the bar, a bar that shone with polished wood. Service was quick, friendly, and competent; we had two samplers and even a fairly decent presentation on the beers. That's amazing for just ten days open.

But I have to be honest: The beer, for ten days open by a brewer who was solo on his first commercial job, simply blew me away. Bill Kroft had managed to put together a full slate of beers that were at least competent, some of which were quite good, and only one clinker, an odd-tasting hefeweizen.

Beers brewed: Year-round: Locke Mountain Light, Marzoni's Amber Lager, Highway 22 Wheat, Patchway Pale Ale, Avalanche IPA, Stone Mason Stout. Seasonals: Emil's Altbier, Campbell's Scotch Ale, Dortmunder, Irish Red, John's Brown Ale, Kölsch, Octoberfest, Raspberry Wheat, Anniversary Ale.

"I'm kind of stuck brewing that with a dried yeast," Bill explained to me six months later, when I told him about my disappointment with the hefeweizen. "The guy we got in to set up the system brewed a batch of hefe with that dry yeast, and people got used to it. I don't really like it, but people drink it, so like I said, I'm kind of stuck."

Bill, buddy, if that's the only problem you have, you're way ahead of the game! Bill gave me his story, and it's a classic. He was a Hoss's employee for years, working his way up from dishwasher to general manager. But he'd also been homebrewing for eight years. "When this concept came up," he said, "I threw my hat in the ring. I couldn't believe it when they let me have the job. I still feel like a kid at play doing this, a homebrewer gone wild."

The Pick: The Dortmunder is a malty, balanced, soft beer that made me want to run out and buy a liter mug; clean, lovely lager. If I had to pick a regular, I'd go with the Avalanche IPA. "I like hops," Bill said with a grin when I looked at him after my first sip, and he sure does. This is a hoppy beer, with the gutsy body underneath to support it. Better hope it doesn't sweep you right off the mountain.

He's completely self-taught, too. "Oh, I talk to Charlie Schnable over at Otto's," Bill said. "I ask questions on the ProBrewer Internet forum, and I do a lot of reading." That's kind of like somebody driving a big rig cross-country after watching *Smokey and the Bandit* three times and hitching a ride home from college on a chicken truck. It only makes the quality of the beer more amazing.

The beer makes the restaurant even nicer, and that's a big job, too. With more than forty restaurants, the people at Hoss's know what they're doing, and while Marzoni's is a new concept and a new menu for them, the basics—solid service and good food value—stay the same. The whole idea of Marzoni's is that the Campbell family figured they had put as many Hoss's as they could into a market that they could realistically control. They wanted to continue to expand but didn't want to go farther from Duncansville than they already had, or "cannibalize" the territory of any existing restaurants. Marzoni's is the possible solution: a completely different menu and image, with a brewery and full bar (the Hoss's restaurants have no booze).

I don't know if it's working for Hoss's or not, but it sure works for me. This is good food and . . . well, you should know by now how I feel about the beer. After tasting Bill's big Anniversary Ale, I assure you: It's only going to get better. Glad I didn't wait three months on this one!

Opened: November 2003.
Owner: Bill Campbell.
Brewer: Bill Kroft.

System: 10-barrel Liquid Asset brewhouse, 1,500 barrels annual capacity.

Production: 700 barrels in 2004 (estimated).

Brewpub hours: Sunday through Thursday, 11 A.M. to 11 P.M.; Friday and Saturday, 11 A.M. to midnight.

Tours: Upon request, subject to brewer availability.

Take-out beer: Growlers.

Food: Brick-oven pizza is the big draw, but the pasta and sandwiches are excellent as well. My daughter was overwhelmed by her meatball sandwich: "It's huge!" she admitted. The portabella parmesan panini is a delicious crusty mouthful of mushroom.

Extras: Seventeen TVs. Private banquet rooms available.

Special considerations: Kids welcome. Handicapped accessible. Vegetarian meals available.

Parking: Large free lot.

Lodging in the area: Comfort Inn, across the parking lot, 814-693-1800; Rolling Rock Motel, 2590 Old Route 22, 814-695-5661; Sunbrook Mansion B&B, 900 Sunbrook Drive, 814-695-6664. The Jean Bonnet Tavern (see below) also has rooms.

Area Attractions: There are two very reasonable family-style amusement parks near Altoona. **Del Grosso's Park** (Exit 41 off I-99, Tipton, follow the signs, 814-684-3538, www.delgrossos.com) has the feel of an old-style "family" amusement park but is fun even for jaded teenagers, with miniature golf, go-karts, and mountains of what is possibly the best amusement park food in the country. (This is the same Del Grosso's as the delicious spaghetti sauce available in local stores; try them, they're very good.) **Lakemont** (700 Park Avenue, Altoona, 814-949-PARK, www.lakemontpark.com) is like a really big county fair, with a lot of older, classic rides, including a large wooden coaster, a gas-powered antique auto ride (running at antique speeds, too), and a very special attraction: Leap the Dips, the world's oldest roller coaster, the last of a once very popular type of coaster known as a side-friction figure eight. No seat belts, no high speeds or huge drops, but my son and I found that the constant side-to-side banging and crashing, and the short, abrupt dips and rises of the tracks, had a quaint but real excitement all their own. Not to be missed and dirt cheap—five of us got in for less than $30. The **Altoona Curve** AA baseball stadium (814-944-9800) is right next to Lakemont and is a beautiful little ballpark.

   The baseball team is named for the famous **Horseshoe Curve National Historic Landmark** (6 miles west of Altoona on local roads, follow signs, 888-4-ALTOONA), the sharp horseshoe-shaped

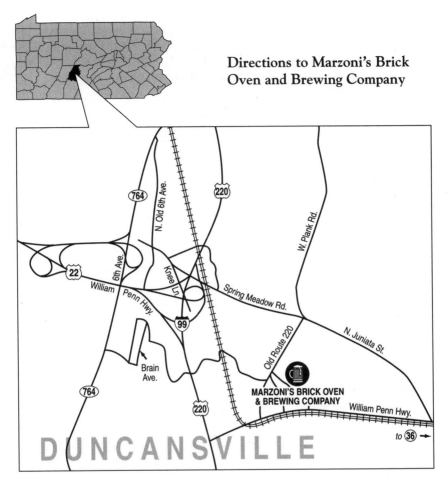

Directions to Marzoni's Brick Oven and Brewing Company

bend that allowed railroad travel over the steep ridges of central Pennsylvania. This engineering marvel and work of surveying genius was considered vital to the country's World War II war effort, and it was a prime target of the German saboteurs who came ashore on Long Island in 1942. There is a funicular up to the tracks, where more than fifty trains pass by each day, diesel-electric engines thundering. Just as vital to rail travel, and an even greater engineering feat, though nowhere near as well known as the curve, are the nearby *Gallitzin Tunnels* (411 Convent Street, Gallitzin, 814-886-8871), dug through the rock of the mountains by immigrant laborers in the early 1850s. This is one of the best sites for train-watching in Pennsylvania, as trains rumble out of the twin-track tunnel into the rock cut. The nearby museum, with restored 1942 caboose, tells their story.

Raystown Lake is the largest lake in Pennsylvania (Lake Erie is on the border), and it supports a wide range of water activities: fishing, boating, water-skiing, swimming. You can rent boats at the **Seven Points Marina** near Hesston (814-658-3074, www.7pointsmarina.com). After you're done jaunting about, come back to Altoona for a snack: Tour the **Benzel's Pretzel Bakery** (5200 Sixth Avenue, 814-942-5062) and watch as 5 *million* pretzels are made every day. Takes a lot of beer to eat those pretzels!

Other area beer sites: The **U.S. Hotel** (401 South Juniata Street, Hollidaysburg, 814-695-9924) is a gem: a real old Pennsylvania hotel bar, complete with massive wood backbar, mosaic and tile floor and walls, some beautiful "bunch o' grapes" lamps over the bar, and an authentic "gentleman's trough" at the base of the bar—a tile trough with running water to take the place of unsightly (and hard-to-hit) spittoons! The beer's not amazing, but the place is great. The **Knickerbocker Tavern** (3957 Sixth Avenue, Altoona, 814-942-0770) is a fun place to eat, drink, and relax. They have great bar food, a beautiful courtyard dining area, a neat little old-style bar, and by far the best selection of beer within 30 miles. But 34 miles away is the **Jean Bonnet Tavern** (6048 Lincoln Highway, Bedford, 814-623-2264), a Colonial-era stone-built tavern that focuses on Pennsylvania drafts, and it has a fantastic selection as well. Protestors of the Whiskey Rebellion raised a liberty pole here in 1794. General/President Washington's punitive expedition to put down the rebellion, the "Watermelon Army," camped here later that year on its way to Pittsburgh. It's a great place to stop after getting off the Pennsylvania Turnpike, before heading up I-99 to Marzoni's.

The regulars at Marzoni's also recommended two places I didn't get a chance to check out: **The Phoenix** (300 Fourth Avenue, Altoona, 814-946-8096) and **Boxer's Café,** over the mountains in Huntingdon (410 Penn Street, 814-643-5013), also recommended by readers of earlier editions.

Johnstown Brewing Company

942 Pinegrove Lane, Johnstown, PA 15905
814-536-3525
www.johnstownbrewing.com

I'd never been to Johnstown before when I came driving in from the northwest. I was looking for a brewery I'd heard was in town. I was not really on a mission, it's just that I was out in Pittsburgh for the Penn Brewery Micro festival that June weekend, and it was a nice day after a week of rain, and I had time, so I went beer hunting.

I stopped in a convenience store on the edge of town and asked. One fellow gave me directions, and I set off. Half an hour later, I was way out of town, headed south at high speed, and I knew something was wrong. I stopped at a local firehall and asked; sure enough, firemen knew where the beer was and had the maps to get me there. Ten minutes later, I was tooling up Menoher Boulevard, still looking for Morley's Dog Brewing.

Imagine my surprise when I found Johnstown Brewing, already up and running as a restaurant and within a month of brewing their first batch . . . and I'd never heard about it! Turns out Morley's Dog was a defunct contract-brewing operation. Some days you just get lucky!

My luck held, too. When I sat down at the bar and asked to talk to the owner, Ralph Lovette was sitting right beside me. We immediately got to talking, and we got along great. Ralph's a real nice guy, pretty sharp, and willing to work.

The first thing he told me was that the building was the old Bethlehem Steel Company's executive club, a kind of country club up on the hill for the upper crust of Johnstown's major industry. "It's where the white hats hung out," Ralph explained, noting that the foremen and bosses wore white hardhats, a symbolic headgear that workers aspired to.

Then he showed me around the place, which is decorated with all kinds of bric-a-brac from the mill: molds, templates, warning signs, protective gear, and lots and lots of hardhats, some of them white. It's touching to Ralph. "Old widowed women bring in

Beers brewed: Year-round: Flood Light, 1889 Amber Ale, South Fork Dam Beer, Stonebridge Brown Ale, Steelworker Stout, White Hat Pale Ale. Seasonals: Twin Piston Pilsner, Wire Mill Belgian White, Lovette Bros. Irish Red Ale, Polska Brewski, Windber Cherry Wheat, Heffly Spring Honey Raspberry Wheat, Patton Punkin Ale, Octoberfest, Winterfest.

their husbands' hardhats," he told me. "'I'd be honored if you'd put it up on the wall,' they say, and they're in tears."

The town has gotten behind the brewpub right from the start, to the point where you have to wonder why the beer distributors in town never picked up on it (and largely still don't; the guys down at the Boulevard Grill have to beg for most of their beers). One of the first things Ralph said to me when I walked in this past summer was "Oh my, Lew, we're selling a lot of beer." Most people think that's a good thing, Ralph!

The Pick: Barrett Goddard learned his lessons well from Ned Strasser, a genius at dry stout: His Steelworker Stout is served on nitro with a big collar, and there is nothing wrong with it *at all*. A real classic, right down to the slight tang of authentic Irish stout. Great rainy-day beer.

Johnstown Brewing kind of eased into the beer thing. Ralph originally hired Brian Neville as his brewer, an experienced brewer who got things set up and running but perhaps took the whole "ease into it" idea a little too far. The beers weren't exactly bland, but they were far from exciting, and there were complaints from the geekerie. Neville left before the first year was up to handle increased responsibilities at another brewery, and Ralph hired Barrett Goddard in February 2004.

Goddard is also experienced, having trained under the well-regarded Ned Strasser at West Virginia Brewing and worked for two years with Andrew Maxwell at John Harvard's, Monroeville. He came in and took charge, and the beers started to perk up immediately. The White Hat Pale Ale (there's those white hats again) is much bigger than it was. "It's right down the middle of the GABF guidelines for pale ale," Goddard said, and grinned. "Which means low-end, these days." He's right—the geeks expect a lot anymore.

They'll get it, too. Goddard is slowly ratcheting things up, getting these drinkers up to speed. One of the biggest steps was his Twin Piston Pilsner, a beer brewed for Thunder in the Valley, a motorcycle rally in Johnstown that lasts four days and sees the town invaded by almost a hundred thousand bikers. Ralph felt they should have their own beer, so Goddard revved up the kettle and blew out a clean, classic pilsner, smoothly shimmering with Saaz hop character. It's a nice one, and I suspect it may be back.

The brewpub seems to have solidly taken hold here, to the point where they've had to expand the deck and are thinking about adding more tanks. The town comes out to eat and drink, the young and old alike. It's not just for the hoity-toity executives anymore; it's for anyone with a thirst.

Time to go, and I didn't even get a chance to tell you about The Underworks lounge downstairs, the terrific food (all the way from a

Directions to Johnstown
Brewing Company

simple salad to the Executive Cut Filet at $40), or the view across the valley. You'll just have to come out to see for yourself; at least you'll be looking for the right brewery!

Opened: July 2003.
Owners: Patrick and Susan Lovette, Ralph and Karen Lovette.
Brewer: Barrett Goddard.
System: 7-barrel Specific Mechanical brewhouse, 1,050 barrels annual capacity.
Production: 950 barrels in 2004 (estimated).
Hours: Monday through Wednesday, 11 A.M. to midnight; Thursday through Saturday, 11 A.M. to 2 A.M.; Sunday, 10:30 A.M. to midnight.

Tours: Monday through Saturday, noon to 9 P.M.; Sunday, noon to 7 P.M. (subject to brewer availability).

Take-out beer: Growlers.

Food: They're serious about steaks here, and they come in a variety of cuts and sizes, all the way up to dinosaur size. There are also a wide variety of salads, a huge pasta buffet on Tuesdays, and some truly delicious sandwiches. Be sure to get the homemade potato chips.

Extras: Live music Friday through Sunday (call for schedule). Lower-Works lounge with TV and jukebox. Large deck overlooking a valley.

Special considerations: Kids welcome. Handicapped-accessible. Cigars allowed. Vegetarian meals available.

Parking: Large on-site lot.

Lodging in the area: Econo Lodge, 430 Napoleon Place, 814-536-1114; Holiday Inn Downtown, 250 Market Street, 814-535-7777; Campbell House B&B, 305 East Main Street, Ligonier, 888-238-9812.

Area Attractions: Admit it: I say, "Johnstown," you think, "flood." Give in: Go to the ***Johnstown Flood Museum*** (304 Washington Street, 814-539-1889) and learn all about the disaster. ***Grandview Cemetery*** is right across the street from the brewpub, with the Plot of the Unknown, the resting place of 777 unknown victims of the flood. Then go see where it started, in South Fork, at the ***Johnstown Flood National Memorial*** (733 Lake Road, South Fork, 814-495-4643), at the site of the infamous South Fork Dam. Exhibits include a "debris wall" that illustrates the water-driven hammer that smashed into Johnstown, and the chilling film story of the flood, *Black Friday*.

But, as the Johnstown Visitors Bureau website (www.visitjohnstownpa.com) says, "The Flood's Over!" Johnstown has other attractions, including the ***Johnstown Inclined Plane*** (711 Edgehill Drive, 814-536-1816), a 72 percent grade incline that was originally built after the flood to evacuate people more quickly from the valley. These days it's all about sight-seeing from the dramatic observation deck. ***The Johnstown Heritage Discovery Center*** (Broad Street and Seventh Avenue, 814-539-1889) is a multimedia, personal look at the life of immigrant workers in late-nineteenth-century Johnstown: the conditions they left in Europe, Ellis Island, tenement life, their work in the coal mines and steel furnaces. The museum is in the former Germania brewery.

Johnstown has created some real attractions out of several events. ***Thunder in the Valley,*** a four-day motorcycle rally in Johnstown, is held in late June. Starting in 1998 with five thousand bikers, it has grown to almost a hundred thousand bikers who come to town, eat, drink, listen to music, participate in a massive motorcycle parade, ride the hills and valleys around Johnstown, and just have a great time. Any bike, any biker is welcome. The *Friendly City PolkaFest* celebrates the town's Polish immigrant families and their beloved polkas. Three thousand people dance, eat, drink, and tap their toes through five days in June filled with clarinets, trumpets, and accordions, the whirl of skirts, and flashing shoes. See the Visitors Bureau website (www.visitjohnstownpa.com) for all the details on these two events. The *Johnstown FolkFest* is a huge free music festival over Labor Day weekend, featuring American roots music and a bit more: jazz, Texas swing, folk, gospel, R&B, honkytonk, big band, Celtic fusion, R&B, blues, and, perhaps inevitably, polka. Something for everyone. See the Johnstown Area Heritage Association's website (www.jaha.org) for details.

Johnstown's setting deep in the Laurel Highlands offers many outdoor recreation opportunities: hiking, hunting, bike trails, fishing, camping. Find them all at the Visitors Bureau website.

If you're still wondering about *Morley's Dog* . . . it's a famous statue in Johnstown (currently under restoration) that has a whole pack of legends around it.

Other area beer sites: The best beer bar in town is the *Boulevard Grill and Warehouse* (165 Southmont Boulevard, 814-539-5805), which constantly tries to get as many good taps as possible. There's a handsome and comfortable front bar, with a big area out back (the warehouse) for live music and dancing. Ralph and Barrett both note the relaxed elegance of the *Ligonier Country Inn* (Route 30, Laughlintown, 724-238-3651), where PJ's Pub is a cozy, wood-paneled refuge for enjoying some good beer and conversation. The inn also has rooms and is convenient to outdoor recreation areas.

Erie Brewing Company

1213 Veshecco Drive, Erie, PA 16501
814-459-7741
www.eriebrewingco.com

It's lonely up in the northwest corner by Lake Erie, where Erie is somewhat isolated by the lake and large swaths of thinly populated territory. It's especially lonely when you're the only brewery around. Erie Brewing Company (EBC) has its work cut out for it, bringing the gospel of good beer to a dry land. It's miles and miles to another production brewery. Only Four Sons and tiny Foxburg are at all near. How does a brewery survive up here without other brewers around to prime the pump for people's tastes?

Pretty well, actually. From EBC's brewpub birth as Hopper's across town in January 1994 through to its new incarnation as a packaging microbrewery, this town has given good support. Erie loves EBC's Railbender Ale. Falling somewhere between an English old ale and a wee heavy, this big malty beer has more than a touch more alcohol than regular beers. At 6.8 percent ABV, it's not your everyday sipping beer, but it is by far the brewery's best-seller. They're a different breed up in Erie, and my hat's off to them.

EBC broke out of the train station brewpub called Hopper's early in 1999 after five years in that location. The new brewery is big and high-ceilinged, with plenty of glass looking out on Twelfth Street. It was originally built as an emissions-testing facility before Pennsylvania canned that program and allowed private garages to do the tests. It worked out well for EBC when it got the place for a discount price. "Our on-premises sales were helped by our no longer being in direct retail competition with bars," noted former president Mark Armbruster.

Erie got off to a good start, selling beer in farther markets such as upstate New York and Pittsburgh. But things faltered a bit, and I noticed it was harder and harder to get through to people at the brewery. I worried about what was going on, particularly when they started going through brewers at a fairly quick pace.

Beers brewed: Year-round: Railbender Ale, Mad Anthony's Ale, Presque Isle Pilsner. Seasonals: Red Ryder Ale, Heritage Alt, German Wheat, ESB, and Golden Fleece Maibock.

Things seem to have settled down, and it's largely due to a change in ownership. Ed Dworke and Andrew Johnson are running things now, pretty much solely directing things. There have been some investments in equipment for expansion, costs are down, and the packaging has a sharp, new, unified look. Self-distribution has been phased out in favor of working with craft-brew focused distributors.

The Pick: Railbender is the obvious choice, and, well, I like it, too: The latest batches of Rail have been tasting great. I find this beer's malty character very appealing after pints and pints of hoppy ales.

The Presque Isle Pilsner is being more heavily supported, a beer that could be seen as severely outgunned when competing in the mainstream. The idea is to bring in drinkers who might be scared of Mad Anthony or a big Railbender. It's a feeder to the other beers.

There's a new brewpub on the way in Erie; it may even be open by the time this book makes it to the shelves. Turnpike Brewing, at 14th and Peach Streets, will have former Erie brewer Gary Burleigh as a brewer. Are the folks at Erie concerned about that? Not at all. It's a case of the more, the merrier. More good beer is good for everyone.

It might seem lonely in Erie, but the people here are loyal. Erie Brewing Company has tapped some of that loyalty for their big beers. Like Erie native Tom Ridge, they have their sights set on wider horizons, but their hometown likely will always be their best market.

Opened: January 1994; brewery opened February 1999.
Owners: Ed Dworke, Andrew Johnson.
Brewer: Shawn Strickland.
System: 20-barrel Price-Schoenstrom brewhouse, 4,800 barrels annual capacity.
Production: 4,300 barrels in 2004 (estimated).
Tours: Saturday, 4 P.M. to 5 P.M., and by appointment.
Take-out beer: Not available; beer is for sale at distributors throughout Erie County, western Pennsylvania, Ohio, and upstate New York.
Special considerations: Kids welcome. Handicapped-accessible.
Parking: Plenty of on-site parking.
Lodging in the area: Spencer House B&B, 519 West Sixth Street, 814-454-5984; Glass House Inn, 3202 West Sixth Street, 800-956-7222; Red Roof Inn, 7865 Perry Highway, 814-868-5246.
Area Attractions: *Presque Isle State Park* (814-833-7424) on Lake Erie is the closest thing Pennsylvania has to a seashore. This sand spit has some beautiful beaches undisturbed by boardwalks or hotels. It is a wildlife conservation area with trails, swimming, boating, fishing, and picnicking areas. Right at the entrance to the park is **Waldameer**

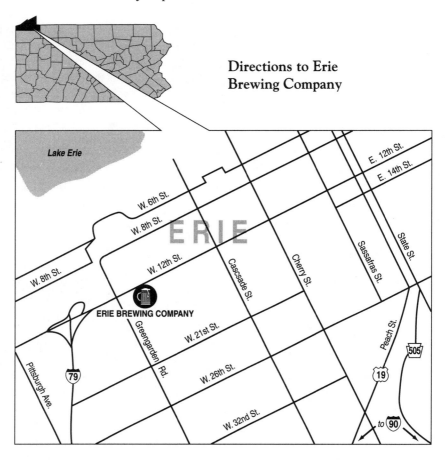

Directions to Erie Brewing Company

Amusement Park and Water World (814-838-3591), an impressive array of traditional amusement park rides and tons of water fun. You might be able to see the reconstructed **Niagara** (164 East Front Street, 814-871-4596), flagship of Oliver Hazard Perry's lake fleet in the War of 1812. The sailing brig has been designated as Pennsylvania's flagship and is sometimes away representing the state; call to see if it is at its dock. The Erie Sea Wolves play baseball in the New York–Penn League; the Erie Otters play hockey at the **Erie Civic Center** (809 French Street, 814-452-4857). You can also call the Erie Area Convention and Visitors Bureau at 814-454-7191.

Other area beer sites: *Sullivan's Pub and Eatery* (301 French Street, 814-452-3446 or 814-459-3222) has the best Guinness in town and fifteen other taps. It's a great old bar to boot, with a tile floor, big carved backbar, and pressed-tin ceiling and walls. ***Oscar's*** (in the plaza at Twelfth and Pittsburgh Streets, 814-454-4325) is Erie's relaxed and comfortable multitap bar. The food's pretty good, and the beer just keeps getting better. **The Docksider** (1015 State Street, 814-454-9700) serves up a decent selection of beer and an excellent series of live blues and folk music, including national acts like John Hiatt; call for music schedule. **Turnpike Brewing** is planned for 1402 Turnpike Road, but don't look for that; Turnpike Road is only thirty feet long! It's on Fourteenth Street, between Peach Street and State Street. Check my website for news on opening and a phone number; Gary Burleigh is planning six house beers, guest taps of Pennsylvania-brewed beers, and Pennsylvania wines.

Four Sons Brewing Company

113 South Franklin Street, Titusville, PA 16354
814-827-1141

And I thought the Bullfrog was pioneering craft brewing in the wilderness.

To get to Titusville, you have to take two-lane roads, no way around it. There are ridges to climb and rivers to cross and woods to pierce, kind of like the musical road to grandmother's house. When the nearest town is Oil City, you know you're getting out there in Pennsylvania.

Yet here is Four Sons, a true state-of-the-art brewpub, sporting schwarzbier, tripel, oatmeal stout, and witbier, a menu that's quite a bit beyond the common fare of Titusville bars, a stylish concrete bartop with an ice rail, waitresses—and waiters!—kitted out in plaid kilts, and a beautiful interior with a parquet floor, lit with clever teardrop light fixtures. What's going on here?

Owner Thom Sauber originally owned radio stations. He sold them to the "Froggy" network of country music stations and made the decision to open a brewpub in this 1840s-era building (thought to have been a bank at one time, where John Rockefeller had an office on the second floor). He named it for his four sons. He then made the very good

Beers brewed: Year-round: Titusville Lager, Plissken Pale Ale, Heavy K, Rebecca's Revenge. Seasonals: Strong Monk, Dim Wit, Monkey Run Oatmeal Stout, Dead Tony's Triple, E's SB, Heifer Weissen, Budgie Brown Ale, Burnin' Iron Horn Ale, Distorter Porter, Noah's Ark Abbey Style Double, St. Cuthbert's Duck Saison, and City Ordinance #905 Amber; many more to come.

decision to hire Matt Allyn away from Erie Brewing to set up the brewery and open the place.

Allyn, who'd brewed at Copper Canyon in Detroit before going to Erie, grew up in nearby Quarry, where he went to high school with North Country brewer Sean McIntyre. The two stay in touch, and along with Sean's buddy Andrew Maxwell at John Harvard's, Monroeville, they refer to themselves as CBC: the Crazy Brewers Consortium. When I asked him why he left Erie for this project, he smiled and replied, "Pubbing's more fun."

He's making the most of that fun with a whole range of beers beyond his four regulars (which aren't "normal" regulars either, including a helles and a schwarzbier). When I first visited, the day before the pub opened, I sampled Dead Tony's Triple, Monkey Run Oatmeal Stout, and E's SB. Three knockout beers, too: Dead Tony's was very creamy-spicy and 9.2 percent, the Monkey Run was unearthly smooth, and the E's SB was a shock—the "ES" in this beer stands for "extra strong," not "extra special."

How does he get away with these beers, in an area that didn't even have a good beer bar, let alone a brewpub? "A lot of people from out of town are real excited: Meadville, Quarry, Oil City," Matt explained. "The university campus in town generates some business. And there are a lot of beer geeks up here, even if they are rednecks."

He was right, too. "Things are going well," he told me six months later. "We're headed for 600 barrels for the year, the mug club's cranking, and people are coming from all around. We've exceeded our original goals on beer and food sales. We just need to stick to the focus: good food, good beer, continually educate the staff."

The good food is chef Jeremy Potocki's job, and he's nothing if not ambitious. The kitchen uses locally baked bread, local specialty pasta, and local produce as much as possible. When the steaks come out, you can cut them with locally made knives, from the Queen Cutlery company. I love to see this kind of community cooperation in businesses.

Matt's jumped right into the community himself. "I think every small town can do this," he said. "There's money in these towns, but people have to go outside to do something nice. They can hang out here and feel like they're in a small pub downtown in some city. They like that. The staff likes it: They're working at the coolest place in town; there's a pride factor. I mean, the guys are wearing kilts; what does *that* say?"

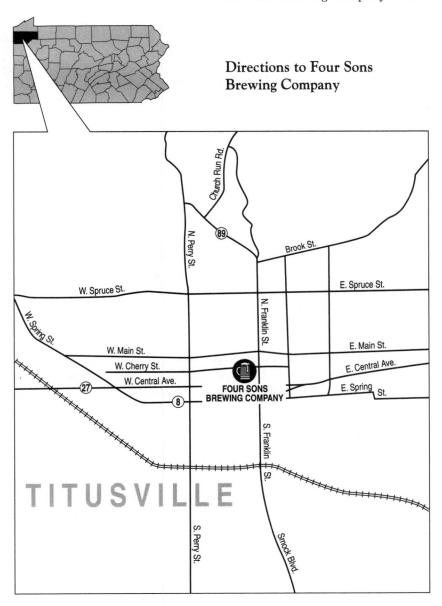

Directions to Four Sons Brewing Company

"All the breweries I've done except for Detroit were in small towns," Matt said. "I brew, I tend bar, and I talk." It may just be as simple as that, and it may just be that Matt Allyn and Four Sons will reenergize this whole town.

Opened: February 2004.
Owner: Thom Sauber.

Brewer: Matt Allyn.

System: 7-barrel Pub Brewing System brewhouse, 900 barrels annual capacity.

Production: 600 barrels in 2004 (estimated).

Brewpub hours: 11 A.M. to midnight, Monday through Saturday. Closed Sunday.

Tours: Upon request, subject to brewer availability.

Take-out beer: Growlers.

Food: I wasn't kidding when I said the menu was ambitious. Strawberry spinach salad, pierogis, Rasta Pub Pork (pork shanks cooked in beer with a jerk glaze), Cuban wraps, scallops in Pernod cream sauce, cedar-planked salmon . . . trust me, these were not meals you'd find in Titusville before Four Sons came to town. The menu offers a number of good vegetarian items as well, beyond simple salads.

Extras: Mug club, and Matt's working on sidewalk dining (that's the message behind City Ordinance #905 Amber).

Special considerations: Kids welcome. Handicapped-accessible. Vegetarian meals available.

Parking: Street parking is pretty easy.

Lodging in the area: Knapping Knapp Farm B&B (43778 Thompson Run Road, 814-827-1092) is a working family farm with packages for hunters, fishers, and stable accommodations for your horse. Shadyside Hotel, 117 East Main Street, 814-827-6923; Cross Creek Resort, 3815 Route 8, 814-827-9611.

Area Attractions: You're in the home of oil. Titusville was where Colonel Drake drilled the world's very first oil well. The **Drake Well Museum** (205 Museum Lane, 814-827-2797) has a reproduction of that first well and pump, as well as other exhibits. **Oil Creek State Park** (305 State Park Road, Oil City, 814-676-5915) has a number of re-created oil field buildings with interpretive signs, plus fishing, canoeing, and picnic sites. The park also has the historic Petroleum Centre train station, which is a stop for the **Oil Creek and Titusville Railroad** (trip starts at 409 South Perry Street, no phone, www.octrr.clarion.edu). The excursion ride is a two-and-a-half-hour trip through "the valley that changed the world," a winding, scenic journey that is always pretty, but truly gorgeous in fall foliage season.

Other area beer sites: Give it up. Sometimes even I can't find a good place for a beer other than the brewpub listed.

Foxburg Inn on the Allegheny

40 Main Street (P.O. Box 362), Foxburg, PA 16036
800-519-6877
www.foxburggroup.com

The first time I visited Foxburg Inn and the Foxhead Pub was in February 2004. My wife, Cathy, and I had been up at Four Sons in Titusville and figured we'd come down and check this place out. I had a map that was just a little too detailed, I guess, and we found ourselves on a dirt road, sliding down hills covered in mud and ice. I gunned the car hard, and we slithered our way up to a real paved road. Then it was down a winding two-lane, past the country's oldest golf course (they're real proud of that here), and out into the river valley . . . where the view just dropped our jaws.

Foxburg sits on the west bank of the Allegheny River, right down on the river, and the inn is a beauty, all ski-lodge angles and big glass walls, with a footbridge over to the upstairs restaurant and steps down to the pub (you can take the interior staircase or the elevator down as well). When you step out on the deck to the cabana bar, the river's edge is about 20 feet away. To your right is a narrow gorge, crossed by an old railroad bridge (currently being converted to a rail-trail). To your left is a long view down a wide river valley, with not another building in sight.

Dr. Arthur and Patricia Steffee have been building a little resort empire here, and they're not showing any sign of stopping. There's the inn, with two large dining rooms; the cozy, well-decorated pub; the brewery, with its growler business; the winery on the other side of the parking lot, offering twenty-six wines made with Erie shore grapes; and the antique shop . . . and that's just what's up and running. Plans include lodge rooms, a dinner-cruise boat, and winter activities, maybe a toboggan run. As part-time brewer, part-time bartender (and aspiring public-relations agent!), Ben Benedict pointed out, "We're perfectly positioned for a weekend getaway!"

That's what Cathy and I were doing, though we had only stopped for dinner. The service (and the view!) made us think seriously about coming

Beers brewed: Allegheny Ale, Dark Bock, Toby Creek Pilsner, Foxburg Lager (mix of Ale and Bock), Allegheny Amber (mix of Pilsner and Bock). Silver Fox Red Amber brewed under contract.

back, though, and the appetizers were outstanding. I'd like to come back when it's warm enough to sit out on the cabana deck and watch the sun drop over the green ridges as the river runs red and gold in the waning light at the end of the day. I've got that view on the brain.

The Pick: Most of the beers are sweet and bland, but tha† kind of works with the Dark Bock. That's the way to bet on this horserace.

The brewery is an add-on, a very simple extract brewery without even a boil in the process. It involves combining hot water, malt syrup (with hop extract added), sugar, and "body enhancer" (I'm not sure what that is, and apparently they weren't either) in a tank, stirring, then running it through a cooler and adding yeast to ferment. Two of the beers, the Foxburg Lager and the Allegheny Amber, are actually mixes of two of the other beers. Dave Colley told me that the beers move much faster in the summer; probably because there's not much going on here in the winter. Whatever the reason, when I visited in winter and spring, there were never more than two house beers on tap.

One time I would like to visit is during Foxburg's annual Oktoberfest. This is prime foliage country, and the valley must look aflame at the peak. Maybe I'll see you there, out on the cabana deck, lost in the view.

Opened: March 2001.

Owners: Dr. Arthur and Patricia Steffee.

Brewers: Dave Colley, Ben Benedict.

System: 5-barrel Specialty Products International brewhouse, 900 barrels annual capacity.

Production: 135 barrels in 2003.

Brewpub hours: Sunday through Thursday, 11 A.M. to 11 P.M.; Friday and Saturday, 11 A.M. to midnight. Open later if busy.

Tours: Upon request.

Take-out beer: Growlers.

Food: Exceptional appetizers. Try anything on the menu that involves mushrooms; the chef has a way with fungus. The Lamb-on-the-Rod is a grilled delight, and ribs, steaks, and the Prime Rib Silver Fox Style are house favorites.

Extras: There is a big-screen TV in the pub. When weather permits, there is a great outdoor "cabana" bar along the river that lets you soak in that tremendous view. There are also weekly open mike (Sunday), cruise (Wednesday), and bike (Thursday) nights. Sunday brunch, 11 A.M. to 2:30 P.M. Banquet facilities available. A dinner cruise boat on the river is planned.

Directions to Foxburg Inn on the Allegheny

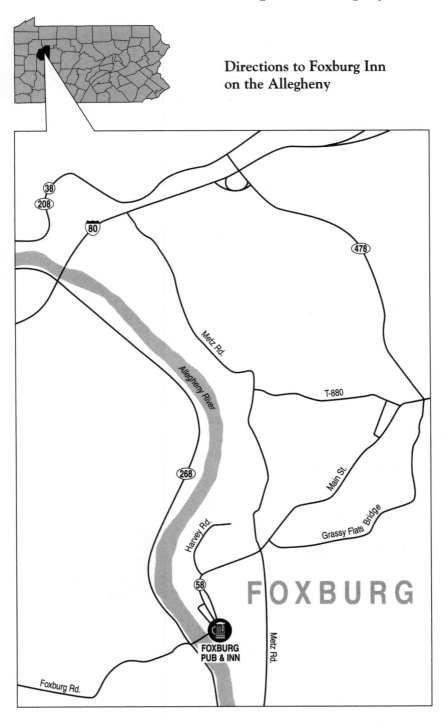

Special considerations: Kids welcome. Handicapped-accessible. Vegetarian meals available.

Parking: Large on-site lot.

Lodging in the area: Barnard House, 190 River Avenue, Emlenton, 724-867-2261; Mitchell Ponds Inne B&B, RR #1, Knox, 800-555-6582 (www.mitchellponds.com); Gaslight Campgrounds, RD #2, Emlenton, 724-867-6981.

Area Attractions: *Foxburg Wine Cellars* (724-659-0021), also owned by the Steffees, is right across the parking lot and makes twenty-six table wine varieties from Erie-area grapes. The *Foxburg Country Club* (Harvey Road, 724-659-3196) is the home of the oldest golf course in continual use in the country, since 1887, and the home of the American Golf Hall of Fame. This nine-hole public course is open from April 1 to October 31. The setting, overlooking the valley, is stunning.

Other area beer sites: Ben Benedict recommended *Otto's Tavern* (618 River Avenue, Emlenton, 724-867-0952) and the *Beer Garden* (2399 Oneida Valley Road [Route 38], North Washington, 724-894-2428). Folks . . . this time, I make no promises. I wasn't able to get to any of these, and I don't know enough about the area to even guess.

North Country Brewing Company

141 South Main Street,
Slippery Rock, PA 16057
724-794-BEER
www.northcountrybrewing.com

Take this on faith, because I am: North Country will open and be open when this book comes out. There are a few reasons to be confident about that. First, Slippery Rock just went "wet" for the first time in its history in 2001, and North Country will be one of two licensed bars in town, which should give it a pretty good edge. Second, Bob McCafferty and Jodi Branem are really determined to get this brewpub open, and they're people who are used to seeing things through. Third, I saw an online poll of Slippery Rock University students last week, and "the brewery opening" was solidly on top of "things you're excited about."

Piff. Facts, who needs 'em? I know North Country's going to open because it's simply too cool-looking not to, and because I've just got to have Sean McIntyre's beer again. If that's not reason enough for you, well, you stay home and drink Yuengling. I'll be drinking your share at North Country's beautifully crafted bar.

I like brewpubs that dare to be different. North Country's all that, a combination of restored antique (the front two rooms date from 1805), log cabin in the woods, hobbit's playhouse, and eco-hideaway. With its determinedly restored rustic look and bold yellow paint, it doesn't fit in on Main Street at all, and doesn't intend to.

Where to start? How about with all the fun stuff woodworker Gregg Kristophel has been doing: the little mouse carved into one table leg and the little mouse footprints on the table; the dragonfly joint at the bar's corner, complete with crushed turquoise eyes (it complements the butterfly joints in the rest of the bar); the wild full-size carvings on the restroom doors. There's more, too, but you'll have to find them; I don't want to spoil the fun. Upstairs is a tiny patio space, with room for perhaps ten people, who can get their beers passed through a purple-painted porthole directly from the upstairs bar. Check out the pattern on the bar, too: Bob and Jodi did that by laying down gunpowder and firing it off!

Come on out back. There's a big patio area out here, surrounded by a fence and shaded by a huge pine tree. You'd hardly know you were in the middle of town. There are Concord grape vines growing over a brick archway, and a stone fireplace-oven that Bob intends to use to make jerky and smoked meats. The coolest planned thing, though, is a big canvas tent roped to a center ring that will girdle the pine tree's trunk and keep rain and pine needles off your head.

It looks like something out of a movie and is proof to me that these people are committed to doing things right. That, and Sean's presence. I loved his beers at Valhalla, and he's really looking forward to brewing here. "I'm going to jump right in with a bunch of beers," he told me.

Beers brewed: Year-round: North Trail Pale Ale, Paddler's Pils, Wolf Creek Red, Stone House Stout, Squirrel's Nut Brown, Friar's Porter, Mac Each Mar Caigh's Mead, Northern Light, IPA. Seasonals: Sleeping Bear Stout, Jenning's Prairie Pils, McConnell's Mill Weizen, Pumpkin Porter.

The Pick: I'll have to go blind on this one, but I feel . . . *confident* about picking the Paddler's Pils after loving Sean's Pillage Pilsner at Valhalla. You can bet it's going to be clean, refreshing, and well structured. Enjoy!

"I'm looking forward to making styles I never had a chance to make at Valhalla. Cellar-aged barleywines, Scottish styles, cask ales." When you try those beers, um . . . just try to forget that the cold room used to be Slippery Rock's morgue. (Don't laugh; the men's room was the embalming chamber!) To 6-foot Sean's discomfort, the coroner must have been a bit vertically challenged; the ceiling's only a little over 5 feet high. I advised him to find a short apprentice ASAP.

North Country is going to set the beer excellence mark high in Slippery Rock. With input from Andrew Maxwell, the beers Matt Allyn is doing up the road at Four Sons, and a couple projects that are cooking in other places, we could be looking at a real brewing renaissance in western Pennsylvania. Judging from the way Four Sons has taken off, I think the area's ready for it. And I'm confident that North Country will be ready. See you upstairs.

Opened: January 2005.
Owners: Bob McCafferty, Jodi Branem.
Brewer: Sean McIntyre.
System: 7-barrel JV NorthWest brewhouse, 600 barrels annual capacity.
Production: Not available.
Brewpub hours: Monday through Thursday, 11 A.M. to midnight; Friday and Saturday, 11 A.M. to 1 A.M.; Sunday, 11 A.M. to 10 P.M.
Tours: Upon request.
Take-out beer: Growlers, four-packs and singles of 32-ounce swing-tops, keggies (self-contained CO_2-pressurized kegs), and five-gallon kegs.
Food: Appetizers, steaks, seafood, wild game and game pies; daily specials.
Extras: Darts. Live music (call or check website for schedule). Hiker "ferry" service for hiking through Jennings Environmental Park and Moraine State Park (call ahead for details).
Special considerations: Kids welcome. Handicapped-accessible. Cigars allowed. Vegetarian meals available.
Parking: On-street parking, plus town lot across the street.
Lodging in the area: Applebutter Inn B&B, 666 Centerville Pike, 724-794-1844; Evening Star Motel, 915 New Castle Road, 724-794-3211; Comfort Inn, 118 Garrett Drive, Grove City, 724-748-1005.
Area Attractions: Slippery Rock has a restored stagecoach tavern, the **Old Stone House** (call 724-738-2408 to arrange a tour). **Jennings Environmental Park** (at the intersection of Routes 8, 173, and 528, 724-794-6011) preserves a rare stretch of Pennsylvania prairie. A variety of programs are presented through the year, including maple sugaring in the early spring. **McConnell's Mill State Park**

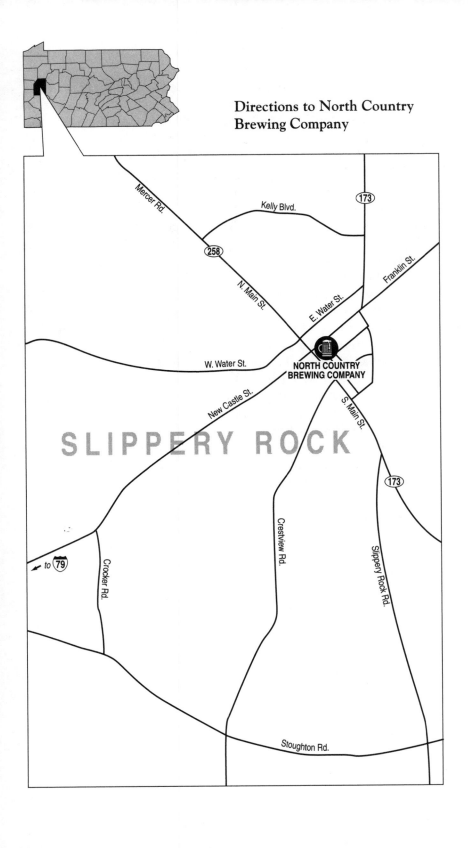

Directions to North Country Brewing Company

Mercer Rd.

Kelly Blvd.

(173)

(258)

N. Main St.

Franklin St.

E. Water St.

W. Water St.

NORTH COUNTRY
BREWING COMPANY

New Castle St.

S. Main St.

SLIPPERY ROCK

(173)

to (79)

Crocker Rd.

Crestview Rd.

Slippery Rock Rd.

Stoughton Rd.

(Portersville, 724-368-8091) and **Moraine State Park** (225 Pleasant Valley Road, Portersville, 724-368-8811) offer many outdoor recreational activities. At McConnell's Mill, there's fishing, hunting, rock climbing, and Class II to Class IV white-water boating through Slippery Rock Gorge, as well as the mill itself, a restored water-powered gristmill. At Moraine, you'll find camping, swimming, boating, windsurfing, biking, hiking, and fishing. The brewpub plans to offer shuttle services to hikers at Moraine; call for information. If the outdoors just doesn't call to you like the indoors, head up the road to **Prime Outlets at Grove City** (Route 208 & I-79, Exit 31, Grove City, 888-545-7221) for 140 stores' worth of shopping, seven days a week. I can smell the credit cards smoking now . . .

Other area beer sites: **Ginger Hill Tavern** (254 South Main Street, 724-794-3504) is pretty much the *only* bar in the area; it's the only other place that has opened since Slippery Rock voted itself wet in 2001.

Sharon is not far away, an industrial town that's mostly known in bar circles for being the home base of the **Quaker Steak & Lube** chain and their award-winning hot wings (101 Chestnut Street, Sharon, 724-981-WING). But there's a surprisingly good array of taps at the **Chestnut Street Café** (23 Chestnut Street, 724-346-1414). Tucked in the first floor of a big brick building, the Café has a high ceiling, a long bar, and a selection of draft beer (and whiskey) that will wow you. Well worth the side trip; probably the best beer bar between metropolitan Pittsburgh and Erie.

Pennsylvania's Regional Foods

Pennsylvania is a patchwork quilt, an assortment of cultures and eth-
nicities that remain strong and clear even in these modern, mobile
times. It probably has something to do with the tendency of Pennsylvanians to *stay*. We have more retirees than any state other than Florida,
and more people living in the same houses in which they were born
than any other state, so there's not a lot of blending going on.

Various snide explanations exist for this phenomenon—too poor or
too stupid to leave being among them—but I think it's because we
know we can't get the right food anywhere else. Pennsylvania has a
plethora of regional foods. Just my home territory, the Dutch Country,
has more well-known and widespread regional dishes than some entire
states. Let's take a look at each area.

Philadelphia loves soft pretzels, hoagies, scrapple, Tastykakes, and the
tasty but odd combination of fried oysters and chicken salad (get it at the
Sansom Street Oyster House), but the food that defines the city is the
cheesesteak, invented at Pat's King of Steaks at Ninth and Passayunk.

You can't get a good cheesesteak if you're more than 60 miles from
here. I know because I've tried, and it's been nothing but a futilely
humorous proposition: The rolls are all wrong, the meat's either too
chunky or ground up, and the stuff they put in them—green peppers,
lettuce, *mint?* I'm sure H. L. Mencken would agree that a man who
would put mint in a cheesesteak would put serpents in a baby's cradle.

A cheesesteak is nature's perfect food. A counterman explained it to
my sister years ago, and she passed it along. "Well, hon," he said around
his cigar, "ya see, your cheesesteak has got your four food groups. Ya got
your bread, ya got your meat, ya got your cheese, ya got your onions,
which is a vegetable." He paused at this point and grinned. "And ya got
your grease, hon, which is *very* important."

I watched my latest one get grilled down at Frusco's in Northeast
Philly (7220 Frankford Ave., not far from the Grey Lodge Pub or the Six-
Pack Store, both of which offer the opportunity for matching your steak
with a great beer; see Philadelphia bar suggestions on pages 27–28). Order
up: "Yeah, a cheesesteak wit', sauce." That's a cheesesteak with onions
and sauce. Shaved, pressed steak goes on the grill, sizzling and popping,

to be turned and lightly chopped with the spatula. A constant pile of onions is kept slowly cooking to one side, glistening and translucent.

When the steak's done, they take the roll, what some people believe is the key ingredient—they're wrong, but their heart's in the right place—a roll that's soft but chewy inside, crusty and tough enough to hold the juices on the outside, and lay it over the steak. (Frusco's gives you the option to pay a buck extra for a roll from the local Sarcone's bakery; definitely take it for their excellent hoagies, but not the steak—too crusty.) Then watch the cook slip the big spatula under the steak, flip it over into his hand, slide a spatula of fried onions on it, and ladle in some hot pizza sauce if you want it. Then spoon a fat stripe of hot Whiz right down the middle.

Because that's what you have here, folks: The classic Philly cheesesteak is made with Cheese Whiz, liquid Velveeta. Oh, you can order it with different cheese if you think Whiz is beneath you; you can even be like John Kerry and order it with Swiss (major *faux pas* for the then-presidential candidate and his handlers, and talked about for days in the Philly press). But Whiz it is, because it's premelted, it blends well with the sauce, and that bright orange just looks good on there.

Where's the best? Good way to start an argument. Eat your way to an answer! Pat's is the classic place to start, then on to Geno's, right across the intersection. Tony Luke's is a perennial favorite (you can also try Philly's secret sandwich there, the roast pork Italian; 39 Oregon Avenue), as is Jim's Steaks (South and Fourth Streets). If you're in the Reading Terminal Market, my sister swears by Rick's.

You'll notice there are no phone numbers. Don't call; these folks are too busy to answer the phone. Go get your steak, and eat it Philly style: on the sidewalk, bent at the waist, the steak angled down and away, so's you don't get that very important grease on your clothes. Get a beer to pound with it: Pocono Pale Ale from The Lion is great, Yuengling Lager is a favorite.

The Philly Suburbs are not as culinarily well defined, and no surprise there; we mostly came either from somewhere else or from the city, so you'll find plenty of good cheesesteak and hoagie joints out here. One thing we do have is a strong tradition of local meat packers in Montgomery County: Hatfield, Leidy's, Alderfer's. There's also an excellent independent German butcher out near Chalfont, Ernst Illg (365 Folly Road, 215-343-0670). They all do meats, but the thing we love out here is *landjaegers*.

The landjaeger is a smoked sausage, with flattened links about seven inches long and maybe an inch across at their widest. They come in pairs, connected by a twist of . . . well, we don't really want to know what that is, do we? Let's just say "casing" and keep our appetite for them. The sausage comes out of the process a dark brownish purple, flecked with white. The ones Ernst makes will keep for a week or so unrefrigerated; the ones from the big packers are more thoroughly smoked and will keep for at least two weeks.

They make an audible *snap* when you bite into them. Each mouthful is pungently smoky; landjaegers will smoke up a car in no time flat. They're chewy, just a little bit greasy, and wonderfully satisfying. There's not much to be said for them as an ingredient; they're just a snack, but most bars and convenience stores have a jar of them handy. You'll need something classically German with these meat sticks: Try a Stoudt's Pilsner.

Pennsylvania Dutch Country is where I grew up, in Paradise, and we've got more regional foods than you can shake an Amishman at. Shoofly pie (wet and dry bottom), chicken potpie, *schnitz* (soft, leathery, dried apple slices), the area's distinctive and individual pretzels and potato chips (see Stackpole Books's *Pennsylvania Snacks* for that whole bounty), red beet eggs (hard-boiled eggs pickled in vinegar and beet juice; they come out purple), and cup cheese.

Cup cheese? Never heard of that one? It's not very common anymore, but once you've developed a taste for it, there's just nothing like it. It's a cheese made by cooking the curds from soured skim milk. In fact, it dates back to German *koch käse*, which means, simply, "cook cheese." One Pennsylvania cheesemaker still makes it, Shenk's Foods (New Danville Pike, Lancaster, www.shenks.com), and they believe it came from Germany with the Mennonites and Amish in the 1600s. Shenk's has been making it since 1929. Oddly, the only other place I could find in the United States that makes anything like it is in Texas.

Shenk's makes it in three levels of sharpness—mild, medium, and sharp—and the sharp is funky enough to stand up to Lancaster Brewing's Gueuze pseudolambic. The cheese is quite runny, stickier than honey, and a light greenish yellow in color. The sharp is flagrantly fragrant, in the limburger range; the medium is quite firm; and the mild is a nose-teasing echo of the sharp. Cup cheese is very low-fat, yet still immensely flavorful. It spreads easily—until you try to get it off your knife, that is—and is delicious even on something as plain as a saltine cracker.

I don't know of any gourmet recipes that use cup cheese, and I don't know of any cookbook authors or "foodies" who rave about it. But every now and then I sit down with a good book, a sleeve of saltines, a glass of something serious enough to defend itself, like a Weyerbacher Blithering Idiot, and eat my way through a little tub of Shenk's sharp. Alone. Just me and the stink.

Northeast Pennsylvania has some Polish and Ukrainian specialties that people grew up with—*bigos* and *crusciki*—and there are the drool-inducing hot dog shops with their individual "Greek sauces" and mustards. But there are two traditions up here I'd like to take a quick look at: Old Forge pizza and Boilo.

Old Forge is a town just outside of Scranton; there's an exit off the far end of the northeast extension of the Pennsylvania Turnpike for it. The first time I came up here was with some friends, one of whom was bent on finding a bar he'd been to, Maxie's. When we finally parked, my pal Rich Pawlak vaulted out of the car and hailed a guy walking toward us with two flat boxes: "Old Forge pizza!" To which the guy replied with a grin, "It's da best!" Huh?

We went into Maxie's (a great little bar, by the way, at 520 South Main Street, 570-562-9948), and Rich revealed all. Old Forge is a little town that has an overabundance of pizza shops, all of which make a unique style of pizza—rectangular, but not the "Sicilian" you find elsewhere. He ordered us some "cuts" (not slices, cuts) and we sampled. You've got a medium-thick crust, but with a crunchy layer on the bottom, about a quarter inch thick; not crispy, but crunchy, almost like zwieback. Then there's a nice, soft doughy layer on top of that, covered with a fairly peppery, onion-studded tomato sauce with lots of mozzarella and American cheese melted right into it all.

Old Forge styles itself the pizza capital of the United States and doesn't really care that hardly anyone outside Scranton has ever heard of the place. After all, they've got that great pizza and we don't. You can find some of the best at Maxie's, Arcaro and Gennell's (443 South Main Street, 570-457-4262), Brutico's (432 South Main Street, 570-457-4166), Revello's (502 South Main Street, 570-457-9843), and Salerno's (139 Moosic Road, 570-457-9920), and they go great with a cold, fizzy glass of Stegmaier.

Now Boilo, on the other hand, is not something you're going to find in a pizza shop or even in a store. Boilo (sometimes spelled Boillo) is something you see in northeast Pennsylvania, and even down into the Lehigh Valley, around Christmastime (or just cold weather). You'll see people at work passing around Ball jars that look like they're full of cider. It isn't quite moonshine, but it's still faintly illegal, though only if you buy it from someone else.

Boilo is a kind of mulled cider, but heavy on the mull. Actually, it's more like spiced whiskey with some juice tossed in. Traditionally, Boilo is made from dirt-cheap blended whiskey (something like Kessler's or one of the bulk-brand Canadians), spiced up with cloves and a cinnamon stick, and diluted with just enough water and orange juice to make it gulpable. We got ours last year in a Ball jar with a rusty lid: classic Boilo. You heat it up to drink it, and it sure does go down easily. Good Boilo's actually pretty decent punch.

I'll share a Boilo recipe passed along to me last year. "From Saint Clair, PA, the heart of the Coal Region, comes a 'Warming Holiday Beverage.' The tradition is to welcome guests with a warm glass of Boilo to warm them up from the cold outside."

Put the following in a pot: 3 cups water, 1 cup sugar, 1/2 cup honey, 1 tablespoon caraway seeds, 4 cloves, 5 sticks of cinnamon, and 3 oranges, cut in quarters (squeeze the oranges over the pot, then put in the pot). Bring it all to a boil, hold at a boil for five minutes, then remove from heat. Add a 1.75-liter bottle of cheap whisky, "the cheaper, the better." Stir well, and return to heat. As soon as it comes to a boil, remove from heat. Cool overnight, then strain into jars. Add used cinnamon sticks to jars and seal. Serve warm, and it will make you warm, but "watch out, it can get you."

The Northwest Corner may have plenty of regional specialties, but the only one I found was bumbleberry pie, a pie we saw at any number of dinors—that's not a typo, that's how "diner" is spelled in the Erie corner. I saw bumbleberry pie as far south as Ridgway, but the best piece I had was at a place in Erie I heartily recommend for breakfast, the Academy Dinor (2516 State Street, 814-461-6611).

Bumbleberry pie sounds like a mistake, and it may have been at one time, but it has become a regional favorite. It is simply a mixed-fruit pie, based on blueberries, but with other fruit mixed in: raspberries, blackberries, pears, apples, whatever the cook has in the pantry and has the courage to add. It's always a little different, but I've never had a bad piece. It also tends to be a fresh fruit pie, because to the best of my knowledge, no one has a commercial prepacked "bumbleberry" can out there!

Pittsburgh has the famous chipped ham that was invented at Isaly's, the hulking huge fried fish sandwiches that are still a Friday staple in Da Burgh, and the "almost famous" sandwiches from Primanti Brothers, a sandwich that got gubernatorial candidate Mike Fisher in trouble in the Philadelphia press during the 2002 campaign. The press asked both Fisher and Philly homeboy Ed Rendell what their favorite sandwich was. Rendell knew the answer to that one straight from his gut: the cheesesteak! But I give credit to Mike Fisher for staying loyal to his Allegheny County roots and telling a dumbfounded Philadelphia press corps that his favorite sandwich was one from Primanti Brothers.

What is a Primanti Brothers sandwich? There actually are quite a few of them: egg and cheese, kolbassi and cheese, steak and cheese, fried baloney and cheese, ham and cheese (and there's a note at the bottom of the menu that extra cheese is available!), and so on. But it's not the cheese that makes it a Primanti Brothers sandwich, or the thick slices of Italian bread, or the paper wrap that is cut with the sandwich. It's the coleslaw and french fries that go *right in the sandwich* that makes it a Primanti Brothers special.

They're in there to save time. The original Primanti Brothers shop was right down in the Strip District, Pittsburgh's food and produce terminal district. Truck drivers back in the 1930s would come rolling in, unload their trucks, and need a sandwich they could eat one-handed as they drove out for their next load. The story is that one driver, who was tired of getting the fries and coleslaw sides and not being able to eat them as they slid around the cab of his truck, asked the counterman to put them right in the sandwich. Genius.

Okay, maybe it's not genius. The sandwiches are huge, and you really have to muckle on to them to get them in your mouth. The coleslaw drips. But they sure are good, and at 2 A.M., when you've been up at the Church all night, there's not much that can beat them. You want a beer suggestion to go with that? Pal, if you're at Primanti's at 2 A.M., I suggest that you call it a night! If you're at the stadium for a game, grab a Penn Dark and dig in. Addresses for all the Primanti Brothers shops are in the Pittsburgh bar suggestions.

Hey, there's a whole other book I could write, full of food from this state! I've barely scratched the surface. Now get out there and have something good—and local!—to eat with all this good local beer!

Pittsburgh

Pittsburgh has come a long way from the days of Carnegie and Frick. The steel mills are silent—or leveled—and the coke furnaces no longer loft their foul stench on the breeze. Pittsburgh went through hard, hard times in the 1970s and 1980s. The population dropped and thousands lost high-wage jobs as the American steel production industry collapsed under the pressure of subsidized overseas competition. Major regional brewer Pittsburgh Brewing—and its Iron City beer—fell into the hands of Australian investors. This city, once a symbol of American industrial might, was turning into a rusty ghost town.

I went to grad school in Pittsburgh in 1982. I treasured visits to Homestead to drink at Chiodo's Tavern. I drank my share of I.C. Light and Straub on my student budget. During that time and in subsequent visits over the next years, I watched Pittsburgh sink into a malaise as dreary as the faded old yellow brick homes peculiar to the city. I didn't know how Chiodo's would survive the demolition of the Homestead Steel Works, a massive structure right behind the bar that was a source of its business and pride.

One of the first harbingers of a turnaround was Tom Pastorius's return to town from Germany in 1985 with his idea for a microbrewery. After testing the waters by having Pittsburgh Brewing contract-brew his beer for a couple years, he started work on his restaurant and Pennsylvania Brewery. Hard work and tight budgets began to slowly pay off.

Similarly, the city started a slow return to health. Pittsburgh gradually let go of the idea that big steel would return, bringing high wages and union power with it, and started to search for its future in other directions. The citizens began to realize their strengths: smaller specialty steel industries, glass and coatings, health care, excellent universities, river trade, and tourism. Local businesses found innovative ways to compete, and employees and city government cooperated to persuade companies to stay in the 'Burgh.

Today Pittsburgh is a hardworking town with its eyes on a new future. This city of fifteen hundred bridges has built on the strength of its past—its museums, fine architecture, and revived industries—to span the abyss left by the departed steel industry. The South Side and the Strip are bustling centers of nightlife, and the suburbs are growing and sprouting new businesses. I was happy to return to Pittsburgh, after years away, and see a cleaner, more confident city with new growth sparking all over.

Pittsburgh Brewing is making moves to regain their market, and Tom Pastorius's lagers are nationally recognized for their excellence. We've lost two brewpubs to the construction work that gave the city its new convention center (and months of snarled traffic), but the Church Brew Works is stronger than ever, and the John Harvard's in Monroeville and Red Star in Greensburg continue the beer evangelization work out in the eastern reaches. There are new beer bars with lots of great taps, and the Sharp Edge—just two blocks from where I used to live—has one of the best selections of draft Belgian beers in the country.

But I'm sad to report that Joe Chiodo has finally retired, and by the time you read this, Chiodo's will be plowed under, replaced by a Walgreen's. I'll miss the vine-shaded deck, the Mystery Sandwich, the best fries, the beers, and the people, and I'll miss Joe. But there are always other bars, new places, old ones, that keep up the spirit of this town: friendly, sincere, and open-hearted.

Go to Pittsburgh as a beer traveler, but don't miss all the other things the city has to offer. To avoid lots of repetition, I have decided to consolidate the **Lodging, Area attractions,** and **Other area beer sites** for the Pittsburgh breweries here. The entry for John Harvard's Brew House in Wilkins Township includes information specific to that area. (My sincere thanks to Tom and Mary Beth Pastorius of Pennsylvania Brewing for their significant help with this section. Thanks also to Paris Lundis of Pubcrawler.com, a Pittsburgh native who gave me a great annotated list of his favorite Pittsburgh bars.)

Area attractions: You may want to come to Pittsburgh just to look at its architectural glories. This city is full of beautiful buildings, both industrial and residential. The Carnegie Museums house just about everything: dinosaurs, Egyptian artifacts, gems and minerals, wind tunnels and earthquake simulations, and Impressionist art. Surely something will interest you or your family. The ***Carnegie Museum of Art*** and the **Carnegie Museum of Natural History** is at 4400 Forbes Avenue (412-622-3131) and the **Carnegie Science Center** is at 1 Allegheny Avenue (412-237-3400). Another Carnegie museum, the **Andy Warhol Museum** (117 Sandusky Street, 412-237-8300), is dedicated entirely to a famous Pittsburgh native's work. The **Frick Art and Historical Center** (7227 Reynolds Street, 412-371-0606) includes the restored mansion of Henry Clay Frick, the Carriage Museum with sleighs and vintage automobiles, and the Frick Art Museum.

See the Pirates or the Steelers at their beautiful new stadiums (both full of Penn beer!). **PNC Park** (412-323-5000, www.pittsburgh.pirates.mlb.com) is right across from downtown on the Seventh Street Bridge, and an easy walk from Penn Brewery. **Heinz Field** (412-323-1200, www.steelers.com) is just downriver. They're both across from **Point State Park,** where the Allegheny and Monongahela Rivers meet to form the Ohio River, a beautiful green spot right beside downtown. The 150-foot spray of the fountain is one of the largest in the country. Don't miss the **Duquesne Incline** (412-381-1665), a Victorian solution to Pittsburgh's steep south shore hills. Ride the incline's hill-hugging cable car up to the aptly named Grandview Avenue for a spectacular view of the Golden Triangle. For just walking around and having fun while maybe buying a few things, you have two great choices: the **Strip District** and **South Side**. The Strip District is Pittsburgh's produce and meat market, north and south of the 2000 block of Penn Avenue. This is a busy, bustling, fun place during the day, and it steams with nightlife after dark. The South Side, on Carson Street around Fat Head's and Smokin' Joe's, is a younger, more fringe scene at night, but a lot of fun, and you can find some great casual food and drink here. The **Pittsburgh Zoo** (412-665-3640) has Siberian tigers, zebras, elephants, and the AquaZoo's shark tank and living coral reef. There is a special kids' zoo with a sea lion pool. For more rousing recreation, **Kennywood Amusement Park** (4800 Kennywood Boulevard, West Mifflin, 412-461-0500) is a national treasure, a well-preserved family-style amusement park, not a fancy theme park, with four roller coasters, thirty other rides, and fourteen children's rides; it was recently rated the fifth-best amusement park in the world. There's also **Sandcastle** (412-462-6666), a water park on the Monongahela with water slides, a huge hot tub, a lazy river, and go-karts. Pittsburgh celebrates in the summer. The Three Rivers Art Festival and the ten-day Mellon Jazz Festival in June start the ball rolling, followed by the Shadyside Summer Arts Festival in July and August. The Three

Rivers Regatta, a wild time in this river city, is held the first weekend in August. For further information on these events and other attractions, call the Greater Pittsburgh Convention and Visitors Bureau (412-281-7711).

Lodging in the area: The Priory—A City Inn, historic B&B, 614 Pressley Street, 412-231-3338; Doubletree Hotel, 1000 Penn Avenue, 412-281-3700 or 800-222-TREE; Best Western, Parkway Center Inn, Parkway Center Mall, 875 Greentree Road, 412-922-7070; Holiday Inn Select, 100 Lytton Avenue, 412-682-6200. Camping: Ohiopyle State Park, 412-329-8951; Raccoon Creek State Park, 412-899-2200.

Other area beer sites: One tip before we start: After you've been out till all hours, go to the "almost famous" *Primanti Brothers Bar and Grille,* where you'll get your sandwich served with fries and coleslaw—right in the sandwich. It's a Pittsburgh tradition after a late night of drinking, and you may see anyone here. The menu's on the wall: roast beef and cheese, fried egg and cheese, kolbassi and cheese, fried bologna and cheese . . . and down in the corner is the note I love: "Extra cheese—25¢." Primanti Brothers can be found in the Strip District at 46 Eighteenth Street (412-263-2142), in Oakland at 3803 Forbes Avenue (412-621-4444), on the South Side at 1832 East Carson Street (412-381-2583), at Market Square at 2 South Market Place (412-261-1599), and at both PNC Park and Heinz Field.

The Strip. *Kaya* (2000 Smallman Street, 412-261-6565) is a cool place with a funky menu of Caribbean fusion and vegetarian dishes, great beer, and a wide selection of spirits. *Roland's* (1904 Penn Avenue, 412-261-3401) is all about seafood to the untrained eye, but a real beer geek will go upstairs and find the massive bottle selection; not what it used to be, but still worth a look. Also recommended: *Aussom Aussie Boomerang BBQ* (2701 Penn Avenue, 412-434-1220; where Vermont Flatbread used to be) got good reports from trusted friends.

Oakland. The *Fuel and Fuddle* (212 Oakland Avenue, 412-682-3473) is a clean, loud, and happy place that's a Pitt favorite, with great taps and bottles and a brick pizza oven. Just a block away is *Mad Mex* (Atwood and Bates Streets, 412-681-5656), a little rough-looking, but the fringey crowd is beer-savvy and drinks good stuff. They eat well, too: big plates of Mexican food. (There are three other Mad Mex's in Pittsburgh: 7905 McKnight Road, North Hills, 412-366-5656; Scott Towne Center, 2101 Greentree Road, South Hills, 412-279-0200; and Robinson Plaza II, Route 60, Park Manor Drive,

412-494-5656.) After drinking in Oakland, I usually—okay, always—
wind up at **Original's** (corner of Forbes and Bouquet, 412-621-0435)
for some fries and one of their great foot-long dogs with chili, cheese,
and onions. And maybe one more beer, if I'm walking.

South Side. Smokin' Joe's (East Carson and Twentieth Streets, 412-
341-6757) has a wall o' taps going, and the bartenders were very
beer savvy the night I was there. **Fat Head's** (1805 East Carson
Street, 412-431-7433) has expanded: They now have thirty-nine
rotating taps, regular cask ale, and an excellent selection in bottles,
as well as the Headwiches, heart-stopping sandwiches the size of
my two fists. Open wide. Across Carson is **Piper's Pub** (1828 East
Carson Street, 412-381-3977), a Scottish-themed bar with a massive selection of single malts (and Irish whiskey as well) and good
beer to boot; you have to love a bar with a dedicated Spaten Opti-
mator tap. Much farther south, in Bridgeville (you'll have to shoot
through The Tubes and run down I-279 to get there), is Pittsburgh's
hottest new beer bar, the **Pittsburgh Bottleshop Café** (1597 Washington Pike [PA Route 50], 412-279-8191), and by the time you
read this, it's just possible that it might be a brewpub as well. The
Bottleshop is the brainchild of Pittsburgh Brewing brewer Mark
Davis, who took an empty strip plaza storefront, filled it with coolers and hundreds of bottles of beer, plus fifteen taps, staffed it with
attractive young men and women, and opened the doors. I tell you,
the place has no atmosphere at all, except what the customers
bring with them, and it rocks. Mark has plans to add a brewpub in
the space next door, with a different feel; watch my website for
details. Once you crawl out of bed the next morning, my favorite
spot for breakfast in Pittsburgh is down here on the South Side:
BOBS (2350 Noblestown Road, 412-922-5828). The breakfasts are
outstanding (try the 12-inch pancakes), as is the service, but it's
worth finding BOBS just to experience the wit of the owner,
Wendy. She'll send you on your way with a grin and her usual
"Welcome to BOBS, now get the hell out." Ah, Pittsburgh!

Also recommended: Paris Lundis at Pubcrawler.com liked **Bado's
Pizzeria and Delicatessen** (307 Beverly Road, Mount Lebanon,
412-563-5300), which has a constantly improving beer selection,
and **Zythos** (2108 East Carson Street, 412-481-2234), with a good
Mediterranean menu. Tony Knipling at Vecenie's Distributing rec-
ommended **Burgh's Pizza and Wing Pub** (533 Washington Avenue,
Bridgeville, 412-257-8767, just up the road from the Bottleshop
Café).

North Side *The Bierhaus* (919 Spring Garden Avenue, 412-231-2498) is an easy block's walk from Penn Brewing and has a tremendous display of breweriana: cans (cone-tops, too), minikegs, tap knobs, trays, wow! Not to mention that the staff is really friendly and fresh Penn Pilsner is on tap. If you like German food and Penn Brewing doesn't fill you up, get yourself to **Max's Allegheny Tavern** (537 Suismon Street, 412-231-1899), where schnitzels, wursts, goulash, and sauerkraut that will make you a believer are served with a great selection of German and local beers. Not far away from Max's is the **Park House** (403 East Ohio Street, 412-231-0551), reputed to be Pittsburgh's oldest bar. It looks it: Park House has that long, narrow, "barrel house" appearance and is well worn and comfortable, with good taps of Penn beers. Over in the quiet Mexican War Streets neighborhood, you'll find a block of homes on Monterey Street that has one brightly lit doorway with an Irish flag: That's the **Monterey Pub** (1227 Monterey Street, 412-322-6535). With a fine backbar, a small but solid tap selection, and a varied clientele that was having real conversations, the Monterey is the kind of bar I wish I had in my neighborhood; this one's a real jewel.

Farther up the Allegheny, in Sharpsburg, is **The Parlor** (1000 North Canal Street, 412-782-7665), which comes highly recommended for good food and a solid beer selection, along with a very friendly staff. Worth a look. Not on the North Side, but right on the river and not far from Sharpsburg is the **Rivertowne Inn** (500 Jones Street, Verona, 412-828-3707), and what a pleasant surprise this place was: a corner bar tucked in behind a supermarket plaza with sixteen excellent taps (*not* the taps everyone else in town had, either), more than two hundred well-picked bottles, knowledgeable staff, and big old plates of fish. You'll want to stay all night.

Shadyside/East Liberty. *The Sharp Edge* (302 South St. Clair Street, 412-661-3537) has great bar food and probably the best selection of Belgian taps in the United States outside of Philadelphia. It alone is worth a visit to Pittsburgh. There's another one if you can't find that one; *Sharp Edge Creek House* is downstream in Crafton (288 West Steuben Street, 412-922-8118) and is just as excellent. **Kelly's Bar and Lounge** (6012 Penn Circle South, 412-363-6012) is a short walk away, with a cool retro feel, a kind of tiki lounge patio out back, and small but solid beer selection. **Bites and Brews** (5744 Ellsworth Avenue, no phone) is new, a pizza and sandwich joint with thirty taps of overly standard micros and imports. I have hopes that the selection will improve.

Just off the stylish block of Walnut Street is the **Pittsburgh Deli Company** (728 Copeland Street, 412-682-DELI), with a deli downstairs and a bar upstairs. There are only four taps, but the bottle selection is eclectic and always changing; "I guess I have 'beer ADD,'" said manager Dave McCombie. "I can't have the same beer twice." The deli also sells its beer to go. That's also the case—in a *big* way—at **D's Six Packs and Dogz** (1118 South Braddock Avenue, 412-241-4666), which is actually over in Swissvale. D's is unique: a small bar with six constantly rotating and phenomenal taps, a tiny menu of hot dogs and sausages, a couple tables . . . and more than eight hundred different bottled beers back in what they call "The Beer Cave." It's amazing! Just a few blocks from Shadyside, you'll find the Squirrel Hill neighborhood and the **Squirrel Hill Café** (5802 Forbes Avenue, 412-5213327). The "Squirrel Cage" has changed from when I used to visit, when it was bright, loud, and young and had a broad selection of nonlocal microbrews. Now it's quieter and older, and carries mostly local beers. Kind of like me.

Lawrenceville/Polish Hill. One night I closed the Church and wanted somewhere else to go. "Gooski's," said the bartender, and I never wrote a letter to thank her. **Gooski's** is in the heart of Polish Hill (3117 Brereton Street, 412-681-1658), and it is rocking, with cheap micros, a big jukebox, and a bargeload of attitude. A must-stop. **Lot 17** (4617 Liberty Avenue, 412-687-8117) is a mix of old-style bar out front and stylish dining room in the back, with an okay tap selection—the best beer on Liberty, along with the **Bloomfield Bridge Tavern** (4412 Liberty Avenue, right at the downhill end of the bridge, 412-682-8611). That's where Stush Frankowski serves great Polish food (get the pierogies or don't bother going), and he's got a good stash of beer, too. Over the hill, down toward the Allegheny on Butler Street, you can find great food of a different type: **Ray's Marlin Beach Bar and Grill** (5121 Butler Street, 412-781-6771) has a kicking menu of Cuban/South Florida goodies that make the whole place smell irresistible around dinner time. Cool the heat with Ray's high-end bottle selection or eight tap beers. There are more bars upstairs, where it's decorated like a hipster's basement. Possibly the coolest beer bar in the 'Burgh.

Pennsylvania Brewing Company

800 Vinial Street, Pittsburgh, PA 15212
412-237-9400
www.pennbrew.com

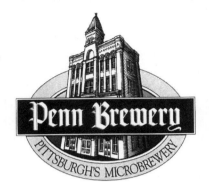

Tom Pastorius once told me a very simple truth about why he opened a microbrewery and why it brews the kinds of beers it does: "Pennsylvania Brewing exists to make beers that I like," he said. Those beers are German-style lagers, and Tom's brewery makes some of the best in the United States.

Lagers are underappreciated by most American beer geeks, though, and that's part of the reason Pennsylvania Brewing had a long, hard climb to their current success as Pennsylvania's biggest microbrewer. This lack of appreciation is a mystery to me. Carol Stoudt blamed it on Budweiser backlash. "Budweiser is the beer that micro lovers hate—for whatever reasons—and it's a lager," she explained. "They throw all lagers together as dull beers."

That makes it particularly tough on microbrewers who want to brew lagers, for not only are lagers less popular, but they are substantially more expensive to brew. They are more labor-intensive than ales, use more energy (cooling costs for the lagering), and they stay in the tanks longer, which means the same amount of tankage produces less lager than ale in a year. And yet a brewer cannot charge more for lagers. The customers don't see or care about the extra costs, so they won't pay more for the beer.

What's more, lager brewers often feel that they brew to higher standards than ale brewers do. Ales are generally more complex and somewhat more eccentric in character than lagers. That gives ale brewers a bit of wiggle room. Lager brewers have very little leeway; their brews are by nature cleaner, purer of essence, a simple yet subtle interplay of hops and malt. As Tom Pastorius

Beers brewed: Year-round: Penn Pilsner, Penn Gold (GABF Gold, 1990, 1993, 1998; Bronze, 1999), Kaiser Pils, Penn Dark (GABF Bronze, 1999), Penn Weizen (GABF Silver, 1997). Seasonals: Oktoberfest, St. Nikolaus Bock, Maerzen, Maibock, All Star Lager, Pastorator Double Bock, Ol' Man Winter Wheat Bock. Some bottled Penn Pilsner also contract-brewed.

put it, "A lager brewer is hanging right out there with nowhere to hide!"

Tom has nothing to worry about from what I've tasted of his beer, and I've tasted my share. His delicately delicious Penn Gold has grabbed GABF Gold three times over nine years. That's proof of Penn's mastery of both the Munich helles style and lager brewing in general, because there's nowhere at all to hide on this pristine, lightly malty beer.

Some of the brewery's flagship Penn Pilsner is still brewed under contract because of the sheer volume it represents. Tom first contracted with Pittsburgh Brewing to make the beer in 1986, and he introduced the beer in his multi-great-grandfather's hometown of Philadelphia (his ancestor founded Germantown).

After two years of selling, scrimping, saving, and sweating, Tom opened his brewery pub at 800 Vinial Street, in part of the old Eberhardt and Ober brewery. Lots of family work went into the brewery; Tom built the sturdy, simple furniture himself. The pub is a beauty of German style and functionality, and Tom has indoctrinated his staff in the Teutonic obsession with having everything just so, *alles in ordnung*. The place settings, tablecloths, and food presentation are uniformly excellent. I can vouch for the food itself: It definitely is not a matter of style over substance. I'd like to eat at Tom's table often, say once or twice a day.

The beer is outstanding. The thing I like most about Penn's beers is their balance. They do not go overboard on anything. Even the doublebock, malty though it is, is kept in a tenuous dynamic balance by malt dryness. That's the mark of a true brewmaster. My hat's off to Tom and his gracious wife, Mary Beth. They have built an honest business and a beautiful one. The service is competent and friendly; the food is fresh and praiseworthy. The beer is clean, pure, and delicious. I don't know what more you can ask of a brewer.

The market, on the other hand, asks a lot. Tom has struggled for years to grow this brand within his resources, to build the brewery to the point where it could support serious growth. It hasn't been easy, though there have been remarkable successes, like the fantastic penetration of PNC Park.

But it took more than Tom and the family could do on their own. He said as much in an interview with *Pittsburgh Business Journal:* "I've

The Pick: The entire Penn line is excellent, but the Pick is easy: St. Nikolaus Bock. Tom Pastorius makes one of the best bocks in the United States. The St. Nikolaus is creamy, smooth, chocolaty, and just rich enough, without stepping over the line into doublebock territory. A beer hearty enough for German food, yet smooth enough to quaff. *Ausgezeichnet!* Excellent! I also recently became much more familiar with Penn Gold, and it is truly a classic helles—imagine those GABF judges being right all those years!

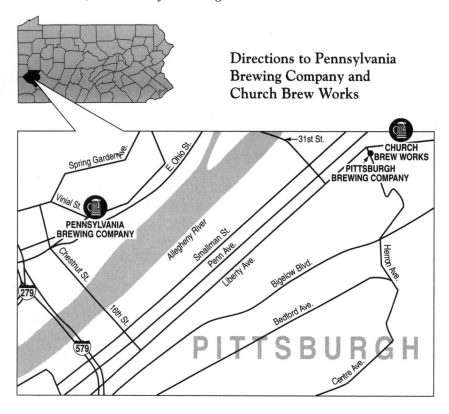

Directions to Pennsylvania Brewing Company and Church Brew Works

been working these 120 hour weeks for 17 and a half years now. Sweat equity has brought us this far, but we could see that we were really up against the wall." In September 2003, he finally sold a majority of the business to Birchmere Capital LP, a local investment group, to raise the money to expand the brand's sales area, and for an expansion. The idea is, as Stoudt's has done, to bring all brewing in-house.

The results remain to be seen, as the expansion is still in the planning stages. But the Penn Brewery finally has the resources to build a strong future, and Tom Pastorius has the experience to make sure those resources are well spent.

Opened: March 1986.
Owners: Thomas V. Pastorius, Mary Beth Pastorius, and Birchmere Capital LP.
Brewers: Tom Pastorius, Paul Shanta, Andy Rich.
System: 45-barrel Jacob Carl GmbH brewhouse, 22,000 barrels annual capacity (plus contracted Penn Pilsner).
Production: 16,000 barrels in 2003.

Brewpub hours: Monday through Saturday, 11 A.M. to midnight; closed Sunday and major holidays.

Tours: Tours by appointment, for groups of twenty or more. (The brewery is visible from the dining room and the Ratskeller.)

Take-out beer: Six-packs, cases, quarter and half kegs.

Food: Penn makes some great German food, but you can also get American food. There is a full lunch and dinner menu of appetizers, soups, salads, sandwiches, and entrées. All desserts are made on-premises. Tom and Mary Beth are just a bit fanatic about the quality of ingredients—you can taste it.

Extras: Full liquor license. Selection includes German schnapps, such as Jägermeister, Killepitsch, and Himbeerngeist. Outdoor beer garden. Live entertainment four nights a week; call for schedule.

Events: Penn hosts the Pennsylvania Microbrewers Fest on the first Saturday of June—a friendly, accessible fest that I highly recommend—and its own Oktoberfest the last two weekends of September. There are parties for St. Nikolaus Day (the first weekend in December) and Mardi Gras, as well as ceremonial tappings of seasonal beers; call for dates.

Special considerations: Kids welcome. Handicapped-accessible. Cigars allowed. Vegetarian meals available.

Parking: Free off-street parking.

Church Brew Works

**3525 Liberty Avenue,
Pittsburgh, PA 15201
412-688-8200
www.churchbrew.com**

Prepare yourself for a shock when you first walk into the Church Brew Works. At least, it was something of a shock to me. Intellectually, I knew that the Church Brew Works was located in a church. As far as I'm aware, this is the only brewpub in America in such a setting.

It's in the former St. John the Baptist Roman Catholic Church, to be specific, just up the street from Pittsburgh Brewing in Pittsburgh's

Lawrenceville neighborhood. I had actually seen the church being renovated some months before the brewpub opened. Even so, it was strange to walk into the place the first time and see a brewhouse, tanks and all, sitting right up on the altar of what was obviously, definitely, for sure, a church. Don't get me wrong. I saw nothing particularly heinous about the fact that it was a brewery. I would have had the same reaction if I had found, say, a beauty salon or a McDonald's.

Beers brewed: Year-round: Celestial Gold, Pipe Organ Pale Ale, Pious Monk Dunkel, Bell Tower Brown Ale. Seasonals: Up to twelve varied seasonal beers per year.

The Pick: I was struck by the Bell Tower Brown Ale the last time I went to Church. There's a twist to this one—Tettnang finishing hops, a most unalelike hop that gives a very bright, spicy, almost minty flavor. This is a real nice beer. (The Pious Monk Dunkel is pretty good, too.)

What's also surprising is that the people who grew up with St. John's as their church seem to be pretty happy about the brewpub in general. That's mostly because the parish had shrunk so much that the diocese had closed it and deconsecrated the church. The building was headed for the wrecking ball when Sean Casey and other local investors bought it to convert it into the brewpub. The friends of the church, people who had been baptized, confirmed, and married there, figured that having the building and their memories intertwined with a brewpub was better than seeing the church leveled to make room for another professional building or minimarket.

Their new faith has been rewarded. The Church Brew Works has certainly brought some excitement to Lawrenceville. Colorful banners fly outside the spruced-up building. People slow down to look and then stop to have a drink. Everyone is doing a little better, including the employees at Pittsburgh Brewing, who now have someplace cool to go for lunch.

And the Church is pretty cool. The stained glass and gold decorations were retained and refurbished, as was the church's lectern, which serves as a hostess station. The ceiling is immensely high, all the way up to the organ loft in the rear. It is one of the most striking brewpubs I've ever seen.

The selection of beers ranges from good to excellent. There is a strong lager component in response to local tastes. Many Pittsburghers are of Eastern and Central European descent, and those folks do love their lagers. You can get a dunkel anytime, festbier in the fall, bock in the winter. That's a nice break from the usual unending brewpub parade of ale, ale, ale. I also like the way brewer Bryan Pearson thinks about his ales. "Anyone can make an overhopped beer," he told me. "It's much harder to make a good golden ale." Amen, brother.

Pearson is also unafraid of trying something different. I had a big beer brewed with quinoa there, called a Turbo Llama. Not sure what the quinoa tasted like, but the beer sure was good. He's made some huge fruit beers, like his Clout Stout, a massive raspberry imperial stout. If you want to take some beer home, they've also started bottling it. There has been talk of a second Church opening, but I have to guess that it's going to take a while to find the right spot!

It does your heart good to see people going to Church during the week. In fact, some Pittsburghers have become faithful and regular Church-goers. It has been a blessing to this neighborhood.

Opened: August 1996.

Owner: Corporation; Sean Casey, president.

Brewer: Bryan Pearson.

System: 15-barrel Specific Mechanical brewhouse, 1,500 barrels annual capacity.

Production: 1,000 barrels in 2004 (estimated).

Brewpub hours: Monday through Thursday, 11:30 A.M. to 11:45 P.M.; Friday and Saturday, 11:30 A.M. to 1 A.M.; Sunday, noon to 10 P.M.

Tours: Monday through Friday at 5 P.M.

Take-out beer: Growlers; kegs by prior arrangement. Bottled Church beer available at the bar.

Food: An eclectic American regional menu that is very popular with the lunchtime crowd. Check out the fun specialties, like pierogi pizza. Some heart-healthy selections.

Extras: Full liquor license. Selection of malts, bourbons, and cognacs. Occasional live music; call for information. Outside patio and hops garden for warm weather.

Events: Oktoberfest. There's a Party on the Patio every Wednesday during the summer, and an anniversary party every August; call for details.

Special considerations: Kids welcome. Handicapped-accessible. Cigars allowed on outdoor patio only. Vegetarian meals available.

Parking: Large off-street lot and plenty of on-street parking.

Rock Bottom, Homestead

171 E. Bridge St.,
Homestead, 15120
412-462-2739
www.rockbottom.com

GOOD FRIENDS. GREAT FOOD. GREAT BEER.

What am I going to do, now that Joe Chiodo has finally called it quits, his tavern finally, aptly, bulldozed like the Homestead steel works that it served for so long and replaced with a Walgreen's drugstore? Will I ever cross the Homestead High-Level Bridge to go drinking again?

Well, yes and no. No, because the bridge has been renamed, so I'll have to cross the Homestead Grays Bridge. And yes, because down there, amidst all the theaters and stores and restaurants of the boomingly popular Waterfront, is Rock Bottom Homestead, where Matthew Carroll brews precisely the way he wants to.

You can read my rants about chain brewpubs and mall brewpubs at the entry for Rock Bottom, King of Prussia (see page 80), but you should know a little something about Rock Bottom, too. It is the second-largest brewpub chain in the country, after the Hops group, with twenty-nine Rock Bottom restaurants and more on the way. They also own the Chop House and Walnut Street brewpubs. Rock Bottom is centered in Louisville, Colorado, but there are Rock Bottoms all across the country, from California to Massachusetts. The chain has expanded both by opening new sites and by acquisition; the King of Prussia Rock Bottom was part of the Boston-based brew moon chain, for instance.

Rock Bottom has changed their emphasis. "We're trying to refocus," said Kevin Reed, who is the director of brewing operations for the whole group. "Most brewpubs that opened in the 1990s were catering to people who wanted beer. Solid food and solid beer did it, without a need for a concept. It's not like that now. We're catching the food-beer pairing wave. I see it like varietal wines. 'Wine and food' is a given now. But some foods are better with beer, and we want to get a piece of that action. We want to educate people, and not just necessarily for Rock Bottom. Whenever they go out, if they're thinking 'beer with

Beers brewed: Year-round: Lumpy Dog Light Lager, Stacks Pale Ale, North Star Amber, High Level Brown. Seasonals: American Dream IPA, Velvet Porter, Maibock, Scotch Ale, Double Bock, Hefeweizen, English IPA, and more.

food,' that helps the production breweries as well; it helps the whole industry."

Things are different at brewpubs, though, according to Reed. "Greg Koch of Stone Brewing in San Diego said that brewers make the beer and wait for people to catch up to them. In the pub business, that's not a luxury we have. We're not quite as aggressive as some of the production brewers. That's a slippery slope: Brewers like to make big beers, but if they don't sell fast enough, it's just tanks taken up. Sometimes you have to stick your toe in the water and see what brings people in the doors."

The Pick: I liked the Velvet Porter, a nitro-driven porter that Matthew had on. It was smooth and mellow, light on the roasted malts, a bit of chocolate, and a dry malt finish; soothing. Good for summer or winter, good with food or without.

Matthew Carroll is on top of that idea. He doesn't brew aggressive beers; he brews drinkable beers with enough guts to them that they satisfy but don't overwhelm. Like all the Rock Bottoms, he has the Lumpy Dog Light Lager, a pale ale, an amber, and when it's IPA time, he does an IPA. He brews the annual red ale that all the Rock Bottoms do to raise money for local firefighters. And he brews some bigger beers in the winter, because he learned quickly that "they hibernate in the winter out here!" as he put it. But he does all the beers his way.

It's always like that at Rock Bottom. I've been to Rock Bottoms all across the country. If the idea of a chain is to provide the customer with a consistent product with no changes, well, Rock Bottom is a half failure, because while the menu's pretty much the same everywhere, the beer's different in every one. Do they all have a pale ale, a brown ale, a kölsch or some other light golden beer? Look around: So do 80 percent of the other brewpubs. I was recently at The Brewer's Art in Baltimore, one of the most different brewpubs around, and they had . . . a pale ale and a brown ale. They're standard beers; people *like* them. But every brewer at every Rock Bottom does it differently.

Rock Bottom is the new place for beer in Homestead. Kudos to Chiodo's, and I'm sad to see it go. I doubt that Matthew Carroll will last more than fifty years like Joe Chiodo did, but while he's here, he'll be making beers you'll drink by the pint . . . after pint, after pint.

Opened: April 2002.
Owner: Rock Bottom Group.
Brewer: Matthew Carroll.
System: 12-barrel JV NorthWest brewhouse, 2,000 barrels annual capacity.
Production: 1,600+ barrels in 2004 (estimated).
Brewpub hours: Seven days a week, 11 A.M. to 2 A.M.
Tours: Upon request, subject to brewer availability.

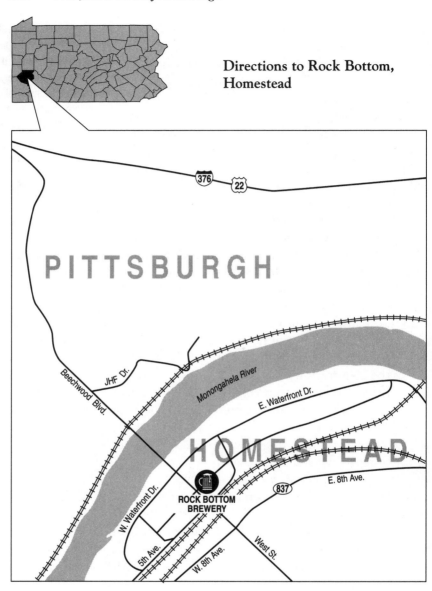

Directions to Rock Bottom, Homestead

Take-out beer: Growlers.

Food: Rock Bottom's menu really has a bit of everything, and everything I've ever had has been delicious. I particularly like their homestyle favorites, like chicken-fried chicken, alder-smoked salmon, jambalaya, and barbecue ribs. Don't miss the white cheddar potatoes, a Rock Bottom signature side.

Extras: Live music on Wednesday nights; call for schedule. Lots of TVs, and a large banquet room for private parties and meetings. The Sing Sing dueling piano bar next door is supplied with beer by Rock Bottom.

Special considerations: Kids welcome. Handicapped-accessible. Cigars allowed. Vegetarian meals available.

Parking: Large on-site lot.

John Harvard's Brew House, Wilkins Township

3466 William Penn Highway,
Wilkins Township, PA 15235
412-824-9440
www.johnharvards.com

It's another John Harvard's Brew House! (You can get the John Harvard's story from the listing for the Wayne Brew House on page 86.) This one is the first brewpub to open in Pittsburgh's suburbs, and still the only one, though the Bottleshop Café in Bridgeville may add a brewery in the coming year.

Like the Springfield Brew House, the Wilkins Township Brew House is boldly staking out nontraditional brewpub space. It is tucked into a shopping center and seems to be doing well there. This Brew House seems more open than the other two, thanks to a glass front wall that came with the storefront space. In a rainy area like this, it is probably a good idea to get as much light as you can when it's out there.

The head brewer here is Andrew Maxwell, who spent some time as Brian McConnell's assistant in Springfield and is now solidly on his own here in Monroeville. What kind of brewer is he? Well, he had to move to a bigger apartment one time because

Beers brewed: The following beers or types of beer are on at all times: John Harvard's Pale Ale, Brown Ale, Duquesne Light, some sort of fruit or wheat beer, varying golden or amber hoppy beers, a varying porter or stout. Seasonals: Mid-Winter Strong Ale, Presidential Ale, Celtic Strong Ale, Big Bad Bock, Bohemian Pilsner, Harvard Hefe-Weizen, Summer Blonde Ale, Queen Bee Honey Lager, Oktoberfest, Pumpkin Spice Ale, Christmas Ale, plus a certain number of "brewer's choice" beers.

of the size of his homebrewing system, so let's just say "dedicated and passionate."

"I brew what people tell me to brew," Maxwell stated as his brewmaster philosophy. "I've got these customers to the point where they know what 'balanced' means, and John Harvard's lets you brew to what those locals' tastes are." The way to get those beers to the right people, of course, is through the service staff, and Maxwell's real big on staff training—something I'm seeing more and more of these days.

If you're headed into Pittsburgh from points east, the Wilkins Township Brew House is a good place to break your beer fast. Monroeville residents must appreciate being able to get fresh, real beer without a trip down to Pittsburgh.

The Pick: Those "brewer's choice" beers sure were int esting! Andrew hit me with Scotch Ale, a pale amber 1(percent deceiver that's age(four months till it's smooth glass and dangerously easy drink. The deep malt charac ter almost drowns the additi of heather, but it's there, flo ing beautifully.

Opened: August 1997.

Owner: Boston Culinary Group.

Brewers: Head brewer, Andrew Maxwell; Sean Hallisey.

System: 15-barrel Pub Brewing System brewhouse, 2,500 barrels annual capacity.

Production: 780 barrels in 2004 (estimated).

Brewpub hours: Monday through Thursday, 11:30 A.M. to midnight; Friday and Saturday, 11:30 A.M. to 1 A.M.; Sunday, 11:30 A.M. to 10:30 P.M.

Tours: Upon request.

Take-out beer: Growlers.

Food: Upscale pub fare, including fish and chips, chicken pot pie, grilled meatloaf, calamari.

Extras: Full liquor license.

Special considerations: Kids welcome. Handicapped-accessible. Vegetarian meals available.

Parking: Off-street lot.

Lodging in the area: Days Inn Monroeville, 2727 Mosside Boulevard, 412-856-1610; Radisson Hotel Pittsburgh, by the Monroeville Mall, 101 Mall Boulevard, Monroeville, 412-373-7300; Harley Hotel, 699 Rodi Road, Monroeville, 412-244-1600.

Area attractions: You'll see the *Sri Venkateswara Temple* (South McCully Road, Monroeville) as you drive along the Penn Lincoln Parkway, and you might as well take a closer look. This gleaming white structure is one of ten Hindu temples in the United States.

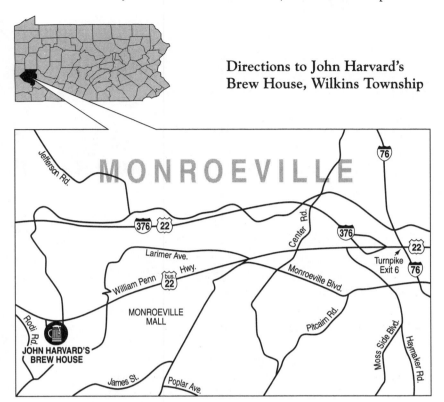

Directions to John Harvard's Brew House, Wilkins Township

See the introduction to this section for other Pittsburgh attractions (pages 222–24).

Other area beer sites: Monroeville has its *own* beer bar now: **Carl's Tavern,** just down the road (3386 William Penn Highway, 412-823-4050), sports a big range of good taps at very reasonable prices and solid food (there's a dining room, too), all in a neatly kept bar that's clean and squared away, but not prissy. One warning: The T-shirts say, "More taps than parking spaces," and they're not kidding! Also, see the introduction to this section (pages 224–27).

Red Star Brewery and Grill

Greensburg Train Station, Ehalt Street,
Greensburg, PA 15601
724-850-7245
www.redstarbrewery.com

We may have lost Hoppers' Erie train station location a few years back, but Pennsylvania gained Red Star Brewery and Grill, situated in a beautiful and operational train station in Greensburg. Red Star opened in October 1998 after two years of restoration at the site. "It was a dump," former brewer Mike Escourt told me. The Westmoreland Trust, a county group dedicated to the preservation of historic landmarks, bought the station and restored it. It is Red Star's landlord.

This is still an operating train station, though. I went all the way up through the station, past the ticket counters and up to the tracks for a look around. You can see into the back of the brewpub from there, under the surprisingly decorative roof of the building.

The brewpub is pretty decorative itself and has chosen a retro look for its printed materials and displays to blend in with the interior architecture of original wooden arches and wood-paneled ceilings. You enter Red Star past a "usable garden" of herbs, peppers, and hops that really are used by both the chef and the brewer. A glass foyer is flanked by fermenters. The brewhouse itself is the centerpiece of the main room. It is impossible to miss, sitting right behind the bar in all its copper-clad glory with no intervening shields of any kind. When you sit at the bar, you're close enough to hear the brewer whistle. There's no doubt: This is a brewery pub.

Jeff Guidos took over the brewing duties a few years ago and made quite a splash with his Voodoo Child Munich Dunkel. Not easy to do when Bryan Pearson has set the local lager bar so high with the success of his Pious Monk Dunkel, but it's hard to argue with the GABF Gold medal Jeff got for Voodoo Child. He's got a knack for lagers, as he

Beers brewed: Year-round: Red Star Golden Light, Canvasback Pale Ale, Swag & Tails Brown Ale, Iron Horse Stout (GABF Silver, 1999). Seasonals: twelve to fifteen per year, often lagers, including Voodoo's Child Munich Dunkel (GABF Gold, 2002), Kat Sass Export, AP-1 Dunke weizen, Altbier, Black Gold Oatmeal Stout, 3 Sheets IPA, Barleywine.

proved to me with a glass of The Kat Sass Export (go ahead, take a second and smile at the name). It was nicely done, maltier than a pils, hoppier than a helles, walking right down the middle: well slotted and good stuff.

The Pick: Jeff had the Black Gold Oatmeal Stout on when I stopped in, and it was solid, smooth, assertive, and just a bit rich; right down the alley on this one.

We were running the taps, as I always like to do at a brewpub, when Jeff suddenly got up and promised to be right back. He was gone for a good five minutes, and my dad got nervous, but then he came walking back with a big smile and a brandy snifter full of dark liquid capped by dark tan foam. "It's a three-year-old barleywine," he said reverently. It was quite impressive, fruity and intense, a 10.5 percent ABV beer worthy of a great deal of respect.

Come hungry—the food's almost as intense as the beer. From down-home western Pennsylvania belly stuffers like the kielbasa and kraut sub to the bolder character of the fire-roasted lamb chops, Red Star's got a dish with your name on it, food that will love being matched with these ales and lagers.

I must admit that I never really had occasion to visit Greensburg before. Thanks to Red Star, I'll be sure to stop in whenever my beer-loving wanderings take me west . . . maybe coming in on the twin steel rails.

Opened: October 1998.

Owners: Al Spinelli, Ernie Vallozzi.

Brewer: Jeff Guidos.

System: 7-barrel JV NorthWest brewhouse, 1,100 barrels annual capacity.

Production: 420 barrels in 2004 (estimated).

Brewpub hours: Monday through Thursday, 11:30 A.M. to midnight; Friday 11:30 A.M. to 2 A.M.; Saturday noon to 2 A.M.; closed Sunday.

Tours: By appointment only, but the brewhouse is right at the bar; how much tour do you want, anyway?

Take-out beer: Growlers.

Food: Red Star's menu has a European influence, but is generally a hearty American table. You won't leave hungry.

Extras: Full liquor license. Techno DJs every Saturday night; call for schedule. Fall Beer Festival; call for details.

Special considerations: Kids welcome. Handicapped-accessible. Vegetarian meals available. Cigars allowed in the bar area.

Parking: Copious free on-site parking.

Lodging in the area: Mountain View Inn, a restored 1920s hotel at 1001 Village Drive, 724-834-5300; Comfort Inn Greensburg, 1129

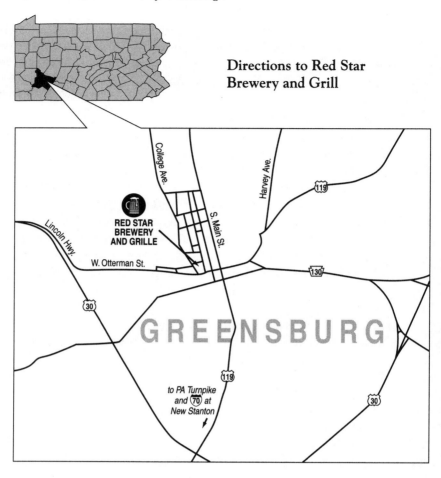

**Directions to Red Star
Brewery and Grill**

East Pittsburgh Road, 724-832-2600; Knights Inn, 1215 Main Street, 724-836-7100.

Area attractions: The *Westmoreland Museum of Art* (221 North Main Street, 724-837-1500) has a surprisingly broad collection, featuring works from John Singer Sargent, Winslow Homer, and the Hudson River School artists, and also a huge toy collection that includes more than 250 Barbies. There is a toy train display over Christmas. *Historic Hanna's Town* (3 miles north of town, just off Route 119, 724-836-1800) is a re-creation of an early trans-Appalachian settlement, featuring an original Conestoga wagon and the reconstruction of Robert Hanna's home/tavern/courthouse. There's a bunch of golf courses around: *Mount Odin Park Municipal,* just west of town; *Valley Green Golf and Country Club,* just south of town; and

Statler's Par 3 course, just east of town. There's fly fishing for trout on the Loyalhanna Creek, and bass and walleye fishing on Loyalhanna Lake. ***Idlewild Amusement Park*** (in nearby Ligonier, 724-238-3666) has rides, miniature golf, water rides, and Mister Rogers' Neighborhood; shake hands with King Friday XIII. Call or visit the website of the Laurel Highlands Visitors Bureau (800-925-7669, www.laurelhighlands.org) for more suggestions.

Other area beer sites: See Latrobe listing on page 8.

BEERWEBS

The Web has become a great place to share beer and bar information. But as with anything else on the Web, you have to use a little wisdom. Websites can be out of date, intensely subjective, poorly edited, and just plain wrong. Let the reader beware.

Here are the websites I use to find beers, bars, and beer geeks from Virginia to New York, and across the country. If I have any reservations about them, I've stated them.

www.lewbryson.com My own website includes frequent online updates to this and my other books, *New York Breweries* and *Virginia, Maryland, and Delaware Breweries*; notes on what I've been drinking; travel notes on my research trips; links to some of my other writing; and "The Buzz," my monthly editorial on what's driving me crazy in the drinks business. I also do an e-mail newsletter, "The Occasional Pint," that has beer news, site news, tips on book updates, and whatever else put a head on my beer that month; you can sign up at the site.

www.Pubcrawler.com Pubcrawler is simply the best brewery and bar locator website in the world. No other site has its combination of completeness, search tools, longevity, and objectivity. You can search more than five thousand North American breweries, brewpubs, and bars by name, city, state, zip code, or area code, and every entry has a map link for directions. You can also sign up for weekly mailings of new reviews in states that interest you. The entries have phone numbers, addresses, links, logos, and, most important, years of patron reviews. You can leave your own as well; you'll find quite a few of mine. My only reservations here are that some of the reviewers are obviously biased. I do my best to keep the website up-to-date in New York, Pennsylvania, Virginia, Delaware, D.C., and Maryland.

www.jackcurtin.com and **www.beeryard.com** Both are written by my colleague and friend Jack Curtin and filled with his trademark blend of humor, rumor, liberal politics, curmudgeonly griping, and well-informed news about the beer scene in Philadelphia and most of eastern Pennsylvania. I check both of these several times a week.

www.BeerAdvocate.com BeerAdvocate is mostly about rating beers and talking about rating beers, which mostly doesn't interest me at all . . . but it is also an online community of people who really care about the beer they drink *and the beer you drink*. So the BeerAdvocate forums are a great place to get inside scoops on what's going on in breweries and bars. Its online directory, BeerFly, has a wide range of listings for breweries, bars, and beer stores. Useful site.

THE BONEYARD

The following breweries that were in the second edition of *Pennsylvania Breweries* are no longer open. They are, for the most part, sadly missed, but some parts of them soldier on in other breweries.

brew moon. Became Rock Bottom, King of Prussia, when Rock Bottom bought out the brew moon chain. Different beer (same brewer!), decor, and food (which is still quite good); same location.

Brick House. Stories abound on why Brick House suddenly closed. The only person who really knows, Joe Grigoli, left for Italy, so it's best to leave it at that.

Buckingham Mountain Brewing Company. Closed after a long downward spiral, largely unmourned. Now houses the completely different Porterhouse.

Dock Street Brewpub. An ignominious end for a grand place. Dock Street was sold to people who styled it as the Dock Street Brewpub and Mermaid Supper Club and tried to make it a brewpub by day, dance club by night. They ran it into the ground in three months.

Foundry Ale House. Closed because of a loss of traffic during the Convention Center construction and uninterested ownership. Some tanks went to Selin's Grove.

Gettysburg Brewing Company. It was sad to see Dave Baker close up shop, a quirky, devoted man who probably kept this place open longer than was wise to do so. Beloved of the geekerie but unable to form a steady clientele.

Independence Brewing Company. A sad, bizarre story of wasted money and wasted opportunities. Independence declined into a whimpering finish despite Bill Moore's heroic efforts.

Jack's Mountain. Still open but had not been brewing for some months as I finished writing. Check my website (www.lewbryson.com) for recent news.

Jones Brewing Company. Hard-headed fighting between management and labor finally did what the competition never could: Jones closed in 2002 after more than a century of keeping southwestern Pennsylvania well watered.

Lancaster Malt Brewing Company. Reorganized and renamed Lancaster Brewing Company, the brewery never missed a day of business.

Mount Nittany Brewing Company. Fell off the radar without a trace. No one I've talked to is sure what happened to Mark Bloom and his dog, Jed.

Mystic Brew Pub. A terribly sad loss. Terry Fies was game right up to the end, and his porter remained excellent, but there was just never enough steady trade to keep Mystic afloat.

Neversink Brewing. Neversink closed (largely under the weight of a recalcitrant bottling line), then reopened with a new brewer and closed again, reopened as Fancy Pants Brewing and closed again . . . and is now being run by Scott Baver and Dave Gemmell—themselves former owners of another closed Reading brewery, Pretzel City—as Legacy Brewing.

New Road Brewhouse. Crashed and burned as a result of absolutely horrible management. Brewer Brian O'Reilly escaped to Sly Fox with his reputation intact.

Old Lehigh Brewing Company. Couldn't make it work as a part-time brewery in the back of a plumbing supply house.

Pabst Brewing Company. Not in the second edition, and since Pabst has sold this beautiful brewery—its last—to Diageo, which is using it to make Smirnoff Ice . . . it's not in this one, either.

Poor Henry's. Henry Ortlieb's shot at reviving his family's brewing heritage foundered, rather spectacularly, right around the same time Red Bell's big brewery crashed and Independence went down. Tough time for Philadelphia microbrewing.

Primo Barone's. Eve Martino quit brewing, and Primo couldn't find a new brewer. The restaurant is still open, but the brewery sits cold and empty.

Red Bell Brewing Company. Red Bell could be said to have sued themselves to death—much of the company's money and energy were expended on fruitless lawsuits, but they were also dissipated in projects that never worked out, like a "planned" State College brewpub and the Center City brewpub that would eventually become the Independence brewpub. The big brewery was closed and the equipment sold off. Red Bell hangs on as a small seasonal brewpub in the Wachovia Center and a contract-brewed brand.

Sunnybrook Beverage. Closed, then reopened as Ortlieb's Brewery at Sunnybrook, Henry Ortlieb's next project after Poor Henry's closed. Henry tried hard to make the grand old place work, with the yeoman help of brewer Bill Moore, but the brewery closed soon after Henry died in a tragic boating accident on July 4, 2004.

Valhalla. Uninterested owners and Convention Center construction killed Valhalla.

Valley Forge Brewing Company, Blue Bell. Continuing construction on Route 202 and contractor problems tolled the bell for Blue Bell.

W. T. Hackett Brewpub. Bad management pulled the rug out from under Hackett's. The brewery remained an eerie time capsule; you could look in the locked front door and still see the place just as it was the day it closed, down to the cheery blackboard with the day's specials.

Whitetail Brewing Company. Wade Keech was spread too thin and finally gave up on Whitetail. It has been reborn as Market Cross.

GLOSSARY

ABV/ABW. Alcohol by volume/alcohol by weight. These are two slightly different ways of measuring the alcohol content of beverages, as a percentage of either the beverage's total volume or its weight. For example, if you have 1 liter of 4 percent ABV beer, 4 percent of that liter (40 milliliters) is alcohol. However, because alcohol weighs only 79.6 percent as much as water, that same beer is only 3.18 percent ABW. This may seem like a dry exercise in mathematics, but it is at the heart of the common misconception that Canadian beer is stronger than American beer. Canadian brewers generally use ABV figures, whereas American brewers have historically used the lower ABW figures. Mainstream Canadian and American lagers are approximately equal in strength. Just to confuse the issue further, most American microbreweries use ABV figures. This is very important if you're trying to keep a handle on how much alcohol you're consuming. If you know how much Bud (at roughly 5 percent ABV) you can safely consume, you can extrapolate from there. Learn your limits . . . before you hit them.

Adjunct. Any nonbarley malt source of sugars for fermentation. This can be candy sugar, corn grits, corn or rice syrups, or one of any number of specialty grains. Wheat, rye, and candy sugars are considered by beer geeks to be "politically correct" adjuncts; corn and rice are generally taken as signs of swill. Small amounts of corn and rice, however, used as brewing ingredients for certain styles of beer, are slowly gaining acceptance in craft-brewing circles. Try to keep an open mind.

Ale. The generic term for warm-fermented beers. (See "A word about . . . Ales and Lagers" on page 21.)

Alefruit. My own invention, so far as I know. I use this term to signify the juicy esters produced by some yeasts, aromas and flavors of a variety of fruits: pear, melon, plum, peach, lemon drop, pineapple. I use "alefruit" when I can't tease out the exact fruits (or when I can but don't want to sound pretentious).

Anheuser-Busch. Anheuser-Busch (A-B) is the world's largest brewer, with approximately half of the U.S. market and 8 percent of the world's market. Its flagship beer, Budweiser, is the world's best-selling beer, and Bud Light is the biggest seller in the United States. Because of this, A-B is often the whipping boy of the microbrewers, but A-B has taken its share of shots at the micros as well. No one disputes the quality control and consistency of brewers like A-B. I've met Augie Busch; he is sharp, devoted to his company and its beers, and driven to improve the company's standing. A-B has more than a hundred highly trained and qualified brewmasters who are fanatical about quality in ingredients and process.

ATTTB. The federal Alcohol and Tobacco Tax and Trade Bureau, formerly part of the ATF, a branch of the Treasury Department. The ATTTB is the federal regulatory arm for the brewing industry. It has to inspect every brewery before it opens, approve every label before it is used, and approve all packaging. The ATTTB is also the body responsible for the fact that while every food, even bottled water, *must* have a nutritional information label, beer (and wine and cider and spirits) is *not allowed* to have one, even though it is a significant source of calories, carbohydrates, and in the case of unfiltered beers, B vitamins and protein. The problem is that sometimes every ATTTB agent and bureaucrat seems to have a different interpretation of the regulations, and sometimes they have a very negative attitude toward the beverages they're regulating. As a brewer once told me, "I'd enjoy this a lot more if [ATTTB] didn't make me feel like I was dealing in controlled substances."

Barley. A wonderfully apt grain for brewing beer. Barley grows well in relatively marginal soils and climates. It has no significant gluten content, which makes it unsuitable for baking bread and thereby limits market competition for brewers buying the grain. Its husk serves as a very efficient filter at the end of the mashing process. And it makes beer that tastes really, really good. Barley comes in two types: two-row and six-row, referring to the rows of kernels on the heads of the grain. In days past, two-row barley was plumper and considered finer. Six-row barley was easier to grow, had a better yield per acre and higher enzymatic power, but had a somewhat astringent character. These differences have been lessened by crossbreeding. Most barley grown in North America is six-row, for reasons of soil and climate. (Incidentally, the grain's kernels, or corns, are the source of the name "John Barleycorn," a traditional personification of barley or beer.)

Barrel. A traditional measure of beer volume equal to 31 U.S. gallons. The most common containers of draft beer in the United States are half and quarter barrels, or kegs, at 15.5 gallons and 7.75 gallons, respectively, though the one-sixth-barrel kegs (about 5.2 gallons), known as sixtels, are becoming popular with microbrewers. See also *hectoliter*.

Beer. A fermented beverage brewed from grain, generally malted barley. "Beer" covers a variety of beverages, including ales and lagers, stouts and bocks, porters and pilsners, lambics and altbiers, cream ale, Kölsch, wheat beer, and a whole lot more.

Beer geek. A person who takes beer a little more seriously than does the average person. I've been chided for using the term "geek" here, but I haven't found another one I like, so my apologies to those who object. I call myself a beer geek, if that's any consolation. Often homebrewers, beer geeks love to argue with other beer geeks about what makes exceptional beers exceptional. That is, if they've been able to agree on which beers are exceptional in the first place. A beer geek is the kind of person who would buy a book about traveling to breweries . . . the kind of person who would read the glossary of a beer book. Hey, hi there!

Bottle-conditioned. A beer that has been bottled with an added dose of live yeast. This living yeast causes the beer to mature and change as it ages over periods of one to thirty years or more. It will also "eat" any oxygen that may have been sealed in at bottling and keep the beer from oxidizing, a staling process that leads to sherryish and "wet cardboard" aromas in beer. Bottle-conditioned beer qualifies as "real ale."

Brewer. One who brews beer for commercial sale.

Breweriana. Brewery and beer memorabilia, such as trays, coasters, neon signs, steins, mirrors, and so on, including the objects of desire of the beer can and bottle collectors. Most collectors do this for fun, a few do it for money (breweriana is starting to command some big prices; just check eBay), but the weird thing about this for me is the number of breweriana collectors—about a third, from my experience—who don't drink beer.

Brewhouse. The vessels used to mash the malt and grains and boil the wort. The malt and grains are mashed in a vessel called a *mash tun*. Brewhouse size is generally given in terms of the capacity of the brewkettle, where the wort is boiled. A brewery's annual capacity is a function of brewhouse size, fermentation and aging tank capacity, and the length of the aging cycle for the brewery's beers.

Brewpub. A brewery that sells the majority of its output on draft, on the premises, or a tavern that brews its own beer. Initially, Pennsylvania law forbade brewpubs to sell anything but their own beer, brewed on-premises. That law has been changed, and now brewpubs *may* obtain a tavern license and serve a full range of alcoholic beverages; not all have done so, and continue to serve only their own beer, though the brewpub license has been expanded to also allow sales of Pennsylvania wines, a nice touch. Anyone ever seen a Pennsylvania winery selling Pennsylvania beers? Just wondering.

CAMRA. The CAMpaign for Real Ale. A British beer drinkers' consumer group formed in the early 1970s by beer drinkers irate over the disappearance of cask-conditioned ale. They have been very vocal and successful in bringing this traditional drink back to a place of importance in the United Kingdom. CAMRA sets high standards for cask-conditioned ale, which only a few brewers in the United States match.

Carbonation. The fizzy effects of carbon dioxide (CO_2) in solution in a liquid such as beer. Carbonation can be accomplished artificially by injecting the beer with the gas or naturally by trapping the CO_2, which is a by-product of fermentation. There is no intrinsic qualitative difference between beers carbonated by these two methods. Brewer's choice, essentially. Low carbonation will allow a broader array of flavors to come through, whereas carbonation can result in a perceived bitterness. Most American drinkers prefer a higher carbonation.

Case law. In Pennsylvania, it is illegal to buy less than a case of beer at a beer store (or, as we call them here, "distributor"). It is also illegal to buy *more* than two six-packs of beer at a time from a bar, though you can buy two, walk out the door, and come back to buy two more. This is very confusing to out-of-staters, and it would be to us as well, if we ever stopped to think about it. Why do we have this law? The wholesalers and the beer stores did it to themselves seventy years ago. They evidently thought it would be great to sell a case at a time without having to break them open and display them. Now they can't get the law changed because the tavern owners jealously defend their six-pack sales rights, and because the antialcohol forces somehow think that the case law keeps people from drinking. Scary, isn't it? Do us all a favor: Write your state legislator and ask them to repeal the case law!

Cask. A keg designed to serve cask-conditioned ale by gravity feed or by handpump, not by gas pressure. These casks may be made of wood, but most are steel with special plumbing.

Cask-conditioned beer. An unfiltered beer that is put in a cask before it is completely ready to serve. The yeast still in the beer continues to work and ideally brings the beer to perfection at the point of sale, resulting in a beautifully fresh beer that has a "soft" natural carbonation and beautiful array of aromas. The flip side to achieving this supreme freshness is that as the beer is poured, air replaces the beer in the cask, and the beer will become sour within five days. Bars should sell out the cask before then or remove it from sale. If you are served sour cask-conditioned beer, send it back. Better yet, ask politely for a taste before ordering. Cask-conditioned beer is generally served at cellar temperature (55 to 60 degrees F) and is lightly carbonated. Cask-conditioned beers are almost always ales, but some American brewers are experimenting with cask-conditioned lager beers.

Cold-filtering. The practice of passing finished beer through progressively finer filters (usually cellulose or ceramic) to strip out microorganisms that can spoil the beer when it is stored. Brewers like Coors and Miller, and also some smaller brewers, use cold-filtering as an alternative to pasteurization (see below). Some beer geeks complain that this "strip-filtering" robs beers of their more subtle complexities and some of their body. I'm not sure about that, but I do know that unfiltered beer right from the brewery tank almost always tastes more intense than the filtered, packaged beer.

Contract brewer. A brewer who hires an existing brewery to brew beer on contract. Contract brewers range from those who simply have a different label put on one of the brewery's existing brands to those who maintain a separate on-site staff to actually brew the beer at the brewery. Some brewers and beer geeks feel contract-brewed beer is inherently inferior. This is strictly a moral and business issue; some of the best beers on the market are contract-brewed.

Craft brewer. The new term for *microbrewer.* Craft brewer, like microbrewer before it, is really a code word for any brewer producing beers other than mainstream American lagers like Budweiser and Miller Lite. (See "A word about . . . Micros, Brewpubs, and Craft Brewers" on page 48.)

Decoction. The type of mashing often used by lager brewers to wring the full character from the malt. In a decoction mash, a portion of the hot mash is taken to another vessel, brought to boiling, and returned to the mash, thus raising the temperature. See also *infusion.*

Draft. Beer dispensed from a tap, whether from a keg or cask. Draft beer is not pasteurized, is kept under optimum conditions throughout the wholesaler-retailer chain, and is shockingly cheaper than bottled or canned beer (each half-barrel keg is over seven cases of beer; check some prices and do the math). Kegs are available in 5-, 7.75-, and 15.5-gallon sizes, and almost all are now the straight-sided kegs with handles. Pennsylvania doesn't have an ineffective and intrusive keg registration law (yet). Kegs are also ultimately recyclable, with a lifespan of forty *years*. Do what I do: Get draft beer for your next party.

Dry-hopping. Adding hops to the beer in postfermentation stages, often in porous bags to allow easy removal. This results in a greater hop aroma in the finished beer. A few brewers put a small bag of hop cones in each cask of their cask-conditioned beers, resulting in a particularly intense hop aroma in a glass of the draft beer.

ESB. Extra Special Bitter, an ale style with a rich malt character and full body, perhaps some butter or butterscotch aromas, and an understated hop bitterness. An ESB is noticeably bitter only in comparison to a mild ale, a style not often found in America.

Esters. Aroma compounds produced by fermentation that gives some ales lightly fruity aromas: banana, pear, and grapefruit, among others. The aromas produced are tightly linked to the yeast strain used. Ester-based aromas should not be confused with the less subtle fruit aromas of a beer to which fruit or fruit essences have been added.

Extract. More specifically, malt extract. Malt extract is kind of like concentrated wort (see below). Malt is mashed, and the resulting sweet, unhopped wort is reduced to a syrup. This is important to know because some breweries brew with malt extract. In extract brewing, the extract is mixed with water and boiled. Specialty grains (such as black patent or chocolate malt, wheat, or roasted barley) can be added for flavor notes and nuances. It is actually more expensive to brew with extract, but you need less equipment, which can be crucial in cramped brewing areas. But the quality of the beer may suffer. Some people claim to be able to pick out extract brews. I've had extract brews that had a common taste—a kind of thin, vegetal sharpness—but I've also had excellent extract brews at various breweries. My advice is to try it yourself.

Fermentation. The miracle of yeast; the heart of making beer. Fermentation is the process in which yeast turns sugar and water into alcohol, heat, carbon dioxide, esters, and traces of other compounds.

Final gravity. See *gravity*.

Firkin. A cask or keg holding 9 gallons of beer, specially plumbed for gravity or handpump dispense.

Geekerie. The collective of beer geeks, particularly the beer-oriented, beer-fascinated, beer-above-all geeks. The geekerie sometimes can fall victim to group thinking and a herd mentality, but they are generally good people, if a bit hopheaded and malt-maniacal. If you're not a member of the geekerie, you might want to consider getting to know them: They usually know where all the best bars and beer stores are in their town, and they're more than happy to share the knowledge and even go along with you to share the fun. All you have to do is ask. See the Beerwebs section for links to the better beer pages, a good way to hook up with them.

Gravity. The specific gravity of wort (original gravity) or finished beer (terminal gravity). The ratio of dissolved sugars to water determines the gravity of the wort. If there are more dissolved sugars, the original gravity and the potential alcohol are higher. The sugar that is converted to alcohol by the yeast lowers the terminal gravity and makes the beer drier, just like wine. A brewer can determine the alcohol content of a beer by mathematical comparison of its original gravity and terminal gravity.

Great American Beer Festival (GABF). Since 1982, America's breweries have been invited each year to bring their best beer to the GABF in Denver to showcase what America can brew. Since 1987, the GABF has awarded medals for various styles of beer; sixty-seven styles were judged in 2004, three medals for each style. To ensure impartiality, the beers are tasted blind, their identities hidden from the judges. GABF medals are the most prestigious awards in American brewing because of the festival's longevity and reputation for fairness.

Growler. A jug or bottle used to take home draft beer. These are usually either simple half-gallon glass jugs with screwtops or more elaborate molded glass containers with swingtop seals. I have traced the origin of the term *growler* back to a cheap, four-wheeled horse cab in use in Victorian London. These cabs would travel a circuit of pubs in the evenings, and riding from pub to pub was known as "working the growler." To bring a pail of beer home to have with dinner was to anticipate the night's work of drinking and became known as "rushing the growler." When the growler cabs disappeared from the scene, we were left with only the phrase, and "rushing the growler" was assumed to mean hurrying home with the bucket. When Ed Otto revived the practice by selling jugs of Otto Brothers beer at his Jackson Hole brewery in the mid-1980s, he called them growlers. Now you know where the term really came from.

Guest taps/guest beers. Beers made by other brewers that are offered at brewpubs.

Handpump. A hand-powered pump for dispensing beer from a keg, also called a *beer engine*. Either a handpump or a gravity tap (putting the barrel on the bar and pounding in a simple spigot) is always used for dispensing cask-conditioned beer; however, the presence of a handpump does not guarantee that the beer being dispensed is cask-conditioned.

Hectoliter. A hectoliter (hcl) is 100 liters, a metric measure of volume used by some brewers with European- or Canadian-manufactured brewing systems. One hectoliter is approximately 0.85 barrels; 27 hectoliters is just about 23 barrels. There are also "half-hec" kegs that hold 50 liters, or about 13.3 gallons, compared with the 15.5 gallons in a half keg. See also *barrel*.

Homebrewing. Making honest-to-goodness beer at home for personal consumption. Homebrewing is where many American craft brewers got their start.

Hops. The spice of beer. Hop plants (*Humulus lupus*) are vines whose flowers have a remarkable effect on beer. The flowers' resins and oils add bitterness and a variety of aromas (spicy, piney, citrus, and others) to the finished beer. Beer without hops would be more like a fizzy, sweet, "alco-soda."

IBU. International Bittering Unit, a measure of a beer's bitterness. Humans can first perceive bitterness at levels between 8 and 12 IBU. Budweiser has 11.5 IBU, Heineken 18, Sierra Nevada Pale Ale 32, Pilsner Urquell 43, and a monster like Sierra Nevada Bigfoot clocks in at 98 IBU. Equivalent amounts of bitterness will seem greater in a lighter-bodied beer, whereas a heavier, maltier beer like Bigfoot needs lots of bitterness to be perceived as balanced.

Imperial. A beer style intensifier, indicating a beer that is hoppier and stronger. Once there was an Imperial court in St. Petersburg, Russia, the court of the czars. It supported a trade with England in strong, heavy, black beers, massive versions of the popular English porters, which became known as Imperial porters and somewhat later as Imperial stouts. Then in the late 1990s, American brewers started brewing IPAs with even more hops than the ridiculous amounts they were already using, at a gravity that led to beers of 7.5 percent ABV and up. What to call them? They looked at the Imperial stouts and grabbed the apparent intensifier: "Imperial" IPA was born. While this is still the most common usage, this shorthand for "hoppier and stronger" has been applied to pilsner and, amusingly, porter. Where it will stop, no one knows, as brewers joke about brewing "Imperial mild" and "Imperial helles."

Infusion. The mashing method generally used by ale brewers. Infusion entails heating the mash in a single vessel until the starches have been converted to sugar. There is single infusion, in which the crushed malt (grist) is mixed with hot water and steeped without further heating, and step infusion, in which the mash is held for short periods at rising temperature points. Infusion mashing is simpler than decoction mashing and works well with most types of modern malt.

IPA. India Pale Ale, a British ale style that has been almost completely co-opted by American brewers, characterized in this country by intense hops bitterness, accompanied in better examples of the style by a full-malt body. The name derives from the style's origin as a beer brewed for export to British beer drinkers in India. The beer was strong and heavily laced with hops—a natural preservative—to better endure the long sea voyage. Some British brewers claim that the beer was brewed that way in order to be diluted upon arrival in India, a kind of "beer concentrate" that saved on shipping costs.

Kräusening. The practice of carbonating beer by a second fermentation. After the main fermentation has taken place and its vigorous blowoff of carbon dioxide has been allowed to escape, a small amount of fresh wort is added to the tank. A second fermentation takes place, and the carbon dioxide is captured in solution. General opinion is that there is little sensory difference between kräusened beer and beer carbonated by injection, but some brewers use this more traditional method.

Lager. The generic term for all cold-fermented beers. Lager has also been appropriated as a name for the lightly hopped pilsners that have become the world's most popular beers, such as Budweiser, Ki-Rin, Brahma, Heineken, and Foster's. Many people speak of pilsners and lagers as if they are two different styles of beer, which is incorrect. All pilsners are lagers, but not all lagers are pilsners. Some are bocks, hellesbiers, and Märzens.

Lambic. A very odd style of beer brewed in Belgium that could take pages to explain. Suffice it to say that the beer is fermented spontaneously by airborne wild yeasts and bacteria that are resident in the aged wooden fermenting casks. The beer's sensory characteristics have been described as funky, barnyard, and horseblanket . . . it's an acquired taste. But once you have that taste, lambics can be extremely rewarding. Most knowledgeable people believe that the beers can be brewed only in a small area of Belgium, because of the peculiarities of the wild yeasts. But some American brewers, Lancaster Brewing, Iron Hill, and Bethlehem Brew Works among them, have had a degree of success in replicating this character by carefully using prepared cultures of yeasts and bacteria.

Malt. Generally this refers to malted barley, although other grains can be malted and used in brewing. Barley is wetted and allowed to sprout, which causes the hard, stable starches in the grain to convert to soluble starches (and small amounts of sugars). The grains, now called malt, are kiln-dried to kill the sprouts and conserve the starches. Malt is responsible for the color of beer. The kilned malt can be roasted, which will darken its color and intensify its flavors like a French roast coffee.

Mash. A mixture of cracked grains of malt and water, which is then heated. Heating causes starches in the malt to convert to sugars, which will be consumed by the yeast in fermentation. The length of time the mash is heated, temperatures, and techniques used are crucial to the character of the finished beer. Two mashing techniques are infusion and decoction.

Megabrewer. A mainstream brewer, generally producing 5 million or more barrels of American-style pilsner beer annually. Anheuser-Busch, Miller, and Coors are the best-known megabrewers.

Microbrewer. A somewhat dated term, originally defined as a brewer producing less than 15,000 barrels of beer in a year. Microbrewer, like craft brewer, is generally applied to any brewer producing beers other than mainstream American lagers. (See "A word about . . . Micros, Brewpubs, and Craft Brewers" on page 48.)

Original gravity. See *gravity*.

Pasteurization. A process named for its inventor, Louis Pasteur, the famed French microbiologist. Pasteurization involves heating beer to kill the microorganisms in it. This keeps beer fresh longer, but unfortunately it also changes the flavor, because the beer is essentially cooked. "Flash pasteurization" sends fresh beer through a heated pipe where most of the microorganisms are killed; here the beer is only hot for twenty seconds or so, as opposed to the twenty to thirty minutes of regular "tunnel" pasteurization. See also *cold-filtering*.

Pennsylvania Liquor Control Board (PLCB). The PLCB enforces the Pennsylvania Liquor Code, including the infamous "case law" for beer sales, and also sells all the wine and liquor in the state. Pennsylvania is a "control state," meaning that the state occupies the place in the market that is normally taken by privately owned liquor stores. The PLCB is not always popular with consumers and retailers, but it is sometimes the only agency regulating the sanitary standards of your local taps . . . not that its agents bother to do that when there are underage-drinking sting operations to run. The PLCB is an agency seriously flawed by divergent missions: make money for the state by selling booze and simultaneously curb consumption of alcohol.

Pilsner. The Beer That Conquered The World. Developed in 1842 in Pilsen (now Plzen, in the Czech Republic), it is a hoppy pale lager that quickly became known as *pilsner* or *pilsener*, a German word meaning simply "from Pilsen." Pilsner rapidly became the most popular beer in the world and now accounts for more than 80 percent of all beer consumed worldwide. A less hoppy, more delicate version of pilsner called budweiser was developed in the Czech town of Budejovice, formerly known as Budweis. Anheuser-Busch's Budweiser, the world's best-selling beer, is quite a different animal.

Pitching. The technical term for adding yeast to wort.

Prohibition. The period from 1920 to 1933 when the sale, manufacture, or transportation of alcoholic beverages was illegal in the United States, thanks to the Eighteenth Amendment and the Volstead Act. (Pennsylvania just barely approved the measure, I'm proud to say.) Prohibition had a disastrous effect on American brewing and brought about a huge growth in organized crime and government corruption. Repeal of Prohibition came with ratification of the Twenty-first Amendment in December 1933. Beer drinkers, however, had gotten an eight-month head start when the Volstead Act, the enforcement legislation of Prohibition, was amended to allow sales of 3.2 percent ABW beer. The amendment took effect at midnight, April 7. According to Will Anderson's *From Beer to Eternity*, more than 1 million barrels of beer were consumed on April 7: 2,323,000 six-packs each hour. Pity poor Pennsylvania: We're still waiting for the full fruits of Repeal. Ask your state legislator why you can't buy beer by the six-pack from distributors. Ask today!

Real ale. See *cask-conditioned beer*.

Real Ale Festival (RAF). An annual Chicago beer festival that celebrates real ale. Medals are awarded to the best bottle- and cask-conditioned beers in a variety of styles. The medals from the RAF are quite prestigious and are of particular significance to brewers.

Regional brewery. Somewhere between a micro- and a megabrewer. Annual production by regional breweries ranges from 35,000 to 2 million barrels. They generally brew mainstream American lagers. However, some microbrewers—Boston Beer Company, Pete's, and Sierra Nevada, for instance—have climbed to this production level, and some regional brewers, such as Anchor, Matt's, and August Schell, have reinvented themselves and now produce craft-brewed beer. The Lion seems to be trying this strategy with its Brewery Hill beers. (See "A word about . . . Micros, Brewpubs, and Craft Brewers" on page 48.)

Reinheitsgebot. The German beer purity law, which has its roots in a 1516 Bavarian statute limiting the ingredients in beer to barley malt, hops, and water. The law evolved into an inch-thick book and was the cornerstone of high-quality German brewing. It was deemed anticompetitive by the European Community courts and overturned in 1988. Most German brewers, however, continue to brew by its standards; tradition and the demands of their customers ensure it.

Repeal. See *Prohibition*.

Ringwood yeast. The house yeast of Peter Austin and Pugsley System breweries. A very particular yeast that requires an open fermenter, it is mostly found on the East Coast. Some well-known examples of Ringwood-brewed beers are Geary's, Magic Hat, and Shipyard; Market Cross in Carlisle uses Ringwood in what was Peter Austin's original brewhouse system. Ringwood beers are often easily identifiable by a certain nuttiness to their flavor. A brewer who isn't careful will find that Ringwood has created an undesirably high level of diacetyl, a compound that gives a beer a buttery or butterscotch aroma. Note that smaller amounts of diacetyl are perfectly normal and desirable in some types of beer.

Session Beer. A beer that is low to medium-low in strength, say 3.0 to 4.2 percent ABV, but still flavorful, designed for what the British call "session drinking," the kind that goes on all afternoon through tons of talk and maybe some snacks, and doesn't leave you knee-wobbling after 4 pints.

Sixtel. A new size of keg developed in 1996, holding one-sixth of a barrel: 5.2 gallons, or about 2.5 cases. Very popular for home use (well, I love 'em!); popular with multitaps as well. The beer stays fresher, and you can fit more different beers in a cold box. The word *sixtel* is of uncertain origin; it was not coined by the developer of the keg, but apparently grew up among the users.

Swill. A derogatory term used by beer geeks for American mainstream beers. The beers do not really deserve the name, since they are made with pure ingredients under conditions of quality control and sanitation some micros only wish they could achieve.

Terminal gravity. See *gravity*.

Three-tier system. A holdover from before Prohibition, the three-tier system requires Pennsylvania brewers, wholesalers, and retailers to be separate entities. The system was put in place to curtail financial abuses that were common when the three were mingled. Owning both wholesale and retail outlets gave unscrupulous brewers the power to rake off huge amounts of money, which all too often was used to finance political graft and police corruption. The three-tier system keeps the wholesaler insulated from pressure from the brewer and puts a layer of separation between brewer and retailer. Pennsylvania's regional brewers generally credit the state's strong three-tier laws with their survival. Recent court rulings have put the future of the regulated three-tier system in serious doubt, however, which may spell paradise or disaster for beer drinkers.

Wort. The prebeer grain broth of sugars, proteins, hops oils and alpha acids, and whatever else was added or developed during the mashing process. Once the yeast has been pitched and starts its jolly work, wort becomes beer.

Yeast. A miraculous fungus that, among other things, converts sugar into alcohol and carbon dioxide. The particular yeast strain used in brewing beer greatly influences the aroma and flavor of the beer. An Anheuser-Busch brewmaster recently told me that the yeast strain used there is the major factor in the flavor and aroma of Budweiser. Yeast is the sole source of the clovey, banana-rama aroma and the taste of Bavarian-style wheat beers. The original Reinheitsgebot of 1516 made no mention of yeast; it hadn't been discovered yet. Early brewing depended on a variety of sources for yeast: adding a starter from the previous batch of beer; exposing the wort to the wild yeasts carried on the open air (a method still used for Belgian lambic beers); always using the same vats for fermentation (yeast would cling to cracks and pores in the wood); or using a "magic stick" (which had the dormant yeast from the previous batch dried on its surface) to stir the beer. British brewers called the turbulent, billowing foam on fermenting beer *goddesgood*—"God is good"—because the foam meant that the predictable magic of the yeast was making beer. And beer, as Ben Franklin said, is proof that God loves us and wants us to be happy. Amen.

Zwickel. A *zwickel* ("tzVICK-el") is a little spout coming off the side of a beer tank that allows the brewer to sample the maturing beer in small amounts. If you're lucky, your tour will include an unfiltered sample of beer tapped directly from the tank through this little spout. Most brewers are touchy about this, as the zwickel is a potential site for infection, but with proper care, it's perfectly harmless to "tickle the zwickel." It's delicious, too: Unfiltered beer is the hot ticket.

INDEX